Understanding Law and Society

This textbook on the sociology of law is organised according to the theoretical traditions of sociology, and oriented towards providing an accessible, but sophisticated, introduction to, and overview of, the central themes, problems and debates in this field. The book employs an international range of examples – including the state, minority rights, terrorism, family violence, the legal profession, pornography, mediation, religious tolerance, and euthanasia – in order to distinguish a sociological approach to law from 'black-letter', jurisprudential and empirical policy-oriented traditions. Beginning with 'classical', 'consensus' and 'critical' sociological approaches, the book covers the full range of contemporary perspectives, including the new institutionalism, feminism, the interpretive tradition, postmodernism, legal pluralism and globalisation. It then concludes with a consideration of current theoretical issues, as well as a reflection upon the importance of a sociological approach to law.

Understanding Law and Society provides a clear, but critical, discussion of the relevant literature, along with study questions and guides to further reading. It is designed to support courses in law and society and in the sociology of law, but will also be of value to others with interests in these areas.

Max Travers is senior lecturer in the School of Sociology and Social Work, University of Tasmania, and teaches courses on sociology of law and sociological theory. His previous publications include *An Introduction to Law and Social Theory* (2002), edited with Reza Banakar.

Understanding Law and Society

Max Travers

Routledge
Taylor & Francis Group
a GlassHouse book

First published 2010 by Routledge
2 Park Square, Milton Park, Abingdon, Oxon, OX14 4RN

Simultaneously published in the USA and Canada
by Routledge
711 Third Avenue, New York, NY 10017

A GlassHouse book

Routledge is an imprint of the Taylor & Francis Group, an informa business

© 2010 Max Travers

Typeset in Sabon by Keyword Group Ltd.,

British Library Cataloguing in Publication Data
A catalogue record for this book is available from the British Library

Library of Congress Cataloguing in Publication Data
Travers, Max.
    Understanding law and society/Max Travers.
        p. cm.
    Simultaneously published in the USA and Canada.
    "A GlassHouse book."
    Includes bibliographical references.
    ISBN 978-0-415-43032-6 – ISBN 978-0-415-43033-3 1. Sociological
jurisprudence. 2. Law–Philosophy. 3. Law–Interpretation and
construction. 4. Postmodernism. 5. Legal polycentricity. I. Title.
    K370.T73 2009
    340'.115–dc22
                                                    2009009056

ISBN13: 978-0-415-43032-6 (hbk)

ISBN13: 978-0-415-43033-3 (pbk)

ISBN13: 978-0-203-87125-6 (ebk)

Contents

Preface and acknowledgements   vi

1   Introduction   1

2   Classical thinkers   17

3   The consensus tradition   39

4   Critical perspectives   65

5   Feminism and law   89

6   The interpretive tradition   113

7   Postmodernism and difference   139

8   Legal pluralism and globalisation   165

9   Conclusion   189

References   201
Index   215

Preface and acknowledgements

This book grows out of two collections, edited with Reza Banakar while I was living in the United Kingdom, aimed at postgraduates and those teaching sociology of law in departments of law and sociology. Our basic puzzle and complaint in those books was that sociology of law, both as a field of inter-disciplinary scholarship and a subject taught at undergraduate level, does not do justice to sociology as an academic discipline. This is evident by the fact that textbooks do not cover the range of theoretical approaches that interest sociologists, or explain the debates between them. Another weakness is that they rarely consider the issue of method, either in the sense of the different techniques used by sociologists, or philosophical debates on how to produce knowledge. We argued in *An Introduction to Law and Social Theory* (Banakar and Travers 2002) that all undergraduate law degrees should require students to do some contextual courses, and preferably give them an opportunity to study sociology of law. In *Theory and Method in Socio-Legal Research* (Banakar and Travers 2005a), we also argued that law students who are interested in doing socio-legal research should have the opportunity to take methods courses at undergraduate level, and certainly before doing postgraduate studies.

After publishing those books, we realised that what was still missing was an accessible introduction to sociology of law for undergraduates. As has happened in other projects, Reza encouraged me to work collaboratively in submitting a proposal to Routledge-Cavendish. Like many sociological jurists in the past, Reza is committed to introducing law students to sociological ideas and perspectives. My own background is complementary in that I qualified as a solicitor in Britain, through the Common Professional Examination route, before becoming a sociologist. We were pleased that the editorial board was persuaded that sociology of law had developed sufficiently as an undergraduate subject to support a textbook. Reza was, unfortunately, unable to write his half, so I have completed the project.

Anyone who has written a textbook will know that it is a difficult task. This is partly because in a subject like this you cannot cover everything, so have to make some difficult choices. In this case, we wanted a book that was about theoretical traditions in sociology of law rather than substantive topics, such as the legal profession or dispute resolution, but was still accessible for students taking undergraduate courses in law and sociology. Getting the level right is difficult. When you try to introduce something simply, much that interests the specialist will be lost. But if you introduce the subject at too high a level, many students will find problems because they do not have the background knowledge to understand basic concepts. The preface to another recent introduction to sociology of law (Milovanovic 2003) justifies the approach taken through a cooking metaphor. It likens that book to the kind of meal you can eat in a leisurely fashion over an afternoon in a Parisian cafe tasting different dishes, as against eating a hamburger where everything has been packaged. Like any textbook aimed at helping the undergraduate student, this book is more like the hamburger, although one that uses the best international ingredients, and tells you where to go for more advanced readings.

I hope that readers will find this book stimulating, and that it will generate interest in law and society studies like the other textbooks published in recent years (for example, Kidder 1983; Cotterrell 1992; Roach Anleu 2000; Sutton 2001; Vago 2005; Deflem 2008). I would like to thank the University of Tasmania for providing an excellent working environment, and supportive colleagues who see the value in publishing textbooks alongside other research activities. I have been fortunate to have been given the opportunity to teach sociology of law, in addition to courses in sociological theory and qualitative research methods. My course is based on reviewing different substantive topics, which is appropriate for those students without a sociological background. I spent only two weeks reviewing the different sociological traditions introduced in this book. Nevertheless, I feel that I could teach an additional course based on reviewing traditions and theories. This book should help students see the relevance of sociological theories and theoretical debates to any field of law and society research.

I tend to get immersed in projects, and not spend as much time with family and friends as I should, which is not made easier by having moved to Australia. In Britain, I would like to thank my parents, Harry Travers, Denise Farran, Anjana Bhattacharjee, Roger Taylor, Wendy Burke, Paul Watt, Paul Elton, Esther Knight, Wes Sharrock, Rod Watson, Dave Calvey, Lee Epstein, Carol Bennett, Monica Mathews, Janet Entwistle, Lyn Burden, Neil Jenkings and Janet Rachel for their support in the last few years. In Australia, I would like to thank my colleagues and students in the School of Sociology and Social Work at the University of Tasmania, David Wearing, Mike Emmison, Robert Van Krieken, Maureen Fitzgerald, Ros Porter, Greg Martin, Hannah Jenkins and Terrie Dempster. In America, Western Europe and Japan, I also have a few contacts: special thanks to Jack and Marilyn Whalen for treating me to some meals in San Francisco. I should also thank the staff at the Nova StarGate hotel in Melbourne since I do some writing there.

Chapter 1

Introduction

The relationship between law and society	3
The view that law is society	5
The view that society is greater than law	5
Approaches to studying law	6
Black-letter law	7
Jurisprudence	8
Policy-oriented research	8
Sociology of law	9
Sociology of law: a debate subject	10
Why sociologists disagree	10
Consensus versus conflict	11
Action versus structure	11
The postmodern challenge	12
Can sociologists address law?	13
The objectives of this text	15
Questions	15
Further reading	16

This introductory text on understanding law and society should interest two types of student readers. Those studying law will already know a lot about the legal system, and legal skills and reasoning, but feel less confident when thinking about the relationship between law and society. Students on social science degrees may know very little about the legal system, but have taken introductory courses in different social science theories and approaches. This in itself suggests that teaching courses in law and society studies, sociology of law, socio-legal studies or the law in context (these are all different terms for the same approach towards law) is not always easy since it involves bringing together different disciplines. Against this, a mix of students on any law and society course can be very valuable, and students often help each other not only with terminology, but in learning how to look at law differently. This chapter will, therefore, need to explain the basics of the legal system (that law students should know in more detail) and the basics of sociology (that should already be familiar to sociology students). To understand the nature of either law or society, you need to know the relevant ideas and concepts from the disciplines of law and sociology. Moreover, the moment you start to think about the relationship, you are starting to explore new territory, and will encounter difficult but interesting questions that cannot be addressed within each discipline.

The relationship between law and society

The first thing that students learn on law degrees are the sources of law as a body of rules that govern different aspects of social life. In the United States, Britain and Australia (the common law world) a significant amount of law is made by judges interpreting precedents handed down from time immemorial. The judgements made by the higher courts are reported in law reports that fill shelves in libraries or can be consulted using search engines in cyber-space. Anyone new to law as a discipline might be amazed, and perhaps disturbed, by the sheer volume of case law being produced by different courts and tribunals, and which lawyers need to know if they are advising clients. Then there is the law made by legislative bodies, such as the American Congress or the British Houses of Parliament, which fills yet more volumes, and may come before the courts generating further case law.

Every area of life is regulated by some form of law, and the amount is increasing exponentially. Criminal law creates offences for which one can be arrested and charged by the police and brought before the criminal courts. Civil law concerns the relationship between citizens. The law student has to learn and be able to apply complex bodies of rules that identify when one can obtain compensation for injury, and the rights and obligations when making a contract. There are, in fact, specialist rules, relating to every aspect of social life, including the ownership of land, different aspects of commerce, the family, the conduct of public bodies and immigration control. The law student learns some of the main areas (tort, contract, criminal and family law) on a law degree but there is too much to learn, and like the medical student, it is often only possible to acquire skills in locating the law, and making legal arguments, rather than obtaining a mastery of each specialist area.

From a sociological perspective, the legal system can also be understood as a number of organisations or institutions that produce, administer and interpret the law. There is the law school itself which maintains law as what the structural-functionalist sociologist Talcott Parsons (see Chapter 3) described as a 'cultural tradition', and trains the next generation of lawyers. There is the legal profession which includes lawyers in private practice, those working for industry and public sector organisations and the judiciary. There are also the criminal and civil courts, and related institutions such as the police. Several thousand people work in these and other specialist organisations concerned with legal affairs in any particular country. In the United Kingdom, both the systems of criminal and civil law are administered and overseen by departments of state, the Home Office and Department of Constitutional Affairs, which are themselves massive bureaucratic organisations. Then, there is the whole political system and legislative process that produces statutory law, which itself consists of numerous organisations, each with its own ways of doing things. To give an example, the British House of Commons is an extremely complex institution with its own procedures and values that exists to review and make new laws. One group of specialists working there are the parliamentary draughtsmen who translate the objectives of legislators into what they hope are effective pieces of legislation.

Outside the nation state, there are organisations that produce and administer laws that shape the relations between states. Many of these are concerned with economic relations in a globalising world, for example, the regular negotiations that have attempted to secure a free trade agreement. Others are concerned with regional affairs, so for example there are many agreements and regulations just affecting the relationship between states in Asia or Latin America. Others are concerned with setting global standards, or attempting to police criminal behaviour. The International Criminal Court in The Netherlands holds trials for those charged with war crimes. The various Conventions that have resulted from the formation of the United Nations, and the many agencies associated with this, on the rights of children, the environment and the rights of prisoners in international conflicts, are not always respected by nation states. Nevertheless, the United Nations will become increasingly important in addressing problems, such as global warming, that can only be solved by co-ordinated, international action.

Understanding law in terms of these organisations and institutions still does not do justice to how law affects us in everyday life (even when we are not aware of it), and particularly how organisations of all kinds, from small businesses to television stations, organise their activities in compliance with external regulations. The term 'legal phenomena' seems to capture how we encounter law regularly in social life, often in dealing with documents such as tenancy agreements, employment contracts or insurance policies, or the liability notices on consumer products. The rights and obligations of the different parties involved in publishing this book (the author and publishers) are governed by a written contract. We may not read these documents closely, but in the modern world they are part of our everyday lives (Friedrichs 2006). It should also be remembered that any organisation by definition will generate its own rules and procedures. This is arguably also law even if it is not recognised as such by the courts, unless they have to intervene when a dispute arises that cannot be settled informally.

How then to understand the relationship between law and society? This difficult question has troubled legal philosophers and social theorists for many years, and there are no easy or simple answers. To get a sense of the difficulties, consider the following positions:

The view that law is society

If society is more than a collection of individuals, there must be some kind of relationship between them, and at the very least a sense of what is right and wrong behaviour. This has led legal philosophers in the natural law tradition to argue that there cannot be society without law (Finnis 1980). From this perspective, social theorists do not usually pay sufficient respect to law. It is central to everything we do, not simply as an external constraint, but because it constitutes and makes possible orderly social life. This involves taking a broad view of law, so any rule or social norm we are following, for example caring for the sick or respecting other people's property, is seen as part of law, even if lawyers or the courts are not asked to intervene, and we are not consulting legal rules. Everything in society is held together, governed and even constituted by law.

The view that society is greater than law

The opposing view, not often articulated by sociologists, but evident when they write about society, is that it is possible to go through life without giving law much thought. A lawyer might need to be consulted when buying a house, or if you are unfortunate enough to be injured in a car accident. For the most part, however, law seems rather a dry, technical subject of interest to a particular occupational group. Legal considerations may be there in the background when you are pursuing your day-to-day work and leisure activities, but they are not central to running a business, getting married, appreciating television drama, ordering from a restaurant menu or conducting a war (to give a few examples). There is inevitably a lot more to any society, whether it is the kind of small-scale group studied by anthropologists, or our own highly complex industrialised society, than law. From this perspective, one can recognise the importance of rules and norms (how people are expected to behave),without seeing them as part of the legal system. Some legal philosophers and sociologists have also argued that we only consult lawyers, and only need law, when things go wrong. Harvey Sacks (1997, p. 43) argued that the emphasis in law on 'written matter, on coherence, clarity, completeness, impersonality [and] predictability . . . provide solutions to matters not treated as problems in the everyday world of others'. It would be intolerable if every aspect of our lives really were governed in fine detail by legal rules.

Even if one accepts that law is only one institution, among many others, it is a particularly important institution, since it is also more or less equivalent to the modern legislative state. Similarly, despite being resented for the amount they charge to resolve problems and conflicts through their knowledge of what to many seem obscure and unnecessary procedures, it would be hard to imagine our complex, industrial society without lawyers. This is why it seems strange that law hardly gets a mention in many sociology degrees, outside the area of deviance. There are likely to be options on class structure and stratification, work and the economy, crime and deviance, the family, the media, education, racial and ethnic relations, perhaps religion and science, but not law. The other side of the problem is, of course, that in many law degrees, students only encounter law as a set of rules, rather than thinking about its character as an institution in broader terms.

The objective of this text is to help you understand the relationship between law and society, without promising there are easy answers even before we look at different sociological traditions. The next section explains what is distinctive about sociology of law through contrasting it to three other ways of studying law which are taught in law schools. It also considers some general debates about the nature of society that have interested sociologists.

Approaches to studying law

Students studying law on university degrees spend most of their time learning and applying what is sometimes forbiddingly called black-letter law. They also usually have to take a course in legal philosophy, and may take courses where there is a focus on how law contributes to the objectives of government. Sociology of law, by contrast, is a subject concerned with thinking about, and investigating using empirical methods, the relationship between law and society.

Black-letter law

'Y receives an e-mail message from X in which he offers to sell his car. The message says that if he hears nothing by the end of that week, X will assume that he is happy with the price. Y does not reply to the message. Does he have to buy the car?'

'Mary is a witness to a car accident caused by Louise in which a child is killed. For the next few months, she finds it difficult to sleep and gets flash-backs. She gets back to normal through seeing a counsellor recommended by her doctor. Can Mary obtain compensation?'

These are examples of the problems given to British law students to test their knowledge of the law and develop skills of legal reasoning. To answer the first question, you need to know the rule or principle established by the case of *Felthouse v Bindley* (1862) 11 CB (NS). You can find the surrounding case law in any British textbook on the law of contract. Since judges follow precedents, this case determines whether a contract has arisen in similar circumstances today, unless a lawyer can make a convincing case that the facts can be distinguished. To answer the second question, you need to be familiar with the case law following the decision in *Donoghue v Stephenson* [1932] AC 562 which created the right of someone to claim compensation if injured by another person or organisation in breach of a duty of care. The issue here is whether you can claim damages for a breach of duty of care resulting in psychological harm or distress. As every law student knows, there are no credits given for providing background information about the origins of contract law, or ethical debates about whether protection against every conceivable type of harm is a good thing. In fact, the flavour of the law school tutorial is that students have to solve problems quickly, with just the rules or principle that is required. Moreover, they have to sit examinations based on large bodies of cases and rules where only the most disciplined, and with good memories, will obtain high grades.

Although one can make fun of how black-letter law is taught in law schools, there is no doubt that knowing the law, or knowing how to find it, has great practical value. It also helps at a later stage of legal training to know about the procedures involved in bring a case to court. Just as medical practitioners need to know about common illnesses and how they are treated, the lawyer needs to know the general principles in a particular area of law, and how to consult specialists when this is appropriate. If cases are appealed, lawyers and judges may have to engage in academic argument over the principles and precedents in a particular area of law. The judgements written up in law reports may in turn form part of legal training for the next generation of lawyers.

Jurisprudence

The only subject outside black-letter law that has become institutionalised in the law school curriculum is legal philosophy or jurisprudence. Many textbooks are quite broad, and include discussion of sociological theorists such as Karl Marx (for an example from Britain, see Freeman 2001). They mostly, however, contrast two philosophical traditions that have been debating the nature of law since the eighteenth century. Natural law theory is the oldest, and argues that law does and should reflect enduring and eternal ideas of what is right and wrong. This view of law originated in Europe during a period when the power of the sovereign or law-maker was seen as having a religious basis: law reflected divine will. By contrast, positivist jurisprudence took the view that law as a set of rules was created by political power, and there should be no room for appeals to moral absolutes.

Although it might seem remarkable to a non-specialist that so much intellectual effort is still expended on debating these philosophical positions and various elaborations or off-shoots, it should be remembered that the objective of this field of legal philosophy is to think through fundamental problems in a systematic fashion. Classic statements by Ronald Dworkin, Hans Kelsen and H.L.A. Hart (different varieties of legal positivism) or by Lon Fuller and John Finnis (natural law theory) repay close study. None of these theorists disagree about what lawyers or judges do in practice and most have little interest in empirical research conducted by sociologists. They are concerned with philosophical debates about the nature of law.

Policy-oriented research

Law has always been an inter-disciplinary subject, and in many law schools there is some focus on teaching the development of social policy either in separate courses ('law and policy'), or as part of courses on black-letter law. Since government agencies providing health and welfare services were established by legislation, it makes sense to explain the purpose behind these on a law degree, and consider the inevitable gap between objectives and achievements. Courses which introduce the 'law in context' often introduce the development of policy in this sense, perhaps combined with some social and political history and a consideration of philosophical principles, and some sociology of law. In the past, they have often advanced a critical view in relation to the welfare state, in the sense of arguing that more can be done to help the disadvantaged. Today, there is a different political climate in that neo-liberal governments have dismantled many of the rights secured in earlier periods through new legislation, and have introduced market principles in the delivery of public services (for an overview, see Harvey 2007).

Some British writers in the law and context tradition have argued vigorously against these developments which have, among other things, made it harder for people of modest means to afford the services supplied by lawyers. There are also, however, many policy-oriented researchers based in law schools who have welcomed the reforms, and accept the current emphasis within government on improving efficiency. This has created many opportunities to conduct evaluations for government departments (Genn et al. 2006). Whatever the policy of the day, it seems inevitable that many law and society researchers will do research for government agencies (Sarat and Silbey 1988), without seeking to raise difficult questions or political objections. There are, therefore, some similarities between black-letter law and policy-oriented research: they each seek to be useful, and speak in the same language as practitioners and politicians.

Sociology of law

Many sociological traditions ask critical questions about society from a progressive or left-wing standpoint, and can be contrasted with policy research that serves the needs of the legal profession or government (for discussion, see Campbell and Wiles 1976). Many of the traditions reviewed in this book speak for subordinate or disadvantaged groups in society (Chapters 4, 5 and 7), and often form the basis of courses in 'critical legal studies' taught in many law schools. However, by no means all sociology is critical. Some theorists and traditions are quite conservative in supporting established institutions, for example, Talcott Parsons (Chapter 3). Others, such as some varieties of interpretive sociology (Chapter 6) or poststructuralist philosophy (Chapter 7), are not interested in advancing a political viewpoint. What all sociological traditions have in common is a scientific interest in studying law. Like any other area of science, this is pursued for its own sake, and for intellectual interest, without assuming at least initially that there will be any practical pay-off.

Another way of putting this is that sociologists of law bring to law the theories and methods that sociologists use in understanding and investigating other areas of society. There are all kinds of theories with different philosophical and political assumptions and debates between them, ranging from structural-functionalism to Marxism and poststructuralism (for overviews, see Cuff et al. 2006 or Ritzer 2004). There are also all kinds of methods that sociologists use in investigating society. Moreover, and to make matters more difficult, good sociological research requires being self-conscious and reflective at all stages of a research project. When they do dissertations, undergraduate students have to write critically about the theories employed, contrasting these with alternatives, in a review of the literature. They also have to write critically about methods, and why they have chosen to use one approach rather than others, in a methodology chapter. This commitment to being self-critical and reflective, and the fact most sociologists are committed to conducting empirical research, characterises sociology as an academic discipline, and distinguishes it from black-letter law, jurisprudence and policy-oriented research.

Sociology of law: a debate subject

A central difficulty in teaching sociology of law is whether to focus on theoretical traditions or substantive topics. There are a number of textbooks on sociology of law or law and society that start by introducing theories, but then concentrate on describing substantive topics, such as the legal profession, judiciary, dispute resolution and international law. The problem here is that the nature of theories in sociology and how they can be applied to law and legal phenomena are not really explained. This text differs in trying to explain the theories, but there is a risk that it will not do sufficient justice to substantive topics. It will, however, include a few empirical studies as examples within particular chapters: you should also be able to see how the same topic (for example, the position of women in the legal profession) can be approached from a range of theoretical perspectives. How though to introduce these perspectives and the debates between them? This section will consider three general debates that characterise sociology as a discipline and relate these to law. To begin with, however, it is necessary to consider why sociologists disagree.

Why sociologists disagree

Sociology has been described as an argument or debate rather than knowledge subject, a discipline more like philosophy than physics or for that matter black-letter law (Anderson et al. 1978). There are many aspects of the world that provide scope for political disagreement: many people, for example, are strongly opposed to the Iraq war, whereas others believe the bloodshed and loss of life has been worth it. Sociologists usually, however, disagree about larger issues than this. Consider, for example, the rise of our advanced, industrialised civilisation over the last 300 years based on a capitalist economy, a world market and the modern bureaucratic state. Some social theorists, such as Auguste Comte, Emile Durkheim and Talcott Parsons, have viewed these developments with hope and optimism: modern law from this perspective is a tremendous achievement. Others, however, believe that we have to a considerable extent lost our freedom: in Max Weber's words that we are reduced to 'cogs' in a machine (Weber 1968, p. iii).

At a different level of society, the same arguments can be made about our experiences of university education, whether in departments of law or sociology. Are the rules and regulations, and the carefully timed ways in which lectures and seminars are delivered, a good thing, making possible education for the masses? Or are we reduced to being cogs in a machine, where the whole experience of education for teachers and students has become deeply alienating? You are not required to take a stand on these issues in every research project as a sociologist of law, but many of the great sociologists have taken a moral and political stand on either side of this debate.

Consensus versus conflict

Although there is less of an ideological divide in sociology following the end of the Soviet Union in the late 1980s, there remains a long-standing debate between those who understand society as held together by shared values, and those who see it as characterised by power relations and conflict. In simple terms, if you believe that society is held together by shared values, you will see it as an orderly place in which conflicts and tensions are signs that something has gone wrong. The mechanisms that Talcott Parsons (1951) identified as holding society together were socialisation, but also the legal system including the coercive forces of the police which could intervene where required. Structural-functionalism was effectively the dominant paradigm in sociology during the 1940s and 1950s but was much criticised in the 1960s and 1970s. Today, to some extent the wheel has come full circle and government ministers in the developed world often employ functionalist ideas in talking about the need to educate deviant groups.

Conflict sociologists, by contrast, believe that conflict and tensions, including crime, are healthy responses to economic inequality. During the 1960s, they believed that mass movements would develop in Western Europe and America that would overthrow existing economic and social elites and redistribute income and wealth (for a British radical text, see Taylor et al. 1973). The obvious difficulty with this position is that, even though they generate periodic recessions, over the long term capitalist societies seem both stable and economically successful. On the other hand, there is growing inequality both between and within countries. In the USA, large numbers of African Americans have a far lower standard of living and education, and are more likely to come into contact with the criminal justice system, than the rest of the population. From this perspective, law is a means of ideological persuasion: it conceals the real economic relationships through which dominant groups exploit the working class. It is also a means of coercion which is apparent whenever the police are used against protestors, for example at the regular demonstrations at international meetings of the World Trade Organisation. This organisation that represents government and business interests seeks to promote and introduce free trade as a means of creating a dynamic capitalist economy internationally. The protestors believe that this will produce even higher levels of insecurity, exploitation and inequality: a major political debate in our times.

Action versus structure

The debate between those theorists who believe that individuals exercise agency and free-will, and those who see their actions as shaped, and even determined by, social structures lies at the centre of sociological analysis. All the classical theorists were aware of, and wrote about, this issue. Talcott Parsons (1937) recognised that it was a central problem for sociology, and that the discipline had to address both structure and agency. The structural-functionalists who took up this research agenda were, however, criticised by interpretive sociologists during the 1960s for their heavy bias towards structural constraint. More recent theorists such as Anthony Giddens and Pierre Bourdieu tend to argue that the debate can be resolved if we recognise that human beings both exercise agency and are subject to constraints (in Marx's words, we choose our own destinies, but not in conditions of our own making). However, this foundational debate tends to surface in different forms. There is plenty of scope for a new generation of theorists to argue that the most sophisticated theories around do not sufficiently address either structure or action. It is, for example, difficult to address or appreciate what people think they are doing in the practical circumstances of their lives, while at the same time believing that they are shaped by forces and structures that are only visible to the sociologist.

As explained in Banakar and Travers (2005a), sociologists can use the same methods, but do so within different theoretical frameworks. Interpretive sociologists, such as symbolic interactionists and ethnomethodologists, try to appreciate the actor's point of view without claiming they know better from having access to a privileged understanding of social structures. Critical researchers, by contrast, when describing what legal practitioners are doing, seek to show how their actions are shaped or constrained by social structures. A central idea or theme in both structural-functionalism and critical sociology is the distinction between 'macro' and 'micro' levels of society: the sociologist has a better understanding of the 'macro' level and how it shapes our everyday actions than the people we study. By contrast, the interpretive traditions reviewed in Chapter 6 do not accept the distinction: they are only interested in how lawyers, judges and the parties to legal cases understand their own activities.

The postmodern challenge

Perhaps the most complex and difficult debates that have taken place in sociology in recent years have been associated with the intellectual movement known as postmodernism (Best and Kellner 1991). This enjoyed immense influence in the humanities and social sciences during the 1990s, partly because it filled a vacuum left by academic Marxism which, outside a few believers, did not survive the fall of Soviet communism in 1989. Postmodernism in its narrow meaning involves making the claim that we have entered a new period of human history, and are no longer in the modern world. Like most sociological arguments, this can be debated, since not everyone would agree that anything substantial has changed. Can one say, for example, that postmodern law is any different to law in the modern period?

In a broader sense, postmodernism is associated with the philosophical arguments of poststructuralist philosophers against the assumptions held by a previous generation of legal thinkers. They have, for example, challenged the view that legal texts represent the world unproblematically. Finally, postmodernism also refers to the work of poststructuralist thinkers who offer an alternative way of thinking about the role of law in society. Michel Foucault (1978, pp. 88–9), for example, argued that it was necessary to 'cut off the head of the king' and recognise that there is more to society than laws made by a sovereign. Chapter 7 will review these ideas and show their relevance to law.

Can sociologists address law?

Sociology of law has not always received a warm welcome from black-letter lawyers or legal philosophers, who have complained about the imperialist ambitions of sociologists, but also the fact that sociology does not address the content of law, and particularly the skills used in reasoning about cases. Although there are institutional reasons why resistance towards sociological insights is particularly strong in law schools (Banakar 2003), it is worth noting that there is nothing new to these arguments. Medical practitioners, scientists, academics working in education and religious studies, and musicologists have made similar objections when sociologists started writing about their fields (see, for example, Martin 1997). The only difference is that sociologists now teach on professional courses in many of these fields, and have influenced the curriculum, whereas few researchers who have done Phds in a sociology department work in law schools.

The charge of 'imperialism' is usually made against the propensity of some sociologists (mainly in structural traditions) to explain what lawyers are doing, or what happens in the legal system, without paying enough attention to how lawyers themselves understand their own activities. Talcott Parsons (1954), who was generally highly complimentary towards lawyers, argued that, even though they might not know it, when they advised clients to settle they were engaging in social control. In this kind of analysis, the content and quality of the legal advice being given was irrelevant. Parsons believed that the sociologist knew more than lawyers about how society worked, and one can see how a black-letter lawyer or practitioner might complain of imperialism. There are similar grounds for complaint against critical researchers or postmodernists who want to show how law represents the economic interests of dominant groups. Sociologists in these traditions often express scepticism towards the claims made by lawyers as a professsional group that they benefit society. From a Marxist perspective, the lawyer serves the economic needs of capitalism (see, for example, Cain 1983). According to Weberian sociologists writing about the professions (Johnson 1972), or Pierre Bourdieu (1987), lawyers are an economic interest group seeking to better their own position at the expense of the public (see Chapter 4).

Black-letter lawyers and jurists have also complained that sociologists do not address the specialist language and technical content of law (Banakar and Travers 2005b). This is largely true in that there are relatively few sociological studies that take us inside the world of law, so we can understand and appreciate how practitioners deal with technical problems. There are also not many studies that do justice to the technical considerations involved in science or music (to give two examples of technical activities). To understand what happens in these fields, one needs some degree of training. One needs to know what is at stake in a scientific experiment, or how one recognises good quality artistic work in a particular field. On the other hand, one might argue that one cannot do a sociological study by staying within the relevances and practical concerns of practitioners. To understand any institution sociologically, one also needs to know its relationship to a wider context, and this inevitably means adopting a critical stance towards law.

To pursue this point, clearly any sociological study about law has to address the detail and content of law, in the same way as a study of science or music has to address the detail and content of these fields. Some sociologists might, however, question whether law needs to have quite so much technical content to be effective at, for example, resolving disputes. Sociologists have criticised lawyers and the courts for mystifying the public through deliberately using obscure and technical language in order to support the professional claims of law as an occupation. Chapter 6 will consider attempts to resolve disputes through arbitration and mediation without using lawyers. Tribunals were initially established as means of resolving problems quickly by lay decision-makers, with the aim of having informal procedures. Another example, where reformers are trying to reduce the role of lawyers, is property transactions. In some countries, this whole area of work has been taken away from lawyers, and to some extent de-legalised by establishing electronic registers of title. Why not go further and de-legalise the legal profession?

Jurists are, therefore, partly correct when they say that sociologists do not address the technical content of law. But from a sociological perspective, the technical content of law can only be a site for argument and debate within different theoretical traditions. Chapter 6 introduces a sociological tradition known as ethnomethodology that is interested in examining the nature of professional knowledge and reasoning in different fields, and has contributed to appreciating language-use in courtrooms. Other sociologists have adopted a critical stance, and sometimes argue that society should be de-legalised or de-professionalised. Then there are the theorists, such as Parsons, who admire the technical character of legal reasoning, and the role of lawyers as agents of social control. In short, the criticism that sociology does not (or cannot) address the content of law does not do justice to the different theoretical traditions in that discipline, or the debates that take place between them. One should add that not every lawyer endorses or approves everything that takes place in the legal system. Without requiring you to support a particular political viewpoint, sociology of law offers a means to reflect critically on professional practice, in the best traditions of the law school.

The objectives of this text

It should be apparent that there are a variety of ways of approaching law within sociology. Chapter 2 introduces the classical tradition in sociology of law and sociological jurisprudence, and more broadly how different theorists have approached law as part of a response to the modern world. Chapter 3 discusses how law is understood by the consensus tradition in social theory, approaches that see society as held together by shared values. Chapters 4 and 5 look at a variety of critical traditions, including Marxism and feminism, but also critical race theory and political movements concerned with improving the position of disabled people and homosexuals. Chapter 6 introduces the interpretive traditions, and focuses on how ethnographic and discourse analytic methods can be employed in researching legal settings. Chapter 7 explains postmodernism and how it has influenced writings on difference and identity in legal texts. Chapter 8 reviews the growing literatures on legal pluralism and also on law and globalisation.

Although not every theorist or theoretical tradition is covered, the text will show how a range of sociological theories can be used in researching law and legal phenomena. Each tradition brings its own insights and questions that can help us understand the relationship between law and society. Each chapter will consider a range of examples, illustrating how theories can be applied to topics. Nevertheless, this text is distinctive in presenting law and society in terms of theoretical traditions, instead of substantive topics. This subject starts to come alive when you start to apply theories and concepts to actual topics, such as what happens when a lawyer advises a client, what happens in a legal dispute, or how laws are made and enforced through the legislative and political process. You should start to look at law differently through considering the different approaches in this book, and find many points of connection with other courses on a law or social science degree.

Questions

1 What do you understand as the distinction between black-letter law and sociology of law?
2 Why is there more to sociology of law than the critical tradition?
3 Why are many sociologists not interested in the content of legal practice or reasoning?

4 'Sociology makes us look critically at institutions we take for granted'. Discuss
   in relation to the legal system.

Further reading

There are several good introductions to sociology of law, including Cotterrell's *The
   Sociology of Law: An Introduction* (Butterworths, London 1992, 2005); Roach
   Anleu's *Law and Social Change* (Sage, London 2000); Vago's *Law and Society*
   (Prentice-Hall, Englewood Cliffs, New Jersey 2005); Sutton's *Law/Society* (Pine
   Forge Press, Thousand Oaks, California, 2001) and Deflem's *The Sociology of
   Law: Visions of a Scholarly Tradition* (Cambridge University Press, Cambridge,
   2008). This book is distinctive in addressing a wider range of sociological tradi-
   tions and perspectives, but you can find useful and relevant materials in all these
   texts.
The *Sage Encyclopedia of Law and Society* (Sage, London 2008) provides overviews
   of substantive topics and theoretical traditions.
For a more advanced discussion of the distinction between law and sociology, see
   Banakar and Travers "Law, Theory and Method" (in R. Banakar and M. Travers,
   eds, *Theory and Method in Socio-Legal Research*, Hart, Oxford, pp. 1–26).
   Harvey Sacks' essay on "The Lawyer's Work" provides an interesting discussion
   about the relationship between law and society in M. Travers and J. Manzo (eds)
   Law in Action (Ashgate, Aldershot, 1997, pp. 43–50).

Chapter 2

Classical thinkers

The classical sociologists and law	19
Marx	20
Durkheim	23
Weber	24
Sociological jurisprudence	25
Savigny	26
Sumner	27
Petrazycki	28
Erhlich	29
The American realist tradition	29
Holmes	30
Pound	30
Llewellyn	31
The relevance of the classical tradition	32
From classical to contemporary sociology	32
Debates about method	33
The legacy of sociological jurisprudence	35
Questions	36
Further reading	36
Boxes 2.1 Marx's base-superstructure model	22
2.2 Llewellyn on the law school	32
2.3 Weber on regulation	34

The most difficult and least inviting part of introductory courses in any academic discipline is often the obligatory introduction to classical thinkers. This is, firstly, because the original writings are hard to follow, often simply because they were written in a different historical period. It requires some effort to obtain sufficient background on the political events and intellectual debates that made them interesting at the time. In my experience, students usually find no difficulty in summarising particular thinkers using the many helpful textbook accounts that have been published (for example, Adams and Sydie 2002). What they are often unable to do is make the imaginative leap that enables one to see that the ideas continue to be relevant to the problems and challenges we face today.

When teaching sociology of law, there is the added problem that theorists have approached the relationship between law and society from within two academic disciplines. Law is the older discipline and was established in universities before the start of the modern period. Sociology was not taught in universities until the early twentieth century, partly through the intellectual and promotional efforts of Emile Durkheim. The term itself was invented in the 1800s by his predecessor Auguste Comte (1975) who was trying to make sense of a century of far-reaching changes in many areas of social life.

Perhaps the simplest way to understand the relationship between the disciplines is to focus on the changes that took place in Western societies during the eighteenth and nineteenth centuries, particularly in relation to law, and then to examine the response of sociological theorists and sociologically minded jurists. One concern that unites them, although it does not cover everything that interested either group of thinkers, is the rise of the modern state which has transformed the legal system. Another question, which sometimes surfaces within jurisprudence as well as among sociologists, is how one can study society scientifically. In each case, and particularly in sociology, thinkers took opposing positions. To give one example, Durkheim took a generally positive view of the modern state, including how law was developing. Weber had a more pessimistic and critical view. Although it would be wrong to see the sociological jurists as concerned with exactly the same issues, many were reacting against the growth of the state in a similar way to Weber.

The classical sociologists and law

One additional difficulty that should be acknowledged from the outset when discussing classical sociological theory in a law and society text is that very few theorists explicitly discuss law. As every law student is taught, law is everywhere and governs all aspects of social life. Marx, Durkheim and Weber would have recognised this. However, they are writing about the modern world as a whole, rather than about the development of modern law which is only one part of society. For Marx (1818–83) and Durkheim (1858–1917), it was decidedly of secondary importance to economic forces in causing social change. Even Weber (1864–1920), who was a lawyer and in *Economy and Society* (1978) provides a detailed history of the development of modern law and the state, saw changes in law as having the same causal importance as changes in religious belief. Introductions to jurisprudence often focus on the specific claims they did make about law, and the subsequent arguments about this. Law students are often asked to write essays about the 'English Question': the apparent paradox raised by Weber as to why the Industrial Revolution happened in a society that had not modernised its legal system. Similarly, jurisprudential writers are understandably interested in Durkheim's views on the relationship between law and morality. This, however, misses what interests sociologists: the classical sociologists were responding in general terms to the modern world, and moreover in ways that are still highly relevant to changes taking place today.

Marx

To understand Marx's ideas, it is necessary to appreciate what was happening during his lifetime. Marx was born towards the middle of what later became known as the Industrial Revolution, in which a series of technological developments in England made it possible to produce cheap cotton clothes on mechanised looms powered by the steam engine. In the 1840s, this industry suffered a severe slump caused by over-production and a falling rate of profit. Manufacturers went out of business, and others were forced to reduce wages and working conditions. There was no social security net. Some workers starved, and others took to the streets campaigning for cheap food (since landowners in the agricultural sector used their political power to prevent imports) and for laws that would prevent employment abuses and provide state support during a recession. These campaigns largely failed since the political system favoured manufacturers: it was not till the early twentieth century that most of the population obtained the right to vote.

The most influential thinkers at this time were generally confident that capitalism, despite its imperfections, would raise living standards. Adam Smith (1970), for example, praised the invisible hand of the market. This was also a period when jurists and political commentators celebrated the rule of law, which had enabled England to avoid violent upheavals elsewhere. Law and public policy were seen as a tool that could achieve the greatest good for the masses. Utilitarian political theorists such as Jeremy Bentham (1973) and sociologists such as Herbert Spencer (1965) presented the political and economic system that had evolved in England as the best imaginable; not least because it respected individual rights and constrained executive power under judicial control. There is a large, nineteenth century literature, now mostly forgotten, that discusses and celebrates law in these terms.

In this context, Marx and Engel's (1967, pp. 99–100) observation that 'Your jurisprudence is the jurisprudence of your class' can be appreciated as a devastating critique of the intellectual establishment. From this perspective, law and the whole political system represented the interests of manufacturers. Whenever a utilitarian thinker, political leader or judge praised the rule of law, they were engaged in promoting a view of society that served their own economic interests. Similarly, the police and army when combating industrial unrest, or even petty crime, were not acting in the public interest, but supporting capitalism. The concept of ideology has been criticised in recent years, by postmodernists and others, as making a naive and even arrogant contrast between what ordinary people believe and the true nature of society as understood by the Marxist theorist. Like all theoretical concepts in sociology, it is complex and has generated many critical debates. Nevertheless, the central idea is easy to understand: an ideology is a set of ideas, widely shared in society, that benefits the economically dominant group, and which is communicated through social institutions such as the legal system.

Marx's central objective as a social theorist was to explain social and economic changes through the whole of human history. This was driven by the optimistic belief that the tensions and contradictions experienced by human societies would eventually be resolved; we would ultimately live in a perfect world (a communist utopia), although only after much conflict and suffering. The driving force in Marx's version of this theory was technological change. This would produce a particular type of economy (the 'mode of production') in each stage of history. Developments in the economy would eventually lead to a transformation of all other aspects of society, including law, the political system and even the nature of religious belief.

Although this theory is complex, the basic ideas are again easy to grasp. In the Middle Ages, the economy was based on lords owning serfs, and each had traditional rights and obligations. This economic system was made possible by laws that enabled lords to own serfs. Marx argued that the development of productive forces in the economy, and the shift to a system where workers sold their labour to employers, required a new type of law. The jurists celebrating individual rights, and who had developed the law of contract, during a two-hundred year period, were not therefore simply promoting their class interests. They were, from a broader perspective, the agents of changes in legal, political and cultural institutions that were required for capitalism to develop. Furthermore, Marx argued that this happened as a result of a protracted crisis that generated class conflict. The struggles by the bourgeoisie to overthrow the old political order were unknowingly serving the need of technological change and economic development.

Introductions to Marx give considerably more detail on his theory of historical materialism (see, for example, Hughes et al. 2003). For the purposes of this text, the key insight or claim (which was disputed by Max Weber) is that law belongs to the superstructure of society, and depends on its

---

Box 2.1 Marx's base-superstructure model

Karl Marx (1818–83) was very much an economic determinist since he believed that everything that happened in society was ultimately caused by the needs of the economy. In his theory of historical materialism, law was part of the superstructure of society and would be transformed when the economic base produced class conflict. He advanced these ideas in the following passage:

> 'In the social production which men carry on they enter into definite relations that are indispensable and independent of their will; these relations of production correspond to a definite stage of development of their material powers of production. The sum total of these relations of productions comprises the economic structure of society – the real foundation, on which rise legal and political superstructures and to which correspond definite forms of social consciousness.
>
> The mode of production of material life conditions the general character of the social, political and spiritual processes of life. It is not the consciousness of men that determines their existence, but, on the contrary, their social existence determines their consciousness. At a certain stage of their development, the material forces of production in society come into conflict with the existing relations of production. ... From forms of development of the forces of production, these relations turn into their fetters.
>
> Then comes the epoch of social revolution. With the change of the economic foundation, the entire immense superstructure is more or less rapidly transformed. In considering such transformations, the distinction should always be made between the material transformation of the economic conditions of production, which can be determined with the precision of natural science, and the legal, political, religious, aesthetic or philosophic ... forms in which men become conscious of this conflict and fight it out'
>
> (Marx 1970, p. iii).

Marx used this theory to explain changes in law that accompanied industrialisation during the eighteenth and early nineteenth centuries. He also predicted that class conflict generated within capitalism would lead to a revolution by the working class, and a further transformation of the superstructure. In some passages, he seems to suggest that law will disappear along with the state after the revolution: this will eventually lead to a utopian society where there will no longer be inequality or social conflict.

---

economic base. The type of law reflects the needs of the economy. Even though Marx's predictions about the self-destruction of capitalism have been proved wrong, the base-superstructure model (Box 2.1) remains useful both in explaining its emergence after the Middle Ages, and also in making us appreciate the distinctive character of law in the modern world.

Durkheim

To understand Durkheim, some historical background is required. He was writing in the late nineteenth and early twentieth centuries at a time when industrialisation and urbanisation had progressed more than in Marx's day. The class conflict that arose during early industrialisation was being managed, partly because labour parties exercised political influence. This was also a period when the state was becoming larger and more powerful in many European countries, and was starting to regulate the economy and society through legislation.

Like all the classical sociologists, Durkheim was a complex, multi-faceted thinker. His response to modernity was generally positive and optimistic. Europe was experiencing a great transition that resulted in temporary problems, such as a rising suicide rate and industrial unrest. Whereas Marx has some resemblance to a dark prophet predicting eventual salvation through necessary trials, Durkheim (1984) writes as a scientist claiming that practical measures can be taken by government to alleviate a temporary crisis. He was a supporter of law and the state as a means of managing the economy. He also believed that the breakdown of traditional communities (what his contemporary Ferdinand Tonnies (1974) called 'gemeinschaft' relations) was necessary, even though those moving to the cities experienced feelings of rootlessness or 'anomie'. Durkheim believed that out of these problems would emerge a new form of civic awareness, suitable for a complex industrial society. The recognition of individual rights was central, and would reduce the tensions generated by urbanisation and industrialisation.

A key concept used by Durkheim in analysing society was social solidarity. He was interested at the most basic level in how societies are formed, as entities that exist separately and independently from individuals. For Durkheim, society consists of shared values or what he termed the 'conscience collective'. Another way of thinking about shared values is that they have a moral or constraining force on members of society (for discussion about his ideas on law and morality, see Cotterrell 2000). Durkheim made a distinction between these informal rules that guide people in their everyday lives, and the laws which are administered by courts. This remains an important sociological insight about the nature of law. Although we often assume that the law must be everywhere, Durkheim recognises that it covers only a limited range of situations. We will see that some European jurists advanced similar arguments, particularly about the limitations of state law as against tradition and customary practice.

Durkheim is, perhaps, best known for advancing the argument that the form of law changed during industrialisation. Durkheim used the term 'mechanical' to describe simpler societies consisting of self-sufficient rural communities, comparing them to gases in which loosely distributed particles did not combine. In these societies, the conscience collective was strong, and there were harsh punishments for blasphemy.

Industrialisation resulted in complex societies with a high division of labour. In these societies, there was 'organic' solidarity requiring considerable co-ordination between groups and individuals. New types of law emerged to meet the needs of the economy, including the law of contract and legislation creating individual rights (Durkheim 1984). Because society was more diverse, criminal law became less punitive, and the prison replaced torture and executions. Despite differing considerably in their understanding of how the modern world would develop, in many respects Marx and Durkheim advanced similar arguments about the relationship between law and society. Each saw law as changing in response to the needs of the economy. Durkheim was particularly far-sighted in predicting that the state would have an increasingly important role in managing the economy, and maintaining economic and social stability.

Weber

Writing at the same time as Durkheim, Max Weber was also centrally pre-occupied with the rise of the strong state. Durkheim's (1984) *The Division of Labour in Society* can be read as expressing the hopes of liberals and progressives during the still insecure Third Republic in France that a strong government would emerge, which could address the problems caused by industrialisation. Weber, by contrast, lived in Germany, a new super-state that, under the leadership of Chancellor Bismarck, sought to overtake England as a world power. In the 40 years before the First World War in 1914, Germany became the first managed economy and welfare state run by large bureaucratic organisations.

Weber's central intellectual problem, like that of Marx and Durkheim, was to explain the immense changes that had taken place in Europe since the eighteenth century. In *The Protestant Ethic and the Spirit of Capitalism* (1930), he argued against the economic determinism of Marx that explained all historical developments as caused by the needs of the economy. Instead, Weber argued that what Marx termed the base and superstructure were inter-dependent. A series of changes in the economy, political system, legal system, religious beliefs and the nature of human organisations together resulted in the modern world. Two organisational changes were the invention of double-entry book-keeping and the introduction of time-keeping in the early factories. Weber argued that these were connected to the religious world view of the first industrialists. They are as much part of capitalism, and central to our civilisation, as the pursuit of profit in buying and selling goods.

Weber's greatest work, *Economy and Society* (1978), is nothing less than a detailed history of how different institutions developed through history.

The underlying theme is that, over time, each sphere of life became more ordered and rationalised. The capitalist limited company run by accountants and managers employing scientific principles replaced the simple enterprises that supplied goods and services in the pre-modern world. Professional bureaucracies replaced the amateurish and ineffective government agencies that had served governments in the past. Weber was also interested in how law had changed in the modern period. His general argument is that discretionary forms of law, such as 'khadi' justice, became rationalised into legal codes. All these developments, happening in different countries in different ways, produced the modern world. Weber, however, differed significantly from Marx and Durkheim in viewing this process with some ambivalence. Like many German intellectuals in the late nineteenth century, he felt that the emerging industrial civilisation was not necessarily superior to previous periods in human history. He remarked, for example, that 'this nullity imagines that it has achieved a level of civilisation never before achieved' (Weber 1930, p. 182). One thing missing was the sense of wonder and spontaneity of the pre-moderns. For all the material comforts achieved through technology, people led empty lives. This dissatisfaction with industrialisation, now fuelled by environmental concerns, is widespread today.

Many law students are still asked to consider the 'English Question' when discussing Weber's work. This arises since the country that industrialised first also apparently had the least modern system of law in Europe. Countries influenced by France had established rational law codes, whereas England still relied on judges making decisions case by case. Even though this remains an interesting question, and makes one wonder whether the British system could have developed differently, it does not really help in understanding Weber's views about law or the modern bureaucratic state. Unlike Durkheim, who saw law positively, and Marx, who believed that it was necessary for capitalism to develop, Weber was darkly pessimistic about the growing power of the state. He was also realistic about how law represents different interest groups, and how the legal profession competes with other occupations for financial rewards and status. Weber saw law itself as primarily a means of legitimating political power. As a sociologist, he did not take the claims made by lawyers or their professional representatives at face value that they were primarily motivated by altruism or public service. Although Weber respected lawyers and government bureaucrats as a necessary part of modern industrial societies, there is nothing celebratory about this hard-headed sociological approach to law.

Sociological jurisprudence

Although the law school primarily views law in instrumental terms as a highly practical discipline concerned with equipping students for professional practice, it has always provided a home for scholars with wide-ranging interests. More than this, law saw itself during the nineteenth and early twentieth centuries as a discipline concerned with understanding society, before the social sciences properly existed as academic subjects. Jurists as much as sociologists were responding to the problems and challenges generated by modernity.

Although jurisprudence is concerned with universal questions about the nature of law, it should not be forgotten that the positions taught on first year legal theory courses today were fashioned during a period of political struggle. The old order or *ancien régime* held onto power in most European countries for most of the nineteenth century and, even when a new democratic society was established, this had to contend with conservative forces seeking to restore the power of the Crown and the Church and defend the power of local landowners or occupational guilds. In this context, theories of natural law (that law reflects god-given principles relating to justice and the social order) were often used to block change: in Marxist terms, natural law was an ideology that served the interest of conservative forces. The positivists in jurisprudence were those who believed that law, particularly in the form of legislation through the democratic state, could be used to engineer a new society. However, there were also political debates within the progressive camp. Many jurists reacted against the growing power of the state, the assault on traditional law and the declining role of the judiciary in relation to the massive government bureaucracies starting to emerge in the most developed countries.

This political reading of nineteenth century jurisprudence has, perhaps, limited value once one starts to study the philosophical arguments in greater detail (although, see Cotterrell 1989). However, it is helpful in understanding what interested the legal thinkers who came to be called the sociological jurists. This section will summarise the ideas of Savigny, Sumner, Petrazycki and Ehrlich. Each advanced a distinctive argument about law and society, which can only be fully appreciated in its own terms. A general theme is that they were reacting against the dominance of legal positivism as a doctrine within law schools, and the growing power of the strong legislative state.

Savigny

Friedrich Karl von Savigny (1779–1861) was a jurist writing in Germany well before it became unified in the late nineteenth century. This was a period when governments across Europe were still responding to the after-shocks caused by the French Revolution. The revolutionary government broke down, and a period of chaos and violence eventually resulted in the rise of a dictator in Napoleon Bonaparte, a war between Britain and France, and the eventual restoration of the French monarchy. Many of the progressive ideas implemented in the early stages of the revolution, and set out in the 1789

Declaration of the Rights of Man, were, however, taken up by Napoleon and imposed by force across Europe. One programme of reform promoted by progressives in the first half of the nineteenth century was for customary laws and judicial precedents across the various small central European states to be incorporated into one law code. This would have become the first step towards unifying Germany, and establishing a strong state. The capacity of governments to collect taxes and redistribute these through the welfare state, which we now take for granted, only became possible through a protracted struggle with local landowners and the church. These institutions, along with regions and occupational associations, also had powers, through customary laws, to collect taxes. A central law code was not, therefore, simply appealing as a modern way of governing: it had many political implications.

Savigny (1975) was a conservative jurist who was opposed to the codification of German law. However, it would be a mistake to see him as a natural law theorist. He believed that law was constructed and arose to serve the needs of particular communities, rather than deriving from universal principles. Like many nineteenth century conservatives, he recognised the need for change, but believed that it should be controlled. Rather than opposing central government, he wanted state law to incorporate and preserve local traditions and customs. These debates are, of course, largely irrelevant to our own times, since we take the existence of a strong state and a unified legal system for granted. It is still the case, however, that legislation to be effective must serve the various communities that constitute society. The remoteness of law, and the oppressive character of impersonal rules and regulations still trouble many legal thinkers today.

Sumner

Writing 50 years later in the New World, the American social theorist William Graham Sumner (1840–1910) came to surprisingly similar conclusions about the potential problems in state law. Sumner had an intellectual interest, as a comparative anthropologist, in what he called 'folkways', the traditions and customs that develop within particular societies (Sumner 1906). Over time some of these became 'mores', moral judgements made within communities. When the state emerged, legislation should emerge out of and respect the folkways and mores. Sumner was a liberal thinker, influenced by the British sociologist Herbert Spencer (an intellectual opponent of Durkheim). He believed that there should be a minimum of state regulation to allow market forces to produce a good society through a process of social evolution. Although not a conservative, he recognised that state law often set itself against the rest of society. As Roger Cotterrell observes:

> Sumner offers a warning about modern forms of law. Legislation can and does diverge from the mores and to the extent that this occurs it

threatens to become divorced from the sources of its authority and potentially ineffective. The legislator, therefore, needs to understand the nature of the complex social ties on which the cohesion of a society depends.

(Cotterrell 1992, p. 20)

Even though he did not have a legal training, Sumner wrote a substantive history of law that continues to influence both legal thinkers and sociologists. Working at the boundaries of law and sociology, he was conscious of the distinction between law and society, not recognised or given much emphasis by positivist jurists, and the limitations of positivist law.

Petrazycki

The Polish jurist Leon Petrazycki (1867–1931) founded a school of sociological jurisprudence that responded to the growth of state law and positivist thought in Eastern Europe. He is significant partly because Adam Podogecki, a sociologist influenced by Petrazycki, made an important contribution in institutionalising sociology of law through, among other things, establishing the Research Committee of Sociology of Law of the International Sociological Association with the structural functionalist American sociologist William Evan in 1962 (Deflem 2008, p. 273). His ideas also became known when the field of sociology of law emerged in the mid-twentieth century through his students Nicholas Timasheff (1886–1970) and Georges Gurvitch (1894–1965) who left Russia after the Bolshevik revolution, and worked in the USA.

Petrazycki developed a complex theory about the origins and nature of law, drawing on the concept of 'impulsion' in which both morality and law were understood as arising out of psychological experiences. Reza Banakar's (2002) summary of these ideas suggests that he had the same concerns about state law imposed over traditional relationships as the other sociological jurists. Petrazycki wrote in *Law and Morality* (1955, p. xvii) that there is much law which 'lies outside the cognisance of the state and does not enjoy positive official recognition and protection, but also much that encounters an attitude of outright hostility on the part of the state and is to be hunted out and eradicated as contrary and antagonistic to the law officially recognized by the state'. This unofficial law existed among traditional groups who still exercised power in Russian society, and had resisted pressures from central government to give up their economic and social privileges since the first attempt to modernise the country by Peter the Great in the seventeenth century. Although some of Petrazycki's ideas are, perhaps, only of historical interest, the central distinction made between 'intuitive' and state law remains relevant for those studying law and society in our own times.

Erhlich

The jurist who went furthest in considering the relationship between state law and how people live in different communities is Eugene Ehrlich (1862–1922). He lived in Austria where the disjunction between numerous ethnic groups and a weak central state trying to exert its authority was particularly acute. Ehrlich contrasted the 'living law', or the norms and rules that operated in different areas of social life, to the laws administered through the courts. He was not, however, thinking only of ethnic or religious groups that were seeking to maintain traditional practices or privileges. Instead, Ehrlich argued that every human activity is governed by informal rules and norms that have nothing to do with formal law. He made the powerful point that ordinary members of society rarely consult lawyers in their everyday lives. People get married and have children, engage in commerce and even settle disputes, without needing lawyers and the courts. All kinds of organisations, including universities, operate by creating their own rules and regulations which exist outside the legal system. Moreover, when lawyers do become involved, this is usually perceived as intrusive and time-consuming: it means that normal social relations have broken down.

If state law is relatively unimportant, what then holds society together? Erhlich (1936) advanced the provocative view, certainly within jurisprudence, that it was more or less self-organising. Although lawyers tend to assume that social life would break down without formal legal rules, Ehrlich believed that there was no need for criminal law or family law. The informal sanctions within communities had worked perfectly well on their own, and could even be harmed or weakened by attempting to regulate through a centralised legal system. It is not entirely clear from the secondary literature whether Erhlich was concerned about the rise of the state, perhaps in the same way as Tonnies or Weber in sociology. He was, however, critical towards positivist jurisprudence for exaggerating the importance and reach of state law. This view remains in the law school to this day: the view that law regulates all areas of human life, and can become relevant at any time. By contrast, Ehrlich and the other sociological jurists believe that there is more to society than law, and that legal education should recognise this.

The American realist tradition

Although they arose in different historical and institutional contexts, the classical thinkers whose ideas have been briefly summarised in this chapter were all concerned with responding to modernity and, in the case of the sociological jurists, the implications for law of the modern state. This also provides a way of understanding the early twentieth-century American tradition in sociological jurisprudence that became known as legal realism.

It is associated with the American judge Oliver Wendell Holmes, the Harvard academic Ezra Pound and the subversive scholarship of Karl Llewellyn and Jerome Frank. This summary will focus on Holmes, Pound and Llewellyn, and on how they understood the distinction between 'law in the books' and 'law in action'.

Holmes

The American intellectual movement known as pragmatism is now largely of historical interest. During the late nineteenth and early twentieth centuries, it was not only intellectually lively and provocative, challenging received ideas from Europe with a genuinely new approach to conceptualising society, but it was also politically radical. This cannot be appreciated without studying American history and politics after the civil war. Even though America was progressive and dynamic by the standards of European countries, there was a feeling among intellectuals that the country needed institutional change. The central principle in pragmatism was that knowledge was produced for practical purposes, rather than reflecting eternal truths. In some respects, this was a version of the debate between natural law theorists and positivists in eighteenth- and nineteenth-century Europe about political and economic changes. America was already a democratic society, but it faced the same challenges from industrialisation, which in the 1930s resulted in a major depression with mass unemployment. There were also distinct problems such as how to absorb millions of migrants from the old world, and give true equality and freedom of opportunity to a large minority of African-Americans who had only recently been freed from slavery in the South.

It was in this context that Oliver Wendell Holmes (1841–1935), an academic and Supreme Court judge, argued against legal formalism, the doctrine that law can only be understood as a system of rules with its own internal logic and procedures. During the nineteenth century, this informed teaching in law schools, and even today the curriculum often assumes that law is primarily a system of rules. Law students are not usually asked to consider how laws arose in a wider context, or the purposes of legislation. Formalism is also a way of promoting a conservative approach to law-making. Most Supreme Court judges believed that the judge should be guided by principles internal to law, and portrayed this as a scientific and rational process. Holmes (1923) argued that judges should draw on their own views on how society should develop. This implied that the whole law school curriculum should change (in our terms it should become socio-legal or contextual), and that judges should have a more political role.

Pound

Roscoe Pound (1870–1964) is significant for developing this new approach to law into a systematic theory. Pound invented the term 'sociological jurisprudence' as a practical part of legal education that would ensure what lawyers and judges thought about the social effects and purposes of law. He encouraged lawyers to study these effects historically with a view to making more effective laws. As an early member of the consensus tradition (Chapter 3), he saw the central purpose of law as maintaining social control, through, among other things, promoting shared values. Unlike Sumner or Ehrlich, he was not concerned about the relationship between law and morality, or in how there can be tensions between established traditions or customs and formal law administered through the state. He did, however, identify a similar problem *within* the legal system. This was the distinction between 'law in the books' and 'law in action' (Pound 1931). By this, he was referring to the fact that reformist judges, such as Holmes who drew on the new social sciences in researching his judgements, were often ahead of the law taught in law schools. The law was more creative and dynamic than the system of precedents and procedures that lawyers were taught to respect.

Llewellyn

The most powerful critique of legal formalism was made by Karl Llewellyn (1893–1962), the founder of the realist movement in American jurisprudence. The political context for his writings was the Great Depression. President Roosevelt had introduced the New Deal as a programme of reform, but this was blocked for many years by the courts which claimed that they were simply following established rules. Llewellyn (1930), like Pound, wanted to undermine the theoretical basis of this position. However, he did so, not by advancing a general theory, but by looking closely at how judges made decisions.

Llewellyn is the first sociological jurist who promoted the use of social scientific methods in investigating how judges made decisions, and also how social behaviour was affected by regulation. Later researchers in the realist tradition pursued an influential programme of research based on collecting statistics on outcomes and identifying causes in the social background of judges. He also argued for reform in legal education (Box 2.2). Law students should not learn what the law says, but about how society produced and was affected by law. This is implied, if not always put forward as a central argument, by all the sociological jurists. In some respects, they had a political agenda, which could be conservative or progressive in different countries. They were also driven by a scientific desire to make theories of law relevant to what actually happened in wider society and in legal practice. In doing so, they were not seeking to develop a science of society, or respond to the modern world, in the same way as the classical sociologists. They did want to change legal doctrine so that it became more relevant to the practical work of judges and lawyers.

Box 2.2 Llewellyn on the law school

Karl Llewellyn advanced a critical view of legal formalism during the 1930s, arguing that legal theory should address and recognise what actually happened in legal practice. He also argued for changes in the law school curriculum. Law students should not just learn legal rules, but how society works. The following extract is part of an address on 'what law is about' to first-year students (Llewellyn 1965, p. 16). From his words, it is apparent that he expected some resistance, and was going against the grain of legal education at that time:

> It has seemed to some students in the past that they had come to law school to 'learn the law', and that the law was made up of legal rules and nothing more, and that all other matter was irrelevant, was an arbitrary interference with their proper training for their profession. I have been told by some that social science was for social scientists in the graduate school; that what law students wanted was the law. I have met with resentment, sometimes bitter, at the so-called cluttering up of our law school curriculum with so-called non-legal material. If I have made my point just now it should be clear to you that this the language of men who do not see far enough beyond their noses to measure even their own job in life. If I have made my point it should be clear that for most lawyers the job of advocates is half, nay, less than half the job they have to do. Even as advocates, I am prepared to argue, they need, desperately, full knowledge of the facts of the life of the community, against which law must play.

The relevance of the classical tradition

Although the classical thinkers can be understood entirely in the light of their own times, it make sense to consider how they have influenced the development of academic disciplines that exist today. This section will approach this question by considering the continuities between classical and contemporary sociological theory as a response to the modern world. It will also consider how research in the contemporary social sciences has been influenced by the writings of the classical sociologists on method. Finally, it will consider the extent to which contemporary jurisprudence and law and society research builds on the legacy of sociological jurisprudence.

From classical to contemporary sociology

The most popular sociological theorists of the last twenty years have included Anthony Giddens, Pierre Bourdieu, Zygman Bauman, Jurgen Habermas, Niklas Luhmann, Michel Foucault, Manuel Castels and Ulrich Beck. Although they differ significantly, each either started by engaging critically with the classical theorists, or has made their ideas relevant to new audiences. Giddens (1999) and Bauman (2000), in particular, advance an analysis of modernity that has many similarities to those of earlier thinkers, who, it should be remembered, were also writing about globalisation and individualisation during the nineteenth century. Even Michel Foucault, by any standards a brilliantly original critical thinker, drew heavily on both Weber and Durkheim.

Sociology has, of course, developed considerably since the time of the classical theorists and, in some respects, is a bewilderingly diverse discipline. Nevertheless, ideas and concepts from the classical theorists remain highly relevant in understanding the contemporary world. Even if Marx's predictions for the violent collapse of capitalism have not taken place, the framework of ideas that he used to analyse economic inequality is widely used, and not only by sociologists. Similarly, bureaucracy has not developed in entirely the way predicted by Weber. However, bureaucratisation and rationalisation are evident in every sphere of life including universities. My own writing on the growth of quality assurance, and its impact on public sector professionals, was influenced by Weber (Box 2.3). Finally, Durkheim's writings about the problems caused by individualism remain highly relevant. They can, for example, be used to explain cultural developments such as consumerism, plastic surgery, the therapy culture and perhaps also the litigious society. This is not really surprising in that the classical sociologists offered systematic, moral responses to the problems and challenges of modernity. We are still grappling with these problems, so their ideas are still relevant.

Debates about method

Another reason why the classical sociologists are important is that they developed the ideas that have come to inform how social scientists today pursue empirical research. In doing rigorous sociology, it is important to think and reflect on how one produces knowledge. Durkheim made a major contribution, building on the work of his French predecessor Auguste Comte, by establishing sociology as a science that could make objective findings and find causal laws in the same way as physics. One of his famous ideas was the view that sociologists should only study 'social facts' (Durkheim 1966). These were defined as features of society that existed separately from individuals, and could therefore be studied using scientific methods. Durkheim was interested in law, partly because it was a good example of a social fact; something that existed before individuals were born and after they died, and constrained their actions.

Sociology is a debate subject, both as a set of responses to the modern world and also about how one should study human beings as a scientific discipline. It should, therefore, come as no surprise that Weber was opposed to the view that sociology should aspire to be like physics. Instead, he advanced the view in *Economy and Society* (1978) that it should be

---

Box 2.3 Weber on regulation

Regulation is a large area of enquiry within socio-legal research, public administration and political science (see, for example, the journal *Law and Policy*). Much of this literature accepts the need for regulation, while acknowledging that it sometimes creates problems. From a sociological perspective, regulation raises wider questions about the rise of the state in the modern world, and the rationalisation of social and cultural life. Max Weber is one of a number of sociological theorists, including Michel Foucault (1977), who have written critically about these developments. Weber (1968, p. iii) believed that 'rational calculation reduces every worker to a cog in this bureaucratic machine'. He also argued that employing scientific methods of calculation reduced the quality of human existence.

From this perspective, the growth of regulation is always accompanied by the rise of bureaucracy. Managers and administrators are required to supervise areas of social life that were previously governed by their own internal rules. A contemporary example is the rise of quality assurance as a field of management in public sector institutions such as schools, hospitals and universities. Max Travers (2007) shows how the legal powers of quality assurers, and the system of inspectorates that report on the public sector in the United Kingdom, come from central government. However, quality assurance also results from new varieties of scientific management being taken up and implemented by public sector managers. These include procedures that quickly have become a taken-for-granted feature of organisational life such as feedback forms and staff performance appraisals.

For the modernist, these are rational measures that improve quality. However, from a Weberian viewpoint they simply create bureaucracy, and may even damage institutions by encouraging professionals working in schools or hospitals to meet centrally driven targets (Power 1997). The sociological jurists expressed similar ideas about the possible dangers of over-regulation, although they believed that the excesses could be avoided if law-makers recognised the dangers.

---

concerned with meaning and interpretation. This, however, does not exhaust sociological views on method, since Marx offers a different way of conducting research to either Durkheim or Weber. Although he did not set this out explicitly in his writings, later critical scholars, from Theodor Adorno (1973) to Roy Bhaskar (1979), have argued that one cannot make sense of social facts without a realist view of the underlying dialectical processes involved in the development of capitalism.

Durkheim was the only classical sociologist who conducted extensive empirical research, and his study *Suicide* (1951) demonstrated the power of comparative statistical analysis. It was, however, only really in the 1950s and 1960s that American sociologists developed the techniques that are used today in investigating society. There are large literatures about quantitative and qualititative methods, each of which have been assisted by technological developments such as the personal computer and the video-camera. This book does not seek to explain or demonstrate how these many techniques can be used in studying law. It is, however, important to recognise that the methods used by sociologists are informed by distinctive assumptions. In simple terms, a positivist influenced by Durkheim, an interpretivist influenced by Weber and a critical theorist influenced by Marx, will understand data collection and analysis differently, whatever method is used. This is why the classical sociologists are still relevant when doing research with a scientific purpose.

The legacy of sociological jurisprudence

In some respects, the sociological jurists have less influence on law and society studies today than the classical sociologists. There have been few contemporary jurists who have expressed similar concerns about the growth of the state, or sought to provide an understanding of law that addresses what happens in practice. One candidate might be Roger Cotterrell (1995), who writes about the relationship between law and community. Critical legal theory admittedly flourished for a time during the 1970s but this drew its inspiration from Marx, who understood society in very different terms to Pound or Erhlich. The sociological jurists are largely forgotten, and do not seem relevant to contemporary political concerns.

Some commentators have argued, more positively, that the interdisciplinary law and society movement, which was founded by lawyers and sociologists in the 1960s, is the contemporary heir to sociological jurisprudence (Garth and Sterling 1998). The law and society movement partly developed because the legal realists took empirical research seriously as part of their commitment to develop a legal theory that addressed or recognised the actual nature of legal practice. Although law school academics started with an interest in quantitative methods, it was natural that they should seek to develop links with social scientists in various disciplines. Since the legal realists were influenced by Pound, who read widely in legal and social theory, one can argue that the law and society movement developed from classical sociological jurisprudence.

Alan Hunt (2006) has argued that the problem with law and society research today is that it does not sufficiently draw on or engage with the classical tradition. It has become empiricist, and serves the needs of the state, rather than treating the state as a central problem. Consider, for example, his complaint about the neglect of Georges Gurvitch, a sociological jurist whose ideas have not been reviewed in this chapter:

> No school applauds his contributions; few commemorative plaques in the form of footnotes in scholarly works record his achievements.

Yet the very causes which underlay the rapidity of his passage into obscurity are the same that mark the theoretical frailty of modern sociology of law.

(Hunt 2006, p. 159)

A sociologist might argue that this presents rather too positive a view of classical jurisprudence, given that Gurvitch, like the other sociological jurists discussed in this chapter, never really addressed the nature of modernity to the same extent as the classical sociologists. One criticism might be that the sociological jurists all belonged to what in sociology would be described as the consensus tradition (see Chapter 3) or had an empiricist view of research as serving government policy. Another would be that, with the exception of Petrazycki, none of the sociological jurists was interested in the development of sociological method or in conducting empirical research. Despite these deficiencies, the sociological jurists did ask critical questions about the relationship between law and society, in a more direct and pointed way than the classical sociologists who were not centrally concerned with law.

Questions

1 'A central issue during the 19th century was the rise of the regulatory state'. Discuss.
2 Why did Marx believe that law represented the interests of the bourgeoisie?
3 How did European jurists in the early twentieth century understand the relationship between law and society?
4 How did Durkheim understand the relationship between law and morality?
5 What do you understand by the distinction between sociological jurisprudence and classical sociology of law?

Further reading

There are many introductory texts that introduce the classical sociologists. Two accessible introductions are Cuff, Sharrock and Francis' *Perspectives in Sociology* (Routledge, London 2006) and Ritzer's *Classical Sociological Theory* (McGraw-Hill, New York 2007). For more depth, try Hughes, Sharrock and Martin's *Understanding Classical Sociological Theory* (Sage, London 2003). Sutton's *Law/Society* (Pine Forge Press, Thousand Oaks, California 2001) provides a thorough study of Marx, Durkheim and Weber's ideas on law in the context of their own times.

For the sociological jurists, the best places to start are Cotterrell's *The Sociology of Law: An Introduction* (Butterworths, London 1992), and Deflem's *The Sociology of Law: Visions of a Scholarly Tradition* (Cambridge University Press, Cambridge 2008). Trevino's *Classic Writings in Law and Society* (Transaction, New Jersey 2006) contains useful essays on the various thinkers. For some general arguments, Hunt's *The Sociological Movement in Law* (Macmillan,

London 1978) offers an interpretation of how sociology of law developed. Garth and Sterling's paper 'From Legal Realism to Law and Society' (*Law and Society Review*, Vol. 32, No. 2, pp. 409–72) discusses the origins of the law and society movement and continuities with sociological jurisprudence. There is a large scholarly literature about particular theorists

Chapter 3

The consensus tradition

Parsons and structural-functionalism	42
The problem of order	43
The social system	44
Parsons on the legal profession	45
The relationship between law and other sub-systems	46
A darker version: autopoesis theory	49
Luhmann as a systems theorist	51
An evolutionary view	51
Law as an autopoetic system	52
Institutionalism	54
Old and new institutionalisms	55
Organisations and their legal environment	57
The consensus tradition and method	59
Measuring the effectiveness of law	59
The normative/positivist debate	60
Assessing systems theory	60
The charge of conservatism	60
An idealised view of law?	61
Questions	62
Further reading	63
Boxes 3.1 Lawyers and social control	47
3.2 The effectiveness of law	50
3.3 The relationship between law and politics	54

The consensus tradition is a general term for a large number of traditions that have been, and remain, influential across the human sciences. The central assumption is that society can be understood as a biological organism, or in some versions a cybernetic entity, held together by shared values. Each social institution has a purpose or function in maintaining social order and in transmitting and maintaining the shared values. Nineteenth-century theorists in sociology include Comte, who also wrote about biology as a new science, and Durkheim, who each developed the view that society had a separate existence and evolved more or less harmoniously from simple beginnings into a complex organism over time. In anthropology, Malinowski saw primitive societies in similar terms with institutions such as the family and legal system maintaining traditional customs and values. In sociological jurisprudence, both Pound and Llewellyn understood law in terms of its functions for society as a whole. Pound saw the main function of law as social control, although this was broadly conceived in terms of transmitting values and providing a framework for resolving disputes, and not just as a means of punishing deviance. Llewellyn, although criticised by Pound (1931) for just focusing on judicial work rather than on the historical evolution of society as a whole, was also a functionalist. He identified 'law jobs' that a society required to be performed for it to operate effectively (Llewellyn and Hoebel 1941).

The central assumption of the consensus tradition is that, in any society, there are strongly held, shared values. This implies that social conflict, whether this means crime or race riots, or the panic of a stock market crash, is both unusual (a temporary episode when order breaks down) and undesirable. The objective of governments should be to combat crime and deviant behaviour, and in the case of political or economic unrest keep the system working for the collective good. By contrast, the approaches reviewed in Chapter 4 see disorder, and even many types of crime, as healthy. They are understood as attempts to resist dominant economic groups, and create a society based on different values and objectives.

This chapter will introduce the assumptions of the consensus tradition, focusing on the ideas of the American sociologist Talcott Parsons between the 1930s and 1950s. His theory of structural functionalism sought to explain systematically how individuals act in accordance with the needs of society. It also provides an analytical framework for understanding the relationship between social institutions, including the legal system. Parsons had the optimistic view that society would become more open and tolerant as the economy developed, and that government could lead this process through progressive legislation.

The rest of the chapter will examine two interesting variants of the structural-functionalist tradition, influenced by Parsons. The first is autopoesis theory which was developed in Germany by Niklas Luhmann (1985). This offers a darker view of society than structural-functionalism through suggesting that institutions are only loosely integrated, and do not work together harmoniously. From this perspective, we should not expect to achieve change in attitudes or behaviour through legislative programmes. The second is a research tradition known as 'institutionalism'. Philip Selznik (1949) developed what is now termed 'old institutionalism', after studying with Robert Merton, a student and associate of Parsons. 'New institutionalism' is a more recent intellectual movement within organisational theory. Although critical towards Parsons and giving a greater role to human agency in responding to structural constraints, it has a similar interest in the relationship between organisations and their wider environment. These traditions in American social science are more optimistic than autopoesis theory. They portray liberal values as becoming institutionalised through society, although not without tensions and obstacles in a similar way to structural-functionalism.

The chapter then considers how researchers in these traditions pursue empirical research and their understanding of method. Although matters are more complicated in the case of new institutionalism, it will be suggested that they mostly have a positivist understanding of method modelled on natural science. The challenge for these researchers is to measure the effectiveness of law, and they often use quantitative methods to test hypotheses within a theoretical model that sees society as held together by shared values. Within this tradition, there is room for researchers to employ a variety of methods, and there have also been some lively debates about whether sociology of law should be an applied or pure science. The chapter ends by reviewing two related criticisms of the consensus tradition: the first that it is rather conservative politically, and the second that it offers an idealised view of social institutions.

Parsons and structural-functionalism

Although politically out of fashion, Talcott Parsons remains the best known and influential sociological theorist of the twentieth century. The amount of criticism generated over his ideas illustrates that there are deep political divisions within sociology, to an even greater extent than within legal thought. Critics have portrayed Parsons as a conservative who opposed the progressive changes that took place during the 1960s, who sided with the establishment, and who did not recognise class and inequality as a political issue. These criticisms are, arguably, simplistic because, like Durkheim, he had liberal political views and believed that the state should regulate the economy and promote social change. Nevertheless, Parsons was a great admirer of institutions like the police and courts, and occupational groups such as lawyers, teachers, those working in business, scientists and politicians. He saw sociologists as a professional group whose scientific expertise could be used to assist society to run smoothly. Sociologists in this tradition during the 1950s even argued, unashamedly, that economic inequality benefits society (Davis and Moore 1945) because it motivates achievement. America was presented as a model for the whole world: a successful society that demonstrated the benefits of capitalism and democracy.

From a different perspective, Parsons offers an unusually systematic scientific theory that seeks to explain the stability of society. He started by considering the problem of order, and this led him to consider the relationship between the individual and society. He then developed an analytic scheme for understanding society as a social system, in a way that made it possible to analyse the relationship between institutions. Parsons was particularly interested in the legal system, and received a warm reception in law schools. His ideas seem naturally to mesh with sociological jurists such as Sumner, Pound and Llewellyn, and even with Ehrlich since he argued that, to be effective, law had to reflect moral values. Parsons' students and associates in studying the relationship between different sub-systems wrote a great deal on law, not least on the difficulties facing legislators who wished to change attitudes and behaviour.

The problem of order

Like many sociological theorists, Parsons was interested in the orderly nature of society. Writing after the violent upheavals and conflicts following the 1789 French Revolution, Auguste Comte (1975) had argued for the establishment of sociology as a new science that could assist governments in helping society to evolve, without returning to the disorder and anarchy of the revolutionary period. Sixty years later, Durkheim (1966) offered similar advice to governments about the many economic and social problems caused by industrialisation. Social pathologies during a time of change were inevitable. However, over time these would disappear as new collective values emerged that would enable individuals to adjust.

As a scientist, Parsons went further than his predecessors in thinking about the mechanisms that produced orderly societies. In reviewing a number of nineteenth-century theorists, including Durkheim and Weber, but not Marx, in *The Structure of Social Action* (1937), he arrived at the view that external force or coercion, or even the popular notion of a social contract, could not account for social stability. More fundamentally, the seventeenth-century political theorist Thomas Hobbes (1996), and later utilitarian thinkers, had been mistaken in seeing society in terms of individuals pursuing their selfish interests. Instead, Parsons, like Durkheim, argued that individuals were already part of society before the state or law regulated their actions. The basic building block of society was the 'unit act' in which the individual was already shaped through socialisation. The choices that people make, and the goals they pursue, came from shared norms and values acquired from other members of society.

The social system

In understanding human societies, Parsons (1951) later developed an analytical model based on the idea that any society or any part of a society could be understood as a social system. The concept of a system comes from biology, although in his later writings he used the metaphor of a cybernetic system. The theory as a whole is abstract and complex, since Parsons also had the grand ambition of combining the human sciences, including sociology, biology and psychology into a general theory of action. These could all be conceptualised as systems, and used to analyse different levels of society, including small and large organisations. A social system could, for example, be a particular person, a family, a small law firm, a university or the large, differentiated institutions that constitute society such as the legal system or the economy. Moreover, for analytical purposes Parsons saw the cultural system (central to his thinking as the source of shared values) and the social system as separate, even though culture is maintained and reproduced through social institutions.

A central idea in structural-functionalism is that any system maintains itself in four ways:

- Adaption: It adapts to its environment, through extracting resources necessary for survival.
- Goal attainment: It sets itself goals and achieves these.
- Integration: It coordinates the different elements constituting the system in pursuit of these goals.
- Latency (also termed pattern maintenance): It transmits the shared values necessary for maintaining the system.

Any organisation can be evaluated, in terms of how well it performs these functions. Parsons is, however, best known for using the AGIL scheme to analyse American society during the 1950s. The economy (A), political system (G), legal system (I) and fiduciary system (L) were conceptualised as sub-systems that performed vital functions for the whole.

The most important sub-system in Parsons' theory was the fiduciary system which maintained shared values. The central processes that allowed society to reproduce itself happened during childhood in the family and through education. Parsons' theory of socialisation drew selectively on Freudian ideas in psychology to explain how norms and values were internalised, and reinforced through approval and disapproval expressed in everyday situations. Another vital social institution for the healthy functioning of society was the economy and, in a similar way to Durkheim, Parsons recognised that this evolved and became more complex over time, forcing changes in other social institutions. A third sub-system required for society to respond to challenges in its external environment was government. In the same way as Comte and Durkheim, and many applied fields in social science today, Parsons saw sociology as serving public agencies that represented everyone in a democracy.

The fourth sub-system required for any advanced society to function smoothly was law, understood as a system of formal rules guiding social behaviour. This was, however, only one sub-system, and analytically separate from the norms and values transmitted through the fiduciary system. Like the sociological jurists reviewed in Chapter 2, Parsons saw law and morality as separate. Law was an instrument that could be used to change moral values, but this was not always effective. It was also needed to combat deviance and crime, but only when the fiduciary system failed to transmit shared values.

Parsons on the legal profession

For Parsons, the main purpose of law was to co-ordinate the many different institutions and organisations in society, which was especially important as this became more complex. One can see here some similarities to Durkheim's (1984) interest in law as providing a framework for social relations in a complex society based on a capitalist economy, and respect for individual rights, steered by an enlightened state. In contrast to some sociological jurists, Parsons was an admirer of government, and the growth of regulation. Nor did he see the purpose of law principally in terms of coercion or social control. Instead, the workings of the courts in applying and interpreting law were viewed as an integrative mechanism, co-ordinating the actions of individuals and relationship between institutions. The evolution of modern, industrialised societies required a larger interventionist state, and more law.

Parsons belongs to a tradition in social science, going back to Comte, that has viewed government, law and the professions as important occupations that deserve respect. Nevertheless, he retained some distance as a scientist from the particular purposes and concerns of different professional groups. Unlike many in the policy sciences today, he did not see academic research as a means of improving government or the provision of legal services. Instead, he wanted politicians, bureaucrats, lawyers, businessmen and others to look beyond the problems and conflicts in their own fields, and to appreciate that they were living in the best possible society. As one ex-student at Harvard put it, you learnt from his lectures that America was getting better during the 1950s 'every day and in every way' (Mayhew 1982, p. 55).

A good example of how Parsons presented this optimistic view to lawyers can be found in a (1954) lecture titled 'A lawyer looks at the legal profession' given at a conference of lawyers and social scientists held at Harvard University. This began by stating what perhaps many social scientists should acknowledge when speaking to a legal audience:

> As a sociologist I am in no sense an expert in the law or the affairs of the legal profession. Worse than that, even from my own professional

vantage point I have never made any special study of the law or of lawyers. ... What I can provide ... is only the kind of perspective an outsider is capable of, not the intimate knowledge that a direct student or participant would have.

(Parsons 1954, p. 370)

After this disarming start, Parsons went on to identify how law performed a number of functions that lawyers themselves did not appreciate because they were not sociologists. Lawyers were presented as technical experts who operate as a 'powerful intermediate mechanism ... between the political organs which carry ultimate legal authority ... and the actual implementation of legal control of ... social processes' (Parsons 1954, pp. 373–4). They were both part of political authority of the state, but also the independent trustees of a 'cultural tradition'. Legal practice involved having to deal with 'what are very often far from easy questions' (Parsons 1954, p. 375). It also required managing conflicting pressures from clients and their obligations under law.

Parsons explained some well-known failings of lawyers as arising from these pressures. One was the temptation to yield to 'financial temptations and pressures from clients'. Another was the practice of many lawyers to retreat into formalism, the tendency 'to exaggerate the importance of being formally 'correct' down to the last detail'. Characteristically, Parsons argued that the cultural stereotype of the lawyer who is obsessed with the detail of the law, and unable to think in broader terms about practical solutions was not 'simply a result of certain types of people 'happening' to become lawyers, but grew out of the situation in which lawyers as a group were placed' (Parsons 1954, p. 377).

Perhaps the most powerful message of the lecture is that lawyers were agents of social control (Box 3.1). Every time they persuaded a client to settle in a dispute, or put pressure on a defendant to accept a plea-bargain, they were unknowingly helping to maintain social order. This, however, continually placed them 'in situations of strain' (Parsons 1954, p. 382) and resulted in professional deviance. One can see here that Parsons recognised the existence of different forms of deviance, including professional misconduct. However, he viewed this benignly as necessary for the healthy functioning of society.

The relationship between law and other sub-systems

The analytic value of the AGIL model of society is that it allows one to think about the relationship between different social institutions explicitly and systematically. As we have seen, sociological jurists such as Pound have always been interested in the impact of law and society, often for practical purposes as much as scientific curiosity. As the state grew during the 1940s

---

Box 3.1 Lawyers and social control

As a consensus theorist, Talcott Parsons saw law as functioning to maintain and reproduce a stable social order. This was not only achieved through the police and criminal law, but also in the everyday dealings of lawyers with clients in civil disputes. In the following passage, he compliments lawyers and other professionals for unknowingly performing this important 'latent function' in their everyday work. Part of legal work involves 'cooling off' clients by persuading them to settle in civil cases, or to accept their guilt when charged with criminal offences if the weight of evidence is against them:

> The professions in this sense may, sociologically, be regarded as what we call 'mechanisms of social control'. They either, like the teaching profession, help or 'socialise' the young, or bring them back into accord when they have deviated, like the medical profession. The legal profession may be presumed to do this but also two other things, first to forestall deviance by advising the client in ways which will keep him better in line, and also 'cooling him off' in many cases and, second, if it comes to a serious case, implementing the procedure by which a socially sanctioned decision about the status of the client is arrived at, in the dramatic cases of the criminal law, the determination of whether he is innocent or guilty of a crime.
>
> (Parsons 1954, p. 384)

---

and 1950s, research on the effectiveness of legislation in effecting social change became a staple part of law and society scholarship. Much of this did not need structural functionalism for scientific legitimation. However, it was natural for social scientists and lawyers to work together, and employ a similar framework, in analysing the impact of law.

Students and associates of Parsons who analysed law and social change include Harry Bredemeier (1962) and William Evan (1980). Bredemeier illustrates how Parsons' approach to understanding the relationships between sub-systems can be refined through employing a cybernetic rather than a biological metaphor. Law was conceptualised as having an impact on other social institutions, but in turn these influenced law through a feed back loop. To complicate the model, there could be both positive and negative feedback loops in any relationship. This enabled society to be represented as a complex, highly abstract set of exchanges that could be measured and analysed by the sociologist.

Functionalist analysts received government funding to measure the impact of law and determine how new programmes could be made effective. William Evan identified seven conditions relevant to legislation on school desegregation which illustrates how functionalists gave practical advice to governments. The first was that 'the source of the new law be authoritative and prestigeful' (Evan 1980, p. 557). He contrasted legislation made by representative democracies with reforms introduced by administrative action and through the courts. This was relevant at the time in that the US Supreme Court had unsuccessfully sought to influence behaviour through interpreting the Constitution. A decision in 1954 supporting the de-segregation of schooling, although controversial, made it easier for Congress to legislate during the 1960s.

Evan's second condition was that 'the rationale of a new law clarify its continuity and compatibility with existing institutionalised values' (Evan 1980, p. 558). The Thirteenth and Fourteenth Amendments to the Constitution already established equal treatment under the law. This meant that the courts and legislature could draw on this cultural authority and 'that the enforcement agents must themselves be committed to the behavior required by the law' (Evan 1980, p. 559). This cautious approach to promoting change has, in fact, some similarities to Comte's advice to the French government after the upheavals of the French Revolutionary period. Comte would have agreed with the third condition, which argues that legislation will be successful where there is some 'model or reference group' that can illustrate that similar measures have already worked. Evan argued that, since desegregation had worked in the armed services, law-makers would know that it was possible to overcome resistance against school desegregation. This gives sociologists a role in policy making through their expertise in understanding the social conditions for effective legislation.

The remaining conditions all related to enforcement. To satisfy the fourth condition, Evan argued that a successful law should be implemented quickly to minimise 'the chances for the growth of organized or unorganized resistance to the projected legal change' (Evan 1980. p. 559). It was also important, as a fifth condition, that 'the enforcement agents must themselves be committed to the behavior required by the law, even if not the values implicit in it' (Evan 1980, p. 559). Evan gave the example of the Prohibition Amendment that sought to make the manufacture and selling of alcohol illegal during the 1930s. Desegregation posed similar problems in that police officers, even though not subject to corruption by organised crime, may have been torn between their commitment to uphold the law and their private views on segregation.

The sixth condition for effectiveness was that there should be positive rewards that follow from compliance, and not just negative sanctions. Evan suggests that this had already been demonstrated by social scientists:

> Legal sanctions are almost invariably negative in character, e.g. fines and/or imprisonment. As the severity of the punishment increases, compliance does not necessarily increase. Severe punishment often affords people the opportunity to neutralize any guilt experienced for their wrong-doing with what feels like justified resentment against punishment.

To encourage the learning of a new pattern of behavior and a new attitude, some positive reinforcement is required, as learning theorists have
found experimentally. We would speculate that as the proportion of
potential resistance to a new law increases, the need for including some
positive sanctions or rewards for compliance also increases.

(Evan 1980, p. 559)

Finally, Evan suggested that as a seventh condition, those who might
potentially benefit need an effective means of enforcing their rights. He
noted that public and private organisations had 'infinitely greater' resources
than individuals. Those affected by segregation should, therefore, receive
'the aid of a public organisation, such as an administrative agency charged
with enforcement of the law' (Evan 1980, p. 560). In this way, law and government grew together during the 1960s in establishing new rights and
making it possible to obtain remedies.

Although each of these conditions or recommendations might seem obvious, they provided scientific legitimation for American governments that
saw legislation as a means of changing values and behaviour, particularly
in the Deep South where there was entrenched institutional discrimination.
Evans, like the structural functionalist tradition in general, recognised that
the moral values in society often lag behind the objectives of legislators.
This was true when Savigny, Ehrlich and Sumner were writing about law in
earlier times. It has been particularly true for America during the twentieth
century, in which politicians with liberal views have experienced many failures and set backs in trying to change traditional values and interests.

Sutton's (2001) extensive discussion of legislation surrounding civil
rights also illustrates these difficulties, as well as the opportunities it
afforded for social scientific research informed by consensus assumptions.
We assume today that de-segregation happened quickly, once laws were
introduced, but it took many years to achieve institutional change (Box 3.2).
This can lead to different political responses depending on the historical
circumstances. Savigny and Ehrlich were conservative thinkers opposed to
the growth of the state, or at least to the radical reforms proposed against
traditional interest groups. The structural-functionalists, on the other hand,
supported the objectives of the state during the 1950s and 1960s in introducing liberal reforms, such as anti-discrimination laws, required for a
dynamic capitalist economy. They were mostly optimistic, and believed that
progressive legislation would ultimately change attitudes, and result in a
tolerant, democratic society.

A darker version: autopoesis theory

Structural-functionalism can be situated, historically, at the peak of social
democracy, a political programme that believed in spending public money

---

Box 3.2 The effectiveness of law

John Sutton (2001) has provided a detailed account of how American law was used during the 1950s to combat segregation in schooling. A two-tier system had been established in the southern states since the civil war, and also existed in several northern states, that effectively denied black students an adequate education. The first move to combat this inequality came through the courts with the Supreme Court's landmark decision in *Brown vs. Board of Education of Topeka* (1954). It was held that segregation violated black students' rights under the Fourteenth Amendment to equal treatment under the law. In a related opinion the next year, the Court required school districts to end segregation 'with all deliberate speed'. Sutton shows how, because it required individual plaintiffs to enforce these rights, the law was unenforceable. There was tremendous political opposition from the southern states which argued in their 1956 Southern Manifesto that it was a 'clear abuse of judicial power'.

The 1964 Civil Rights Act was considerably more successful. This made it possible for litigants to take class actions, assisted by new government agencies. However, Sutton argues that a key factor was not the law, but political will. There was a major programme of investment in education, and recalcitrant school boards were offered the incentive of receiving funding in return for ending segregation. At the same time, the government was more committed to taking legal action to ensure compliance. Sutton reports that this combination of stick and carrot was 'stunningly successful', although less so in the northern states for administrative reasons. However, this example should not be taken to mean that legislation is always more effective than decisions by the courts in changing behaviour and attitudes. Sutton concludes that:

> Under the right circumstances, administrative agencies can achieve dramatic results, but enforcement efforts can fade dramatically when the political winds change; courts move more slowly and tentatively and they only have weak capacity to enforce their own mandates, but they tend to be less vulnerable to political pressure.
>
> (Sutton 2001, p. 183)

The implementation of the 1964 Civil Rights Act depended on having a political party in power sympathetic to these social goals. Progress was made under the Johnson administration, but the programme 'stalled' when Nixon became president. During the 1970s, cases brought before the courts were again important in maintaining political pressure on those still resisting desegregation.

---

through the state to stimulate the economy, and establishing trade barriers to protect full-employment. This became discredited, following a sustained economic crisis during the 1970s, and out of resentment at what many perceived to be high-handed, expensive and inefficient bureaucracies. During the 1980s, many Western governments placed their hopes in reducing public spending, and opening up economies to global competition. The pendulum may yet swing back in favour of greater state regulation of the economy following the 2008 financial crisis that has led many governments to nationalise banks.

Nevertheless, the enthusiasm with which governments and academic commentators viewed the state as a mechanism for transforming society between the 1940s and 1960s, now seems naive and misplaced. This offers one way of understanding the ideas of Niklas Luhmann (1985), a German systems theorist who has developed a distinctive theory about the relationship between law and society.

Luhmann as a systems theorist

In a similar way to Parsons, and most theorists who have sought to develop a scientific, logically consistent understanding of society, Luhmann can be demanding for the general reader. There is no equivalent to Parsons' (1954) lecture which was addressed to ordinary members of the legal profession, although this may be because most of his work has not yet been translated for an English readership. Although his ideas have not been particularly influential in the USA, Luhmann should, arguably, be regarded as a major late twentieth century theorist of the same stature as Bourdieu, Habermas or Foucault (see Chapters 4 and 7). They were each, in different ways, responding to a changed political climate in which social democratic governments had become frustrated and disappointed over their inability to manage the economy or steer society through legislation.

Luhmann had studied with Parsons at Harvard in the 1950s, and responded to the changing political and economic climate through developing and revising systems theory. *A Sociological Theory of Law* (1985) offers a systematic attempt to explain the origins of law as a distinct institution with important functions for society, building on insights from the classical sociologists and Parsons. He later modified his ideas, responding to developments in systems theory, and advanced the more pessimistic view that law is an autopoetic system, only loosely integrated with other social institutions.

An evolutionary view

A Sociological Theory of Law bears comparison with Weber's (1978) *Economy and Society* as a detailed account of how law has developed during the modern period. It also draws on Durkheim, Parsons and jurists including Pound, in seeking to explain at a theoretical level the importance of law for all societies. Like these thinkers, he was impressed by the rise of law as a specialist, technical occupation that has become differentiated from other social institutions:

> . . . our functional concept of law makes it clear that law fulfills a necessary function in every meaningfully constituted society and must

therefore always exist. The development of law is not to be understood as the step from the pre-legal to legal forms of societies, but as a gradual differentiation and functional independence of law.

(Luhmann 1985, p. 83)

One part of this evolutionary process was the emergence of separate institutions such as the courts and the legal profession:

To this end, a special order of behaviour develops in the form of process which segregates itself from everyday life with the aid of particular situations, formulae and symbols, places, roles, and finally, even particular norms. It becomes independent, and can therefore be concentrated on legal decision-making, above all on the resolution of normative conflicts.

(Luhmann 1985, p. 111)

One important argument advanced by Luhmann is that the growth of legal rules and the methods of reasoning used in law, what he calls 'positivity', should be taken more seriously by sociologists. Unlike some sociologists and sociological jurists, Luhmann did not see judges being displaced by the administrative state. Nor did he approve of socio-legal research that studied lawyers as an occupational group, or even particular ways in which law was politically interesting, without addressing what he saw as more important theoretical questions relating to the function of law in modern societies. He complained that 'it is exactly in this way that law itself is eliminated as a totality in its complexity . . . and disappears from the sociology of law' (Luhmann 1985, p. 3).

Law as an autopoetic system

During the 1970s, Luhmann became interested in a variety of systems theory developed by a Latin American biologist and social theorist called Humberto Maturana (1981) who has attempted to unify the human sciences through writing about the nature of living systems. In this theory, every system, whether this is a biological organism or a social institution, seeks to thrive and prosper within its environment, to sub-divide and become more complex over time (the meaning of the term autopoesis in biology). Because of this, it can only be loosely integrated with other subsystems, even if this integration is necessary and generally beneficial.

Although this theory has particular implications for understanding the relationship between law and society, it is important to remember that it applies to each and every system. Lawyers can be criticised for developing a technical language that no one else understands, which is taught to law students on courses in black-letter law. Each subject on the law school curriculum can be accused of developing its own specialist terminology and jurisdictional claims, so there is limited communication, and considerable miscommunication, between them. However, the same process of sub-division and the construction of barriers occurs in any field. Politics is its own world, along with the economy, and institutions such as universities and the mass media that constitute the fiduciary system. Autopoesis has particular implications for those who would like a steering role for academics in spreading knowledge. From this perspective, the specialisation of academic life, and its institutionalisation through higher education, prevents it from communicating with wider publics.

Luhmann (1985) views law as a 'normatively closed system', meaning that it has distinctive values and concerns, and a way of communicating within itself, that is closed to other groups and institutions in society. It can, for example, only answer questions in 'binary' terms (whether something is legal or not legal) within its own categories. At the same time, it is a 'cognitively open system' that draws on information supplied from its environment. There is, therefore, integration as understood within Parsons' structural functionalism, but more emphasis on the tensions that can arise between law and other social institutions. Luhmann uses the term 'structural coupling' to characterise these relationships. There are no 'causal relations', such as one finds portrayed in the feedback loops used in cybernetic models. Instead, change in one part of society is understood as an 'irritant' forcing change elsewhere (Box 3.3), often with unpredictable consequences.

A central idea in this re-working of structural-functionalism is that sub-systems are only loosely integrated. Law cannot bring about changes in the rest of society. Moreover, Luhmann tends to emphasise the negative features of law and regulation rather than its role in co-ordination. As the custodian of a cultural tradition, the legal profession is most concerned with maintaining its own autonomy while imposing unnecessary demands on other institutions. Nevertheless, Luhmann does not see either the state or law as being completely dysfunctional; he may simply be offering a realistic corrective to optimistic versions of systems theory in the past. Some have interpreted the theory as being critical towards lawyers for not sufficiently being open to other social institutions and ways of thinking. It can also be read as supporting the professional ideology of lawyers (as custodians of a cultural tradition) against attempts to regulate or remove judicial discretion.

Autopoesis has mainly been advanced as a theoretical position in jurisprudence, rather than informing an empirical programme in sociology of law (although, see King and Piper 1980 and Paterson and Teubner 2005). Luhmann's ideas have, for example, been taken up by the German jurist Geunter Teubner (1993). Roger Cotterrell (1992, p. 168) sees the ideas as supporting the positivist tradition in jurisprudence that law should

---

Box 3.3 The relationship between law and politics

Klaus Ziegert (2002) offers this summary of the relationship between law and the political system, as understood by autopoesis theory:

> Political systems, and above all governments, put pressure on the legal system, through their legislative programmes. These cannot, however, control legal operations. At best, they can motivate legal operations and, at worst, irritate the legal system.... As there is no communication between the political system and the legal system (but only communication in the respective systems), there is no relationship, and certainly not a hierarchical one, between these systems but rather a functional cooperation in which each system controls its own operations... For instance, the 'irritating' political intentions in the legislative programmes (eg. 'tougher law') are subject to legal filtering in the periphery... [through] legal academic debates and doctrinal dissertations and the highly selective operations of legal decision-making in the centre of the legal system. In turn, the 'formalistic' or 'legalistic' application of legal norms in the legal system, and especially in the courts 'irritate' the political system and motivate changes in the legislation or even law reform, and so on.
>
> (Ziegert 2002, p. 69)

According to this passage, the relationship between government and law is by no means harmonious in an advanced industrial society.

---

only be concerned with interpreting rules: 'Justice, moral worth, scientific truth or even economic efficiency are revealed, in this view, as wholly inappropriate criteria for judging the content of modern law'. From a sociological perspective, autopoesis theory can make one think about the relationship between lawyers and other social institutions in concrete terms. It makes visible how problems in different areas of social life are translated into legal categories, and the practical difficulties and 'irritations' experienced when the ordinary citizen has dealings with law.

Institutionalism

Although autopoesis theory has become influential in Europe, the main heir of structural functionalism in the USA is a variety of traditions that have developed in sociology, organisation studies, management and political science known as 'institutionalism'. This is, perhaps, a contentious statement in that proponents of what is called the 'new institutionalism' present themselves as critics of Parsons, not least because they disagree fundamentally with how he understood the relationship between the individual and society (DiMaggio and Powell 1991a). This section will attempt to explain the assumptions informing different varieties of institutionalism, and to identify the similarities and differences to functionalism (and also autopoesis theory). It will also examine how this theory has been used to investigate the relationship between organisations and their legal environment.

Old and new institutionalisms

The term institutionalism has been used to describe a wide range of theories, some with opposing assumptions, which have been advanced within different disciplines. Rational choice traditions are the latest version of utilitarianism, the nineteenth social philosophy that saw society as consisting of individuals seeking to improve their own position through assessing the costs and benefits of their actions. Other traditions are closer to Durkheim and Parsons in arguing that society exists separately from individuals as shared values maintained through social institutions. The field of institutionalism is exciting because it brings together these different ideas to look at the relationship between organisations and institutions (terms used interchangeably by some writers but given technical meanings by others). On the other hand, it can be confusing because there are so many sub-traditions, and an enthusiasm for generating new theories. Philip Selznike (1996, p. 276) has complained of 'an undesirable preoccupation with polarities and polemics' that has interfered 'with a steady, problem-centered approach to the advancement of our understanding'. Such debates are, perhaps, inevitable in an inter-disciplinary field that seeks to promote new and interesting findings to business and government.

One introductory text in political science offers the following summary of what institutionalist approaches have in common:

> The most fundamental point is that scholars can achieve greater analytic leverage by beginning with institutions rather than with individuals. Further, all the approaches point to the role that structure plays in determining behavior, as well as its role in determining the outcomes of political processes. In addition, all the versions of institutionalism argue that institutions create greater regularities in human behavior than would otherwise be found. At a practical level institutions do have the capacity to mold individual behavior and to reduce (but not eliminate) the uncertainty that otherwise dominates much of social life.... Finally, institutions are seen in all but the most extreme conceptualisations as the results of purposive human action, so that the fundamental paradox ... of institutions being formed by human agents yet constraining those same actors arises in all versions of the new institutionalism.
>
> (Peters 1999, p. 141)

The main theorist in what has become known as the 'old' institutionalism is Philip Selznik, who was influenced by Parsons. Selznik was interested in how organisations develop their own culture and values in response to pressures from other organisations, and how this can often have unintended or adverse consequences for their original objectives. His best known study, *TVA and the Grass Roots* (1949), demonstrated how this happened to an agency concerned with environmental protection as groups with opposing interests and values were incorporated in an attempt to create a political consensus. Within the theoretical framework of structural-functionalism, it can be understood as investigating the problems that arise in attempting to change behaviour and values through legislation. However, Selznik looked at how these difficulties arose within an organisation. This led to the interesting general observation that practices and procedures are 'infused by a value beyond the technical requirements of the task at hand' (Selznik 1996, p. 202). In other words, they survive and are vigorously defended long after they have outlived their usefulness.

New institutionalism is the theoretical tradition founded by James March and Johan Olsen in the 1980s and developed by DiMaggio and Powell in the 1990s. It was partly a sociological response to rational choice theories that had always been influential in economics and political science as a means of studying organisations (DiMaggio and Powell 1991a; March and Olsen 1984). Perhaps the main difference to old institutionalism (remembering that older theorists dispute that there are significant differences) is that the new institutionalists placed more emphasis on how individuals and organisations responded to, as against being shaped by, their environment. Nevertheless, one still finds statements that could have been written by Parsons while advancing his concept of the unit act against utilitarianism. According to DiMaggio and Powell (1991a, p. 11), 'this perspective emphasizes the ways in which action is structured and order is made possible by shared systems of rules that both constrain the inclination and capacity of actors to optimize as well as privilege some groups whose interests are secured by prevailing rewards and sanctions'.

To understand what is at issue, it is worth noting that many sociological theories start with either a view of society that emphasises the importance of agency (the ability of social actors to influence their environment) or structure (the constraint on individuals from social institutions or structures). Parsons is a structural theorist because he sees individuals as largely shaped by society with little opportunity to make choices. By contrast, interpretive approaches such as symbolic interactionism and ethnomethodology, reviewed in Chapter 6, place more emphasis on individual agency: on how people actively interpret and construct the world around them. The most popular sociological theories in recent years have sought to combine both approaches. They want us to appreciate that individuals are both shaped and constrained by society, but also that we exercise free will. New institutionalists often draw on ethnomethodology in arguing that the study of organisations has to address how individuals make sense of structural constraints. However, like most sociologists, they tend to favour the structural perspective. Despite apparently embracing ethnomethodology, they are primarily interested in the relationship between organisations, rather than how individuals understand and experience institutional constraints.

New institutionalists have developed some general theories on how organisations are shaped by, or respond to, their environment and tested these through conducting empirical research. The best known is DiMaggio and Powell's (1991b) use of the concept of 'isomorphism' to understand institutional change. Isomorphism had been used in the field of human ecology to describe the 'constraining process that forces one unit in a population to resemble other units that face the same set of environmental conditions' (DiMaggio and Powell 1991b, p. 66). DiMaggio and Powell argued that three 'mechanisms' were at work in organisational change. First, 'coercive isomorphism' results from 'both formal and informal pressures exerted on organisations by other organisations upon which they are dependent and by cultural expectations in the society within which organizations function' (DiMaggio and Powell 1991b, p. 67). Second, 'mimetic isomorphism' occurs when organisations copy other organisations in response to uncertainty. Third, 'normative isomorphism' takes place through professionalisation: this is why management has a similar character in different organisations. From this model, DiMaggio and Powell developed a series of hypotheses and invited researchers to test these in different organisational fields. To give an example, they predicted that 'the greater the extent to which the organizations in a field transact with agencies of the state, the greater the extent of isomorphism in the field as a whole' (DiMaggio and Powell 1991b, p. 76). This process of change is not, however, conceptualised as the top-down internalisation of values as in structural-functionalism, but as an active process in which organisations are shaped by, but also influence, their environment.

Organisations and their legal environment

As Lauren Edelman and Mark Suchman (1997) have noted, many of these ideas are relevant to understanding the relationship between law and society. A central problem raised by classical thinkers such as Ehrlich and Pound is the effectiveness of law in changing existing social practices. They saw organisations and social groups as enjoying some independence from the state: they were well-placed to resist and subvert either judicial activism or government programmes that attempted to protect individual rights. Although more optimistic about the prospects for social change in America, Parsons also recognised that there was a tension or lag between different sub-systems. Selznik recognised that agencies established to counter existing values and practices were often co-opted by vested interests. Similarly, structural-functionalists such as Evans and Breidemeir were not surprised at the slow pace of civil rights legislation during the 1960s and early 1970s. In writing about these issues, they did not, however, focus on the response to law from inside particular organisations.

In the past few decades, civil rights legislation has enjoyed more success in changing behaviour and attitudes across American society. Nevertheless, many organisations have found it possible to protect themselves from close scrutiny by either the courts or regulatory agencies. Edelman and her associates have examined the effect of equal employment legislation on private companies and public agencies, drawing on the new institutionalism as an analytic framework (Edelman, et al. 1993). The researchers found that employers set up their own internal grievance procedures, drawing on the language used in the national statutes. This has happened partly through 'coercive isomorphism' as managers responded to the threat of legal action by providing potential claimants with a speedier, informal remedy. It has also happened through 'normative isomorphism' and 'mimetic isomorphis' as managers introduced procedures that were becoming institutionalised. They also found that 'those organizations that were closest to their institutional environments – whether because of dependence on government contracts or because of higher visibility – responded earlier ... than others' (Suchman and Edelman 1996, p. 924).

One can see from this summary how the new institutionalism offers some useful resources for studying the relationship between law and society through focusing on how organisations respond to external constraints. Whereas the structural-functionalists saw this as a top-down process, there is more room to appreciate how internal processes within companies can shape the development of regulation. Suchman and Edelman (1996) have shown not simply how law is incorporated, and subverted by organisations, but how management ideas and practices are taken into account by judges when making decisions about equal employment:

> At the organizational level of analysis, organizations reciprocally define the law through their practices regarding compliance. Responsive to their cultural environments, organizations often voluntarily seek to comply with legal change. However, the socially constructed nature of legal constraint implies that these effort, themselves, can mold the meaning of the mandate. Courts frequently measure compliance against 'industry standards' or 'business necessity'... and all these yardsticks, in one way or another, embody the institutionalised expectations of the organizations supposedly being regulated.
>
> (Suchman and Edelman 1996, p. 939)

The consensus tradition and method

Although this text will not provide a systematic introduction to either the philosophy of social science or the different data-collection techniques used by sociologists, it is difficult to understand any research tradition without considering these issues. In the case of the consensus tradition, the founders of the tradition, Comte and Durkheim, developed the epistemological position known as positivism. Put simply, this is the view that sociology as a science should become like physics. Its assumptions and methods should be modelled on natural science. It is worth noting, in passing, that other traditions reviewed in this text were founded in sociology in opposition to positivism. Interpretivists (Chapter 6) believe that natural science is an inappropriate model since it does not recognise that humans live in a meaningful world. Critical theorists (Chapter 4) argue that framing research questions in this way cannot address the underlying social processes that really matter. There are also postmodern thinkers (Chapter 7) who seek to question the concept of truth on philosophical grounds. Positivism, by contrast, claims that one can establish the truth, and make objective findings in the form of scientific laws, through conducting empirical research.

Measuring the effectiveness of law

A variety of methods have been used in the consensus tradition, including historical research, ethnographic fieldwork and interview studies. Studies in this tradition by no means always take the form of testing hypotheses or finding causal connections. They often simply involve describing social processes and relating these to the wider view of society afforded by a particular theorist or tradition. This is probably the best way to understand the qualitative research conducted by Philip Selznik or Laura Nader: these studies are informed by the view that society as a whole shapes and influences organisations, even though this is not a smooth or predictable process. It should also be noted, as an aside, that Luhmann was critical towards quantitative methods, favouring the thick description used in the grounded theory tradition in symbolic interactionism (see Chapter 6).

With some exceptions, most researchers in the consensus tradition, particularly in America, have employed quantitative methods within a positivist framework modelled on natural science. A common research design is to measure two variables and identify a causal connection using statistical techniques. The theorist who has employed this methodology in its purest form in law and society studies is Donald Black (1989). He has sought to accumulate general scientific findings about the nature of law through measuring such variables as the severity of punishment. The methodology has been influential across the consensus tradition, and was employed by sociologists associated with Parsons. Because it modelled itself on natural science, a central objective of structural-functionalism was to generate hypotheses that could be tested using the most advanced methods available, and in this way refine and develop systems theory.

The normative/positivist debate

The liveliest debates in social science often result from disagreements about how to pursue rigorous, scientific research. This happens rarely in law and society studies, suggesting that most researchers are seeking to escape from these disciplinary constraints, or perhaps that they share broadly the same assumptions. There are, however, sometimes debates which reveal a great deal about law and society studies as a field. One of these arose within the consensus tradition, when Donald Black (1972) roundly criticised Philip Selznik and his associate Philippe Nonet for not doing scientific research.

This debate echoes an earlier exchange between Pound (1931) and Llewellyn (1931). Although these thinkers opposed legal formalism, they had significantly different hopes for sociological jurisprudence. Pound believed that the objective should be to assist governments in implementing progressive legislation. Llewellyn, on the other hand, wanted to understand the work of judges out of scientific interest. Matters are perhaps more complex in that the legal realists tended to debunk the myth of law as a disinterested and scientific pursuit, whereas Pound was respectful towards the legal establishment. However, the main point of disagreement was whether law and society studies should be a value-free science or seek to advance the researcher's political views. Writing 40 years later, Black criticised Selznik from a positivist perspective for advancing a moral viewpoint, rather than developing sociology as a science. Nonet replied by stating that the pursuit of pure science would result in 'intellectual sterility'. Instead, sociology of law should both describe and evaluate, taking its example from jurisprudence.

Assessing systems theory

During the 1970s and 1980s, sociology textbooks often presented structural-functionalism as a dead tradition. It was roundly criticised by critical theorists for not addressing or even recognising the existence of inequality and power relations. It also came under attack from interpretivists for not adequately addressing meaning, or human agency. These criticisms are worth reviewing since they demonstrate what makes the consensus tradition distinctive as a sociological perspective, and how other traditions reviewed in this book have substantially different assumptions, both about the nature of society and how one should pursue empirical research.

The charge of conservatism

The central objection to structural-functionalism from critics during the 1960s is that it supported capitalism and liberal democracy uncritically.

Popular versions that appeared in textbooks were, invariably, highly supportive towards social institutions such as the police, government, the corporations and the professions. The theory lent itself to conservatives seeking to defend the family against women's liberation and to portraying counter-cultural groups such as drug users, or those with a different life-style, such as homosexuals, as deviant. Structural-functionalists also defended and justified inequality on the grounds that it motivated people to achieve through the educational system, while ignoring or down-playing the power of organised groups to obtain an unfair advantage.

When one reads Parsons himself, it is hard to make this criticism. This is because he has an evolutionary view of society. He saw the values of individualism and democracy as spreading or becoming institutionalised through the social system to support the needs of a dynamic capitalist economy. While accepting the need for some degree of social inequality, he supported taxing the wealthy and companies to make possible the welfare state. Nor was he opposed to social change. In marked contrast to classical thinkers in the consensus tradition, such as Comte and Durkheim, who believed that women were biologically inferior, Parsons (1967) wrote sympathetically about the tensions and conflicts created by these changes. It will also be apparent from this chapter that American researchers influenced by this tradition have whole-heartedly supported civil rights. They have always had the optimistic view that behaviour and values can be changed through legislative programmes.

One could, therefore, argue that there is nothing conservative about structural-functionalism or the consensus tradition in general. This, however, only holds if you believe that there is no alternative to liberal capitalism, and are generally satisfied with the distribution of income, wealth and power in society. Anyone with radical political views will find all the traditions reviewed in this chapter to be deeply conservative. For one thing, they tend to present lawyers, business people and bureaucrats in a positive light. As Alvin Gouldner (1970) noted, in a critical review of American sociology in the early 1970s, the structural-functionalists represented the establishment, and their optimistic studies celebrated the achievements of liberal capitalism both at home and abroad (where America was fighting the Vietnam war). They were incapable of recognising the need for radical, structural change that would combat poverty or help the disadvantaged. The same charge of conservatism can be made against different varieties of the consensus tradition today. They have a natural affinity with those in positions of social and political power, including government officials, business leaders and those many lawyers who serve the needs of public and private sector organisations.

An idealised view of law?

The other main criticism of structural-functionalism advanced during the 1960s was by interpretive sociologists in the symbolic interactionist tradition.

This was partly a criticism of the positivist assumptions informing those many empirical studies that sought to measure causal connections between variables. Herbert Blumer (1969) argued that this missed what was most important about human group life: how individuals made sense of the people and objects in different social worlds. He advocated that sociologists should investigate organisations and institutions using ethnographic methods, and that there was too much emphasis in structural-functionalism in producing abstract theory (see also Mills 1959).

Although there was no direct contact between the two traditions, and many differences between them, this has some similarities to the critique of formal jurisprudence by the legal realists. Interactionists had a similar debunking intent in showing what actually happened inside social institutions that was concealed or idealised within general theories. Perhaps the clearest example can be found in the field of medical sociology. Researchers influenced by Parsons had portrayed the socialisation of medical students as happening smoothly, so that values were internalised that served the needs of society (Merton et al. 1957). Interactionists, by contrast, revealed how young medical students actually learnt medicine.

Similarly, in the case of law, the general message in structural-functionalist studies is that despite occasional deviance lawyers are primarily motivated by altruism and follow legal rules. Interactionist studies, such as Jerome Carlin's *Lawyers on Their Own* (1962), present lawyers in a more realistic and unflattering light by describing practices such as ambulance-chasing. David Sudnow's (1965) ethnomethodological study on plea-bargaining showed that informal rules developed in courts faced with high case-loads that were not recognised in official law books. The structural-functionalists tended to see these practices as examples of professional deviance rather than as part and parcel of organisational life. For their own theoretical and political purposes, they often provide an idealised view of law.

Questions

1 Why are consensus theorists admirers of law and the legal profession?
2 How does Parsons understand the relationship between law and the economy?
3 'Autopoesis theory offers a pessimistic view of the prospects of using law to change society'. Explain and discuss.
4 How does the new institutionalism differ from structural-functionalism in understanding law?
5 'Consensus traditions often rely on quantitative methods to test the hypotheses generated by their models of society'. Explain and discuss.

Further reading

The best way to approach Parsons is through a sociological textbook such as Cuff, Sharrock and Francis' *Perspectives in Sociology* (Routledge, London 2006) or Ritzer's *Sociological Theory* (McGraw-Hill, New York 2007). Trevino's collection *Parsons on Law and the Legal System* (Cambridge Scholars Press, Cambridge 2008) brings together his main writings on law. The most accessible piece is probably the lecture 'A Sociologist Talks to the Legal Profession', also published in Parsons' *Essays in Sociological Theory* (The Free Press, New York 1954, pp. 370-85). For applications of structural-functionalism, see Evan's *Law and Sociology* (The Free Press, New York 1962).

Autopoesis theory is difficult, but Luhmann's own text *A Sociological Theory of Law* (Routledge, London 1985) is worth trying. See also Philippopoulos-Mihalopoulos' *Niklas Luhmann: Law, Justice, Society* (Routledge, London 2009). For an interesting debate between autopoesis as a structural theory and interactionism (reviewed in Chapter 6), see the chapters by Ziegert and Flood in Banakar and Travers' *Theory and Method in Socio-Legal Research* (Hart, Oxford 2005). For some practical applications, see the chapter by Paterson and Teubner in that volume, and King and Piper's *How the Law Thinks about Children* (Gower, Aldershot 1980).

For old institutionalism, Selznik's classic study *TVA and the Grass Roots* (University of California Press, California 1949) is worth consulting. Several statements and some empirical studies by new institutionalists are contained in DiMaggio and Powell's *The New Institutionalism in Organizational Analysis* (University of Chicago Press, Chicago 1991). For discussion of how this framework can be used in law and society studies, see Suchman and Edelman 'Legal-Rational Mythws: Lessons for the New Institutionalism from the Law and Society Tradition' (*Law and Social Inquiry* 1996, Vol. 21, No. 4, pp. 903–41).

Chapter 4

Critical perspectives

The critical tradition and law	69
Developments and debates in Marxism	69
Habermas and legitimation crises	72
Bourdieu and the legal field	74
Law, power and ideology	75
Two central concepts	75
Employment law	76
Same-sex marriage	80
Critical perspectives on the legal profession	82
Sociologists and the legal profession	82
Hierarchy and change within the profession	83
The law school and the reproduction of ideology	85
Assessing critical theory	85
The problem of rights	85
Critical theory after the fall of communism	87
Questions	88
Further reading	88
Boxes 4.1 Ideology and legal consciousness	77
4.2 The 1984 Miners' Strike in Britain	79
4.3 The American courts and same-sex marriage	81
4.4 Heinz and Laumann on the legal profession in Chicago	84

Consider the following criminal hearings that took place recently in Australia. The millionaire businessman, Alan Bond, who had made his fortune through the construction industry, was charged with defrauding his company out of 1.2 billion dollars (Drummond 1996). Represented by one of the top criminal law firms in Sydney, he was jailed for two years, but served his term in relatively comfortable conditions in a minimum security prison. After being released, he returned to live in his luxury home, and became a consultant advising new companies. In the second hearing, an aboriginal defendant was convicted, after pleading guilty to the theft of items in a supermarket worth $35. He was represented by Legal Aid, a public agency providing free legal advice and representation. This defendant was sentenced to probation but, because he could not provide a surety, had already spent a month on remand in an ordinary prison with rather less pleasant conditions. He was homeless when arrested and needed help from social services to find housing after being released.

Each defendant committed a crime and was punished following due legal process and procedure. Nevertheless, there is clearly a difference between their personal and financial circumstances, and how they experienced the law. Moreover, if one takes a larger picture, prisons in Australia and elsewhere are full of people from low-income backgrounds, with low education and often mental health problems. Relatively few millionaires, like Alan Bond, come before the courts.

This disparity of wealth and life chances, well-documented by sociologists, does not pose a moral problem for the theoretical traditions reviewed in Chapter 3. This is because they see society as held together by shared values. One of these values in Western capitalist societies is that everyone should have the opportunity to work hard and make money through selling goods and services in a free market. It is assumed that there will always be some inequality, but that everyone has the opportunity to become wealthy, and the capitalist system will raise living standards for everyone. Another is that theft and violence is frowned upon, and anyone who acts in this way has committed a criminal offence and may be brought before a court and punished. These shared values explain why conflict, in the sense of large-scale civil disturbances or riots, rarely happens.

Structural-functionalists influenced by Parsons did recognise, even in the 1950s, that criminal or deviant behaviour can threaten social order. However, in normal circumstances, these could be explained as an illness or pathology that did not threaten the smooth functioning of society as a whole. There are, of course, hard empirical questions one can ask about this theoretical perspective both historically (consider, for example, the American civil war) or in our own times since there are many regions of the world that have experienced massive upheavals and unrest. Nevertheless, most readers of this book will live in prosperous, orderly societies in which everyone shares common values.

This is not, however, how a critical theorist would understand stable, and generally peaceful, countries such as the United States. From this theoretical perspective, it seems odd that everyone should believe that it is possible to become wealthy, while a large proportion of the population is on welfare or struggling to make a living. The reason why people appear to hold shared values is because they are influenced by what they are told at school or by the media, powerful institutions which are run by members of the economically dominant group. The most disadvantaged groups in society, who are unemployed or work long hours for low wages, have little choice other than to accept the situation, and submit to social workers and other welfare professionals. To put matters starkly, if you make trouble at work by asking for higher wages and conditions, an employer might quite reasonably prefer to hire someone else, and in many circumstances is legally entitled to do so. Far from being characterised by consensus, societies are better understood as a power struggle for advantage. In a stable society, the dominant groups hold and maintain their economic position without difficulty. However, there is always the potential for opposition and, given the right conditions, for a revolutionary movement to emerge that overthrows the existing order.

There have not been revolutions of this kind in recent years, where mass groups demonstrate on the street, and attempt to form a new government, except those that have established capitalist democracies in Eastern Europe and the old Soviet Union in the late 1980s. It is easy to forget, however, that there were a number of revolutions or successful 'liberation' movements in the twentieth century, including in China, Russia, Vietnam and Cuba. The Russian revolution took place in 1917 when industrial workers and peasants, led by a revolutionary party influenced by Marx's ideas, overcame the old regime and established a socialist society in which only the state owned property and controlled the economy. This became the Soviet Union, the second largest country in the world next to China, and a nuclear superpower committed to promoting and supporting revolution in Western countries. The capitalist, democratic societies of Western Europe were defended against invasion and occupation by the NATO military alliance. The Berlin Wall symbolised Europe and the world at this time: there was an economic, military and ideological struggle (in the sense of a war of ideas) between the free world and communist countries.

The Soviet Union collapsed in the late 1980s, after experiencing internal economic and political problems, but also because it ultimately lost this ideological struggle. Today, given the triumph of capitalism as a social and economic system in most countries across the world, there seems little prospect of a revolutionary movement emerging in Western countries that is committed to a socialist re-distribution of income and wealth. This is why Francis Fukuyama (1992) proclaimed at the time that we had reached the end of history. On the other hand, there are still wide disparities in wealth and power across society, and in some countries economic inequality has increased.

There have also been other conflicts and power struggles taking place in society since the 1960s. The sociologist Max Weber had argued in the early twentieth century that these would be more important and consequential than class in mobilising political action. Many movements have emerged that speak on behalf of minority or disadvantaged social groups, such as women, racial and ethnic minorities, homosexuals and the disabled, or about issues such as the environment or the treatment of young people or the elderly. This chapter will introduce these critical perspectives, focusing on how critical theorists understand the role of law in maintaining the dominance of established elites or social values.

The critical tradition and law

Critical theory can become confusing since there are numerous varieties, and many sub-traditions, and they are often combined. The Marxist tradition alone includes all kinds of thinkers and traditions, some of whom have significantly altered Marx's ideas with the aim of making Marxism relevant to their own times (Fine 2002). This section will start by considering a debate within Marxism over the role and importance of law. This is between those who see law and the state as important, against those who place more emphasis on culture in explaining the stability of capitalism. It will also summarise the critical theories of Jurgen Habermas and Pierre Bourdieu and discuss how these thinkers understand law.

Developments and debates in Marxism

Marx's ideas were introduced, in the context of his own times, in Chapter 2. The central problem for Marxist theorists after the death of Marx has been to explain why there has been no working-class revolution. There have been various traditions, but two of the most influential have been the structural Marxism developed in France by Louis Althusser and the humanist Marxism advanced by various thinkers, including the Italian theorist Antonio Gramsci and the Frankfurt School. Broadly speaking, these twentieth century Marxist thinkers became more interested in the superstructure of society than its economic base. Althusser (1984) was most interested in the role of the state, and humanist Marxists in the role of culture in maintaining capitalism. This shaped how they were interested in law.

Structural Marxism

Althusser was an important Marxist theorist during the 1970s, the last decade when Marxism was arguably in good health as a critical theory.

This was partly because European societies were experiencing economic difficulties. Unemployment was rising, governments faced difficulty in maintaining the welfare state, and there was growing industrial unrest, including national strikes by workers in key unions in some European countries. Marxism has always benefited as an intellectual project when capitalism appears to be in trouble, but Althusser was also responsible for the revival in its fortunes through re-fashioning and promoting it as a scientific theory (Althusser 1969). Structural Marxism offered a convincing explanation of why revolution had not taken place as Marx predicted, while still offering hope to those concerned about growing economic inequality.

There has always been a philosophical debate within Marxism between humanists and scientific determinists (Gouldner 1980). Humanists take their inspiration from Marx's early writings when he was influenced by the philsopher G.W.F. Hegel. The central assumption is that human beings have themselves created capitalism, and the conditions of their alienation, but through an act of will could change things. At the centre of society was the human agent, who in theory could exercise free-will. Determinists, on the other hand, took their inspiration from Marx's later writings, and particularly *Capital* (1976), where he claimed to have discovered a science that could predict the future of capitalism. There was little room for free-will in this theory since human history was driven by economic forces, concealed from ordinary people, but understood and amenable to analysis by the Marxist theorist. Althusser is most associated with this second version of Marxism, and claimed to have discovered an 'epistemological break' in Marx's thought where he abandoned his youthful humanism and became a scientist. However, he understood the relationship between the economy and other elements of society, such as law and the state, differently from Marx.

Althusser's version of Marxism was to replace the base-superstructure model (see Chapter 2) with the concept of a society as a system or 'structural whole' in which three elements were in dynamic tension. One of these elements was the economy, which was 'determinant in the last instance'. This retained the central, distinctive feature that makes Marxism a critical theory concerned with social transformation. Over time, conditions would arise in the economy that would lead to a working-class revolution. There were, however, two additional elements, what he called the Repressive State Apparatus and the Ideological State Apparatus (Althusser 1984). The Repressive State Apparatus comprised the organisations and agencies that make up the state, including the police and courts.

Althusser was writing at a time when riot police were used to break up workers' protests, and he viewed law as a coercive force that protected employers and property owners against the working class. However, he placed greater emphasis on the Ideological State Apparatus. This encompassed a variety of institutions, including the family, the educational system and the mass media, which Althusser saw as created by, and serving the interests of the state. In a similar way to Parsons, although with a very different political slant, Althusser saw these institutions as securing consent for capitalism. In Marxist terminology, they promoted capitalist ideology, a set of ideas that benefited the ruling class. Althusser also identified the legal system as part of the Ideological State Apparatus. When an unemployed worker was punished for stealing, perhaps to feed his or her family, the court was not simply exercising force, but also promoting or reproducing the ideological view that everyone is supposedly equal, so it is entirely fair that this individual should be punished. This happened both through what was said in court about criminal responsibility, but also through judges or magistrates never considering the economic forces that cause unemployment or low wages.

Althusser's theory is distinctive in allowing no place for the individual, since we are all products of the Ideological State Apparatus (ISA), which itself is one element in the social whole. It is also distinctive in emphasising the relative autonomy of the ISA and Repressive State Apparatus from the economy, and how within each element or 'practice' there were tensions and contradictions. This allowed Althusser and associates such as Nicos Poulantzas (1978) to analyse actual processes, and the complex relationships, that exist in society in some detail. Instead of simply being a descriptive theory, it was still claimed, however, that tensions and contradictions could build up, and cumulate in such a way that there was a transformation of society as a whole. This kind of analysis eventually became unsatisfying as a means of explaining or predicting how capitalist societies were actually changing during the 1970s. There was also the problem, shared by previous economic determinist versions of Marxism, that there was no need for the activist to do anything: it was simply a matter of waiting for structural forces to work themselves out. Nevertheless, for a relatively long period Althusser's re-shaping of Marxism was highly influential across the social sciences and humanities. Whereas Marx himself was most interested in the economy, structural Marxists wrote a great deal about law and the state.

Humanist or cultural Marxism

Althusser is not the only Marxist thinker to have viewed culture as important. Writing in a prison cell in the first years of the twentieth century, the Italian revolutionary Antonio Gramsci (1971) believed that Marx had under-estimated the capacity of the dominant economic group to influence public opinion. Unlike Althusser, however, Gramsci believed that revolutionaries should not simply sit back and wait for economic discontent to produce class struggle. Instead, they should try to win the war of ideas, and expose the lies promoted by the media and entertainment industry. A key term was that capitalist institutions had secured 'hegemony' through making inequality seem normal and natural, even though it would be possible to organise society differently. This does not mean, however, that Gramsci saw law as unimportant. Rather, in the same way as Althusser, he understood it as a cultural institution, in addition to one that exercises force and power through the police and courts. This means that anyone who exposes the hidden meaning of legal texts, or shows how apparently neutral concepts in legal philosophy really support economic inequality, is engaged in political struggle against capitalism.

The variety of cultural Marxism that has become most influential in universities is the Frankfurt School. This was a group of German thinkers who came to America during the Second World War and became interested in, and horrified by, the success of consumer capitalism. They were more pessimistic about the prospects of a working-class revolution than either Althusser or Gramsci. They also placed even more emphasis on cultural institutions, and in particular advertising and the entertainment or culture industries (Adorno 1973; Marcuse 1964). There is very little in their writings about the economy, law or the state, but instead they were concerned with the nature of consciousness in an advanced, affluent society. They argued that, while we believe we are content, in fact we are alienated and repressed.

It might seem strange in a textbook about law and society to include a tradition in which law and the state are seen as of marginal interest. Nevertheless, it seems important to recognise that the study of culture has always been popular among progressive intellectuals when the prospects for a working-class revolution look remote, which is certainly the case in the developed world today. Cultural Marxism encourages us to examine films and advertisements as cultural products that promote ruling class ideology. The Critical Legal Studies movement that flourished in America during the 1980s adopted this approach in analysing legal texts (see, for example, Unger 1976), and postmodernists, who are often leftists, are also influenced by Gramsci and the Frankfurt School.

Habermas and legitimation crises

Another important critical thinker who has written extensively on law is the German thinker, Jurgen Habermas between the 1960s and 1980s. His ideas are hard to summarise, since Habermas (1984, 1986a) synthesised a wide range of ideas from different theoretical traditions in social science. In some respects, it is a systems theory, like the theories of Parsons and Luhmann reviewed in the previous chapter. However, there is also a strong critical element: it is informed by the belief that an ideal world is possible in which human beings can live better lives guided by reason.

Habermas' contrast between what he called the 'lifeworld' and 'system' has some similarities to Ehrlich's ideas about the living law, discussed in Chapter 2. The lifeworld encompasses how we live our lives through associating with and interacting with others. Habermas suggests that whenever we engage in activities for their own sake, whether in commerce, sport, art or intellectual activities we are participating and reproducing everyday society. By contrast, the system means the activities of government, including the rules and regulations, and many institutions and agencies that have grown up to regulate the lifeworld. In his early work, Habermas (1986b) was highly critical toward the state and law. He argued that the system is governed by a desire to accumulate or maximise efficiency, which is ultimately bad for human beings.

A key idea was that the welfare state had developed as a redistributive mechanism to reduce economic inequality, and address the social problems created by capitalism. However, the state itself had become a problem both because it could not deliver what was promised, and because it created resentment among those dependent on professionals and bureaucratic agencies. This is what Habermas (1986b) called a 'legitimation crisis': widespread discontent with organisations and the political system. He also coined the term 'juridification' to refer to a legal system out of control, so that more and more activities become subject to expensive and burdensome regulation. Like Althusser, Habermas did not believe that these tensions and contradictions would necessarily lead to social transformation. He was, however, interested in the social movements that emerged during the 1970s, such as the Campaign for Nuclear Disarmament, and believed that it was possible to achieve renewal through the political process, and engaging in rational discussion about problems.

In his later work, Habermas (1996) has written positively about law and liberal democracies, and would probably support the slow but steady progress being made in addressing the problem of climate change through international agreements such as the Kyoto Protocol. This illustrates that there is no need for human beings to accept what the Frankfurt School described as 'instrumental reason'. Instead, Habermas believes that through creating democratic spaces where we can engage in rational discussion, it is possible to fashion policies that address collective problems created by capitalism and industrialisation. This optimistic view of capitalism and democracy might seem at some distance from his earlier predictions of a legitimation crisis. Nevertheless, Habermas is still more aware than most of the problems that arise in liberal democracies. He would recognise that well-intentioned attempts to regulate the environment might lead to resentment against excessive bureaucracy and widespread protest, when it becomes clear that international agreements cannot address the underlying problems (which are from a critical perspective caused by capitalism). He, therefore, poses an important set of questions. Is law and regulation the solution to our problems, assuming we can establish an effective democracy? Or is it a problem in itself: and, if so, Is it possible to create a society where there is a smaller state and less law?

Bourdieu and the legal field

Another critical theorist who has written a great deal about law is the French sociologist, Pierre Bourdieu (1930–2002). One way to understand his project is that it combines ideas from Marx and Weber. Like Marx, he is interested in capitalism as an economic system, and how this generates inequality. He also, however, agrees with Weber that there are multiple groups competing for economic resources, and cultural status. Bourdieu is best known for employing the concept of cultural capital, in addition to economic capital, to explain why the middle classes secure the best jobs. Being able to appreciate high culture, speak well and appreciate academic books will help you get into university, and when applying for professional jobs. Bourdieu has a rather bleak view of society where those with money and power maintain their position, through passing on different forms of capital to their children. However, making this distinction also enables him to identify factions within the middle class (Bourdieu 1984). Those working in business and commerce are more significant and have more power in society than writers or artists, even though these have higher levels of cultural capital.

Bourdieu was interested in law as a remunerative and high status occupation that has developed with the state. His writings on sociology of law consider, among other things, how law schools in the nineteenth century produced experts and specialists necessary to build a strong state (Bourdieu 1987). He employed the term 'field' and 'habitus' in analysing what lawyers do in society: this is intended to make us think about how lawyers are socialised, what legal practice involves, and how lawyers assist or intervene in other areas of society. Lawyers are portrayed as an elite occupation, even though the profession is internally stratified. The profession is also centrally involved in making capitalism work, a central theme in Marxist sociology of law (Cain 1983).

In a series of books and pamphlets published during the 1990s, Bourdieu adopted a critical stance towards contemporary social change. *The Weight of the World* (Bourdieu et al. 2000) contains interviews with those affected by neo-liberalism and globalisation in France and makes a political case against neo-liberal policies. School teachers have, for example, to cope with government cut-backs, and workers with unemployment or restructuring. Although this book is not directly about law, one can see that lawyers are working behind the scenes serving the companies and government agencies promoting these changes. Moreover, one can also see how law as a field is being affected, so many professionals working for the state or providing legal services to the poor are also faced with changes in their conditions of work. This makes Bourdieu sound like a Marxist, but he is also interested in how occupational groups compete for power and influence, and how the legal profession developed to serve the needs of the state (Madsen and Dezalay 2002).

Law, power and ideology

The central assumption in critical theory is that dominant groups exercise power over subordinate groups, and that these accept their subordination through the influence of ideological ideas about their place in society. From this perspective, law is both a means of exercising power, and also one means through which ideological ideas are promoted. Marxism is the oldest critical theory and is concerned with social class as a line of division in society (Chapter 2). There are, however, other lines of division in addition to class, and many critical theorists have employed similar ideas in writing about the discrimination faced by different groups or other social issues. This section will explain the concepts of power and ideology in more detail, and consider how they can be applied to political campaigns concerned with laws relating to the employment relationship and same-sex marriages.

Two central concepts

Marx emphasises the importance of economic relationships, and how these shape every part of society. He was centrally interested in employment which he viewed as inherently exploitative. Most workers, aside from well-remunerated managers and professionals, are not paid the real worth of their labour. They also have no real job security since they can be laid off if demand falls for their product, replaced by machines, or find that their jobs have been moved overseas to developing countries where it is cheaper to hire and train workers. From this perspective, employers exercise power over workers: they tell them what to do, extract what Marx (1976) called 'surplus value' and can dispense with their services when necessary. Any critical analysis is, firstly, looking to discover or expose this kind of power relationship.

Workers do not engage in overt resistance against poor conditions or the power of the dominant economic class, partly because it would take a great deal of courage and sacrifice to do so, but also because they are persuaded by capitalist ideology. This key term in the Marxist tradition at its simplest means a set of ideas that support the dominant economic group and those who benefit from the capitalist system. To give an example, the British Prime Minister Margaret Thatcher observed during the 1980s that there was no alternative to economic restructuring in the face of global pressures even if this resulted in mass unemployment. From a Marxist perspective, this is an ideological viewpoint. Those doing well from capitalism, both in Britain and internationally, benefit considerably if governments accept that there is no alternative to increased levels of economic inequality.

The employment relationship produces both income and status inequality, in that workers on low wages are treated with less respect than people who have amassed great wealth through commerce or even the professionals, like lawyers, who work for them. However, critical theorists in recent years have become increasingly interested in lines of social division in which there is no direct economic exploitation. This is partly because the hopes of activists that a mass, working-class movement would develop have not been realised. The proportion of the population working in manual industries, the traditional basis for class politics, has steadily declined, and there is far less industrial unrest today than during the 1960s and 1970s. Since the 1960s, there has also been an explosion of what are often called 'new social movements', political campaigns designed to improve the position of minority groups. These include the civil rights movement in America, the feminist movement, and movements representing young people, the elderly ('gray power'), homosexuals and disabled people. Like the trade unions and socialist political parties, they sought to improve the status of marginalised and low status groups, and combat dismissive or discriminatory attitudes. They also sought changes in the law so these groups acquired equal rights as citizens.

Critical theorists are, therefore, interested both in economic relationships involving exploitation, and status differences where some group suffers from discrimination or a lack of respect. In each case, law is a central site for struggle. Legislation provides the mechanisms in which the dominant group exercises power and constraint. It also provides an important way in which ideological ideas about the relationship between dominant and subordinate groups are promoted, often unconsciously, by lawyers and judges, or at least how they support prevailing views in the media and politics (for a contemporary statement, see Box 4.1). The critical theorist, in alliance with the political activist, seeks to change the law, and combat the cultural assumptions that allow it to exist without being questioned or challenged. This can be illustrated by considering the continuing struggle by labour unions against industrial relations laws that favour employers. This will be contrasted to campaigns by gay activists to secure equal treatment in allowing same-sex marriages to be recognised in law.

Employment law

Since the early years of capitalism, there has been a struggle by the labour unions to improve working conditions. Countries like Britain and America are currently regulated by numerous health and safety laws, enforced by inspectorates that visit workplaces and fine employers for submitting workers to potential harm or injury. Citizens in these countries take these laws for granted to the extent that one might assume they have always existed. In fact, there was a protracted political campaign in Britain during the first half of the nineteenth century in which the labour unions, supported by some manufacturers, tried to raise awareness about the plight of workers, subject to terrible conditions during periods of high unemployment. Engels, who documented these problems in graphic detail in his book *The Condition*

Box 4.1 Ideology and legal consciousness

The critical researcher starts by describing how ordinary people think about law, and then reveals its ideological nature by showing how it maintains economic inequality and other forms of power relations. One of the best studies of this kind in recent years is Patricia Ewick and Susan Silbey's (1998) *The Common Place of Law*. This is based on conducting in-depth interviews with 430 people, seeking to address their experiences of, and attitudes towards, law. Many interviewees were respectful towards the legal system, and saw it as means of solving problems. Others viewed it with suspicion, or attempted to make the best of having little power in relation to lawyers and well-resourced organisations.

Although Ewick and Silbey, like most critical scholars today, make little reference to Marx, their theoretical framework is influenced by his ideas on power and ideology. They are interested in how members of marginal groups develop an oppositional consciousness and the extent to which they can resist the 'hegemony' of law by telling stories about their experiences. They also argue that most people take law for granted, although when it does intervene in our lives, we experience it as a disturbing force that does not always meet our hopes or expectations:

> Occasionally...the law seems to intrude into the 'lawless' everyday world, often displacing our very experience of mundaneity. Normal appearances are shattered when our motives, relationships, obligations, and privileges are explicitly redefined within 'legal' constructs and categories.... The tragic, but sadly commonplace, aspects of life become strangely refigured through law: harsh words between feuding co-workers become harassment, or the brutal violence committed by a husband against his wife is euphemistically labeled a domestic dispute. In short, when we confront our own lives transposed within the legal domain, we often find ourselves subject to a mighty power that can render the familiar strange, the intimate public, the violent passive, the mundane extraordinary, and the awesome mundane.
>
> (Ewick and Silbey 1998, pp. 15–16)

of the Working Class in England (1993), found workers in the cotton industry were placed in conditions where they became deformed or blind through poor lighting, or lost their hearing through the deafening machinery, and were not given adequate breaks during the working day. Horrified officials from London complained about finding young children working in the same conditions, for even lower wages, or being put to work down mines. The employers could do what they liked, and the workers had no choice other than to accept the conditions or lose their jobs, and at this time they were not entitled to social security payments from the state.

Historical studies of this period portray health and safety legislation, and later the whole raft of laws that created the welfare state, as a compromise between the forces of capital and labour. The working class accepted capitalism as a system that could and did lead to improved living standards for everyone. The wealthy families who had made massive profits from industrialisation accepted the need for some constraints on how they employed labour. Both groups accepted the power and authority of the state as an independent force that made law and regulated the economy. This is not to say, however, that there has ever been a truce between employers and their workers. In fact, capitalists have always argued that they need flexibility to make profits, and so create wealth for everyone, and that too much regulation makes this difficult. This is one reason why many industries in Western countries have moved, or been 'outsourced' to countries in the developing world like India or China: wages are lower, but there are also fewer government regulations. This does not necessarily mean that people are working in unsafe or unhealthy conditions, although concerns have been raised in some industries that there is a price paid by Asian workers for the cheap clothing or electronic goods available to Western consumers.

To understand what is at issue in these debates, and how law becomes an issue for struggle and conflict, it is necessary to consider some concrete examples. A dramatic example is the 1984 Miners' Strike in Britain (Box 4.2). This illustrates how the ordinary criminal law can be used to break a strike, and how this plays an ideological role in securing and maintaining consent for the right of capitalists to close down whole industries when it suits them. Protracted strikes of this kind are relatively rare. This is, however, partly because most developed countries have changed their employment legislation in recent years so that it has become more difficult to take industrial action.

To get a sense of how these legislative changes affect working people, it is worth considering the far-reaching programme of reform introduced briefly in Australia during 2007 known as Work Choices (Stewart and Williams 2007). Like any piece of employment legislation this had complex objectives, but it is worth focusing on two changes to the employer–employee relationship. Previous legislation had given workers protection against being unfairly dismissed, so that employers were often put to great expense and difficulty if they wished to terminate the contract of a difficult employee. The Work Choices legislation removed this protection for workers employed in small companies with less than one hundred workers. These companies no longer required a good reason when dismissing employees. Another significant change was brought about by the new AWA agreements. Previous agreements had contained a large number of safeguards for workers, and entitlements such as the right to sickness and holiday pay, minimum rates of pay and maximum hours. The AWAs, however, only provided certain basic protections. This meant that, when an old

Box 4.2 The 1984 Miners' Strike in Britain

In 1984, the British Coal Board announced numerous pit closures on the economic grounds that coal could be obtained more cheaply from open-cast mines in Eastern Europe. The National Union of Miners, led by the socialist Arthur Scargill, called a national strike, and half the miners joined this, particularly those from areas where there was most risk of pit closures. The result was a long and bitter industrial dispute which eventually resulted in the miners going back to work, with promises of compensation, and a victory for the National Coal Board and Conservative government.

The most memorable images from the strike were the battles that took place outside working pits where the miners had chosen not to strike. The Union organised pickets, and this resulted in large crowds attempting to block pit gates. Police forces from around the country worked together to ensure a strong police presence. Officers were equipped with riot shields, helmets and truncheons. There was a high level of violence during these encounters, and many miners were arrested for common law offences including assaulting the police and criminal damage, but also riot, conspiracy to riot and affray. This level of force gradually wore down the striking miners. They also faced a challenge through the civil law over how the ballot had been conducted, which was in breach of an Employment Act introduced by the Conservative government before the strike. The National Coal Board succeeded in obtaining an injunction freezing the union's assets.

From a Marxist perspective, it would be hard to find a clearer example of how law is employed in the interests of a dominant class. It was used during this strike to control and discipline the workers, so anyone travelling to a picket line ran the risk of being stopped by police on motorways (Green 1990). It was also used to protect capital, or the economic interests of the National Coal Board, through protecting working miners.

There was also an ideological battle being waged, and the National Coal Board was largely successful, with the help of the government and sections of the British media, in portraying the striking miners as selfish bullies or common criminals. This is a good example of how ideas promoted about law are ideological. Marx argued that, whereas the law is often understood as benefiting everyone, in fact it benefits the economic interests of the ruling class.

agreement ended, an employer could offer workers a contract offering lower wages and no sick pay.

Although it is easy to exaggerate the changes, the unions in Australia claimed that this shifted the balance between employer and employee back to the nineteenth century. Employers' groups, however, presented it as necessary for the health of the Australian economy, and as offering workers greater freedom of choice, since there was currently a labour shortage in many industries. There were mass protests, and this was one reason why the

Australian Labour Party won the 2007 Federal election which led to a partial repeal of the legislation. However, the opponents of Work Choices have not decisively won the battle of ideas. Many Australians, and certainly those who vote for the Liberal Party, accept what for a Marxist is the ideological view that everyone benefits from having the freedom to negotiate their individual employment agreements, even if companies can dictate the conditions.

Same-sex marriage

In many Western countries, there were laws criminalising gay and lesbian sex until relatively recently, and all kinds of direct and indirect discrimination. This did not necessarily affect individuals economically, since it is possible to conceal one's sexuality. The dominant heterosexual community was, however, exercising real power over this minority group. It forced people to engage in same-sex relationships 'underground', and required them to conceal their sexual preferences and identity at work, in churches or when holding office. There were often cruel attempts made to force young people to behave or think 'normally'. Homosexuality was largely invisible in the mass media, which promoted and maintained the view it was a deviant activity. Politicians, church leaders and newspaper editors sometimes made moralistic and disparaging statements, and scientists portrayed same-sex preferences as an illness. Although Marx only used the term in relation to economic exploitation and power relations, it seems appropriate to describe this set of heterosexist ideas and prejudices as an ideology. The dominant group, heterosexuals, benefit because their values and lifestyle is promoted as normal and natural, and homosexuality as morally wrong.

Since the 1960s, the Gay Rights movement has achieved considerable success in changing attitudes and securing legal rights and protections for lesbians and homosexuals. They have, for example, secured anti-discrimination legislation, so a worker sacked because an employer disapproved of his or her sexuality, can obtain compensation. Consensual private sexual acts between adults have been de-criminalised, and the age of consent has been raised. There have also been effective campaigns by lobby groups within organisations. The police have, for example, come under pressure both not to harass gay people, but also to take legislation on hate speech seriously. Companies have started to recognise long-term same-sex relationships among employees, and to give partners the same rights to a pension or other contractual benefits as enjoyed by those in heterosexual relationships.

Although not without opposition, these campaigns have been accepted in most Western countries as protecting lesbians and homosexuals from unfair and discriminatory treatment. There is, however, now a fierce debate, particularly in America, since pressure groups have gone a stage further and demanded the right to get married in the same way as heterosexual couples (Hull 2006). The first country to recognise these marriages, which should be distinguished from mere civil partnerships, was the Netherlands in 2001, and since then same-sex marriages have been recognised in Canada, Belgium, Spain, South Africa and the American state of Massachusetts. There has been a lot of legal activity in America where the courts have allowed same-sex marriages only to have the decision over-turned on appeal, so many marriages have since been annulled (Box 4.3).

Returning to the concepts employed by critical theorists, one can see that religious or conservative opponents of same-sex marriage have successfully used their political power, including pressure on an elected judiciary, to prevent legal change. They are, therefore, exercising power over gay and lesbian couples who wish to marry, as well as depriving them from some benefits that are only available to married couples. They have also so far been successful in waging an ideological battle to define what is acceptable behaviour in America. This is a highly symbolic issue, particularly given that any American government needs the support of Christian religious groups (which explains why even the Democratic Party has been reluctant to campaign vigorously on this issue). Moreover, even if gay marriage were to be permitted, this would not be the end of the struggle. It would simply be a

---

Box 4.3 The American courts and same-sex marriage

The Netherlands was the first country to recognise same-sex marriage in 2001, and several European countries have passed similar legislation, or permitted civil unions for same-sex couples. In America, where fundamentalist Christians can influence the outcome of national and state elections, there has been considerable opposition to attempts by couples to secure these rights. During the 1970s, the Hawaii Supreme Court decided that same-sex marriage should be allowed under the state's equal rights amendment prohibiting gender discrimination. Opponents countered by amending the state's constitution, making same-sex marriage illegal. Similar struggles took place in other states, leading to the Federal government led by President Clinton to enact the Defense of Marriage Act in 1996 that allowed states not to recognise same-sex marriages performed in other states.

The issue re-surfaced during 2004, when the mayor of San Francisco issued marriage licences to same-sex couples as an act of civil disobedience, in defiance of state laws prohibiting state marriage. The Supreme Court of California later invalidated these marriages, but this sparked a further wave of constitutional amendments at state level, and also a proposal by President Bush to amend the American Constitution. Nevertheless, the Gay Rights movement did achieve some successes. In 2004, the state of Massachusetts recognised same-sex marriages. The state of California also enacted a Domestic Partnership Act in 2005, which gave same-sex couples the same rights as married couples. The issue continues to generate strong passions, and has created a great deal of work for lawyers and legislative assemblies in America.

step towards what campaigners hope will eventually be a different kind of society. This might seem hard to imagine, but there are plenty of societies historically where there was not simply greater openness and toleration toward homosexuality, but it was portrayed positively as a life-style choice. Those campaigning for law reform are asking us to question our still rather conservative attitudes towards sexuality.

Critical perspectives on the legal profession

Sociologists in the Marxist tradition have asked difficult questions about the content of law and its role in supporting the position of economically and culturally dominant groups (Bankowski and Mungham 1976). There have also been sociologists influenced by Marx and Weber who have asked critical questions about the legal profession. This section will consider the arguments advanced by Weber about the power of lawyers as an occupational group. It will then examine arguments about a class and racial divide in the legal profession. Finally, it will consider the role of the law school in reproducing law, both as a discipline that assists dominant groups maintain their position, and the privileged position of the legal profession.

Sociologists and the legal profession

Some sociological theorists have been highly complimentary towards lawyers and the legal profession. Parsons (1954), it will be remembered, saw them as an important agent of social control in persuading clients to settle, and as the custodians of shared cultural values passed on through generations in law schools. He also believed that this is why lawyers, but also other professionals such as doctors and politicians, should be well-rewarded. It was important that the most talented people in society are motivated to pursue the study necessary to occupy these important positions.

Critical sociologists, as one might expect, have a different view towards the professions. Weber (2007) was interested in the way particular occupations had discovered a way to increase their status and incomes through controlling the supply of a particular skill. Even though by no means every lawyer earns a high salary, it remains true that the legal profession can control supply in a way that is not available to many occupations. A good historical example is the specialism of conveyancing in Britain. For much of the twentieth century, solicitors enjoyed a monopoly from the state in providing these services. Because of this, it was possible to make a comfortable living from conveyancing, in addition to providing other legal services. During the 1980s, the Conservative government removed the monopoly by making it possible for anyone to become a property conveyancer without a legal training. The result is that the fees charged for conveyancing dramatically decreased, and many lawyers who had previously relied on this income, had to find other areas of work. Weberian sociologists, such as Johnson (1972), have argued that all professions rely on state monopolies or other restrictive practices to boost their incomes. They can, therefore, be viewed as an interest group in competition for power and status with other occupations and the state.

Hierarchy and change within the profession

From a critical perspective, the legal profession offers a fruitful site for investigating power relations. The next chapter will discuss what a feminist would describe as the subordination of women in the profession. It is also clear that in America, there are more African-Americans and minorities working for smaller firms than for large commercial firms, and it is harder to become a partner in a predominantly white firm if you are from an ethnic background (Pierce 1995). What is also striking, however, is that the profession is highly stratified. The American sociologists John Heinz and Edwin Laumann (1994) conducted what remains the most complete survey of the profession in an American city (Box 4.4) and found there were huge differences in income between lawyers working in the legal aid sector and those in large commercial firms. Each segment of the profession (to use a term employed by Bucher and Strauss 1961 on differentiation in medicine) represented different types of clients. Other researchers have shown how lawyers themselves are highly conscious of status differences, even within segments (Travers 2002). There is, for example, a pecking order or hierarchy among large commercial firms in the City of London, and competition in annual rankings. It is this hierarchy that makes possible systematic discrimination, so there are fewer women or ethnic minority lawyers working for large commercial firms.

A Marxist would also be interested in how law firms in different segments of the profession are changing. Firms have been traditionally organised as partnerships that employ lawyers who have the opportunity to buy into the partnership during their careers. Richard Abel (1988) in his study of changes in the legal profession of England and Wales has shown that it has become increasingly difficult to buy into a partnership. The result is that larger numbers work for a salary through their careers. This is not necessarily exploitation, but it can be argued that the gap in income within particular firms has grown at the same time as that between different segments. One related development is that small firms or sole-practitioners have disappeared. Governments funding free legal services to the general public prefer these to be delivered by large organisations. These large firms often employ professional managers with the aim of increasing the productivity of staff, and in the case of legal aid franchises deliver a standardised product through new technology.

Some researchers have likened these changes to mechanisation in the cotton industry during the early nineteenth century, and even argued that

---

Box 4.4 Heinz and Laumann on the legal profession in Chicago

The most thorough study of the structure and composition of the legal profession in a particular city was conducted in Chicago during the 1970s by John Heinz and Edwin Laumann (1994). This was based on interviewing 777 lawyers, randomly selected from the Chicago bar. Their central finding was that the legal profession was divided into two 'hemispheres' in terms of income and status:

> Lawyers who serve major corporations and other large organizations differ systematically from those who work for individuals and small businesses, whether we look at the social origins of the lawyers, the prestige of the law schools they attended, their career histories and mobility, their social or political values, their networks of friends and professional associates, or several other social variables. Though there certainly are distinctions that cut across the line between the two broad classes of clients, this fundamental difference in the nature of the client appeared to be the principal factor that structures the social differentiation of the profession.
> (Heinz and Laumann 1994, pp. 127–8)

One question they address is the nature of segregation on ethnic or religious lines. They found, for example, that Protestants from high status backgrounds (a group sometimes described colloquially as WASPS or White Anglo-Saxon Protestants) were over-represented in finance and banking. Catholics who included Polish and Italian Americans were most likely to be found doing litigation, in either hemisphere. Jews tended to work for personal clients in fields such as criminal defence or personal injury plaintiff's work (Heinz and Laumann 1994, p. 136).

Since the study was conducted many changes have taken place, including a steady growth in the market for legal services, and the admission both of substantial numbers of women and previously excluded minority groups, such as African-Americans, to the profession (Heinz and Laumann 1994, p. xix). Re-visiting their data in the 1990s, Heinz and Laumann argued that, despite these developments, not much may have fundamentally changed: 'Increasing specialization in the practice of law might drive the two sectors further apart, or it might divide each of them into several smaller clusters' (Heinz and Laumann 1994, p. xxii).

---

lawyers are facing proletarianisation (Abel 1988, pp. 21–5). This is a good example of how critical theory makes one think about the legal profession differently, and also illustrates how, at some point, the sociologist will need to conduct empirical research to test a theoretical viewpoint. To make this case, one would need to show a dramatic decrease in job satisfaction, control of work, and increase in job insecurity among lawyers working in high street firms.

The law school and the reproduction of ideology

Although critical researchers are interested in divisions within the legal profession, they always remain conscious that law itself, as a set of institutions and procedures for punishing criminals or settling disputes, benefits economically or culturally dominant groups in society. This is the key point made by Marxists, and also by those campaigning for the rights of minority groups such as homosexuals, the elderly or disabled people. Law either directly discriminates or oppresses (consider how employment law is used against workers) or it is a vehicle for promoting ideological ideas that benefit the dominant group.

Whether or not one agrees with this theoretical perspective, it should be apparent that the law school plays a major part in reproducing law as an ideology. The American critical legal anthropologist, Elizabeth Mertz (2007), has made this case through describing how black-letter law is taught in undergraduate tutorials. There is also a large body of critical legal scholarship that criticises or seeks to make us question the assumptions that underpin different areas of black-letter law (for example, Mansell et al. 1999). Although these perspectives are taught in some contextual law degrees, for the most part law students learn legal rules without considering how law benefits dominant groups in society. They also never question whether lawyers are really necessary, or whether there might be too great a reliance on law. It will be remembered that Habermas advanced this argument, suggesting that there is something wrong with the large, bureaucratic state serviced and maintained by lawyers that manages and regulates every aspect of our lives. From a critical perspective, it makes sense to start close to hand and challenge what students learn in law school.

Assessing critical theory

Critical theory was for a time the largest field of contemporary law and society scholarship, and led to the establishment of journals, such as *Social and Legal Studies* and *Law and Critique* that exclusively publish critical studies about different areas of law. It is still highly influential, but also faces considerable challenges. These were evident in the Marxist tradition even before the collapse of the Soviet Union in debates over the problem of rights, or whether law benefits or oppresses subordinate groups. Since the fall of the Soviet Union, it is arguable that most critical research conducted has a reformist, rather than revolutionary intent, and effectively accepts that there is no alternative to capitalism. At the same time, new social problems have emerged that cannot easily be understood or addressed by existing critical theories.

The problem of rights

In an examination of how law developed in capitalist societies, the Soviet jurist Evgeny Pashukanis (1978) argued that it mainly served the needs of the middle-class or bourgeoisie. After a socialist revolution, law in the form of judges who acted independently from the government, and a body of rules that protected individual freedoms, would no longer be required. This was because everyone would finally have economic equality and an equal say in how society and the economy was organised. It is unclear whether Marx also believed this, but his writings on communism do not mention the everyday problems that concern people in capitalist societies, ranging from noisy neighbours, to racial discrimination. He had the utopian belief that all conflicts would be resolved and the state would 'wither away'. This suggests that in this utopian, technologically advanced society, there would be no need for law.

In reality, the Soviet Union quickly became a totalitarian dictatorship, in which the secret police could arrest critics, and detain them in concentration camps or psychiatric hospitals, without a proper trial or right of appeal. A deep, moral distaste towards actually existing socialism informed the British historian Edward Thompson's writings on law. Thompson (1975) wrote about the Black Acts in England during the eighteenth century, harsh laws designed to stamp out poaching in forests around London. He was interested, among other things, in how the local police did not fully enforce these laws, and magistrates and juries often sided with the poachers. This was partly because they were honouring and upholding legal rights and obligations that, although never written down as state law, were respected by those living in the forests. Thompson argues that ordinary people at this time, the small folk living in these forests, were protected against a rapacious, capitalist regime by the rule of law.

Many other Marxist writers have come to accept that law benefits subordinate groups, and that any society requires a legal system. Moreover, critical theories concerned with non-economic forms of disadvantage also recognise the importance of law. Critical theorists today often argue that it is only possible to achieve a better society through giving rights to subordinate groups. Many support, for example, the view that a world government should agree and enforce a set of universal, human rights eliminating poverty or discrimination. There are, of course, great political obstacles to this project, but it is seen as having the potential to create a perfect society. The difficulty with this project from a Marxist perspective is that it requires abandoning many of the key assumptions that make it a critical theory (Benton 2006). Marx argued convincingly that the real enemy of workers, which generated economic inequality and insecurity, was capitalism. From this perspective, it is hard to see how giving different minority or disadvantaged groups rights can be anything more than palliative or tokenistic. A version of the same argument can be used about non-economic forms of discrimination since there is usually a side to any social movement that seeks rather more than the right to exist as a tolerated minority. Some gay couples are, for example, uncomfortable with the idea of securing the right to marry since this accepts heterosexual marriage as a model for family relationships. Some queer theorists believe that everyone is partly homosexual, or at least could choose this lifestyle given encouragement and tolerance. They do not simply want the right to be different, but would like homosexuality to be promoted as a positive life-choice in schools, and through the media. Although they have little chance of realising this goal politically, it demonstrates the limitations involved in securing rights. There is a difference between reforming the system, and struggling for revolutionary change.

Critical theory after the fall of communism

Since the collapse of the Soviet Union, there have been few progressive intellectuals advocating revolutionary change, and most acknowledge the success and stability of free market capitalism. Although Habermas and Bourdieu remain influential in universities, it seems apparent that many of the radical social movements that sought to transform society during the 1960s and 1970s have run out of steam, or become content with advocating liberal reforms. It seems unlikely that this period of political quiescence will last forever, but for the moment critical theory seems in retreat, and in some cases is only kept alive in universities as a specialist academic pursuit.

The rise of postmodernism, which immediately filled the vacuum left by Marxism, illustrates the disillusionment of many progressives. Postmodernism as a philosophical movement questions and problematises the idea of truth. This makes it difficult to argue persuasively against economically or socially dominant groups, although in practice many postmodernists also have a commitment to critical politics. It would also be fair to say that postmodernist writings are often inaccessible to wider audiences. University researchers are, these days, more likely to be doing consultancy work for government agencies or the police rather than working with community groups or social movements campaining for social or legal change.

Finally, it is worth noting that new issues have emerged in recent years which were not predicted by critical theorists, and cannot easily be addressed from a Marxist or post-Marxist perspective. Consider, for example, the effects of the terrorist attacks of 9/11 which have resulted in governments across the world legislating to remove civil liberties. None of the critical theorists reviewed in this chapter expected or can explain the success of Al-Qaeda in recruiting suicide bombers in the Arab world and in Western countries such as Britain. Similarly, progressive theorists such as Habermas and Bourdieu did not write about global warming during the 1960s and 1970s because this was not recognised as a problem. This does not mean that the plight of workers who will lose their jobs in a global recession, or the continuing struggles of minorities such as homosexuals for equal treatment, are not important and worthy of study. However, it explains why we may need new critical theories that explain the social and economic basis of unanticipated problems.

Questions

1 'Critical theorists are still coming to terms with the triumph of capitalism following the end of the Soviet Union in the late 1980s'. Discuss.
2 How does ordinary legal consciousness support capitalism?
3 'Legislation in itself cannot solve the problems faced by homosexuals'. Discuss.
4 Evaluate the view of law advanced by either Louis Althusser or Jurgen Habermas.
5 'Lawyers have high incomes because they have secured a monopoly from the state in providing legal services'. Explain and discuss.

Further reading

There is an extensive literature on Marxism and different varieties of critical theory in relation to law. Good introductions include Collins' *Marxism and Law* (Oxford University Press, Oxford 1982), and Mansell, Meteyard and Thompson's *A Critical Introduction to Law* (Cavendish, London 1999). For a more systematic introduction to debates within Marxism, and different critical traditions, you should consult a text on sociological theory, for example, Cuff, Sharrock and Francis' *Perspectives in Sociology* (Routledge, London 2006). There are chapters on Bourdieu, Habermas and different critical traditions in Banakar and Travers' *An Introduction to Law and Social Theory* (Hart, Oxford 2002).

For critical discussion of how law was used during the 1984 miners' strike, see Green's *The Enemy Without* (Open University Press, Milton Keynes 1990). Hull's *Same-Sex Marriage* (Cambridge University Press, Cambridge 2006) provides an overview of the campaign for same-sex marriages. Abel's *The Legal Profession of England and Wales* (Blackwell, Oxford 1988) considers how one can understand change in the legal profession from a functionalist, Marxist and Weberian perspective. For some interesting reflections on the state of Marxism today, see Fine's chapter in Banakar and Travers' *An Introduction to Law and Social Theory* (Hart, Oxford 2002, pp. 101–18). For a review of Pashukanis' writings on law, see Head's *Evgeny Pashukanis: A Critical Reappraisal* (Routledge, London 2007).

Chapter 5

Feminism and law

Feminism as a social movement   92
  The struggle for legal rights   92
  Economic and cultural objectives   93

Feminism and jurisprudence   94
  Liberal feminism   95
  Radical perspectives   96
  The feminist critique of law   98

Empirical studies of legal practice   100
  How women experience divorce   100
  The experiences of indigenous battered women   101

Women in the legal profession   103
  A two-tier occupation   103
  Experiences of sexism   105
  An ethnographic study   107

Some critical issues   109
  A different way of doing law   109
  Understanding the backlash   110

Questions   110

Further reading   110

Boxes 5.1 Catherine MacKinnon and Andrea Dworkin's
            pornography ordinance   97
       5.2 Fertility treatment as a feminist issue   99
       5.3 Feminism as method   101

There will be younger readers of this book, living in Western democratic societies, for whom the term 'feminism' may have little meaning, or seem either irrelevant or even vaguely threatening. This is interesting because, between the late 1960s and 1980s, feminism was highly influential, not only in universities, but across society as a social and political movement. There were campaigns that changed the law so this benefited women, or particular groups of women, in a way that we now take for granted. There was a transformation in the cultural life of society so that women could express themselves in the arts. Moreover, women have been the main beneficiaries of the expansion of higher education that took place during this period. Whereas in the 1950s, most students in universities were men, today there is a majority of female students outside some scientific subjects and mathematics. The legal profession itself was almost exclusively a male occupation. Today, equal numbers of men and women enter the profession and, in theory, have an equal chance of becoming judges. There are also more opportunities for women to enter politics and make law through the political process. Prominent female politicians such as Condoleeza Rice, the American Secretary of State during the George W. Bush administration, and Hillary Clinton, who lost to Barak Obama in the 2008 contest to become the Democratic presidential candidate, demonstrate that women can occupy the highest positions in government.

This being so, it is understandable that some readers may see feminist jurisprudence and sociological studies about inequality in the legal process as of historical interest: about a period of campaigning and political struggle that has achieved its goals. Feminists who were active during this early period can, however, easily show that there is still some way to go before achieving economic and social equality. As we will see later in this chapter, legislation intended to improve the position of women has not always achieved its aims, raising similar issues to those one finds in the Marxist tradition about the limitations of law in achieving social justice. Although there are many women lawyers, few have succeeded in breaking through the 'glass ceiling' to senior positions. Even Hillary Clinton faced what sounded like misogynist criticism from some sections of the American media: criticism directed towards her, not because of her politics, or her association with Bill Clinton, but because she was a capable woman (Kaufman and Hymowitz 2008).

The chapter starts with an overview of feminism as a social movement, and its fight for legal rights for women, including the right to vote, and economic and cultural objectives. It is easier to appreciate its current and future prospects through appreciating the history of feminist struggles for equality, which have been achieved only in recent times. The chapter will then provide a brief overview of some theoretical positions in feminist jurisprudence, seeking to distinguish liberal from radical perspectives. The next section will discuss the influence of feminism in sociology, and review some empirical studies of how women experience the legal process. The chapter will also consider the quantitative and qualitative evidence for discrimination against women in the legal profession. It will conclude by asking what has happened to feminism and where it is going. These questions are important since, after three decades of campaigning by feminists, many women apparently accept a different role in society from men, and are not seeking radical change.

Feminism as a social movement

The modern struggle for women's emancipation began during the eighteenth century. Revolutionary thinkers were proclaiming the Rights of Man in new democratic societies. Women, however, were almost universally seen as incapable of benefiting from those rights or making a contribution to society beyond child-rearing. There have, therefore, always been two sides to feminist political activity. There have been campaigns, first by individual writers and thinkers, and then by organised groups, over many years to change the law, and achieve equal rights for women. There have also been campaigns aimed at improving the economic prospects and cultural status of women. How this has happened has varied between countries. This section draws mainly on the well-documented history of feminism in England, although there have been similar movements around the world.

The struggle for legal rights

The fight for individual rights and freedoms against the power of absolutist monarchies and the church is a central theme in modern European history during the late eighteenth and nineteenth centuries. This is what intellectuals, such as Voltaire, Condorcet, Rousseau and Montaigne in the eighteenth century movement known as The Enlightenment were arguing for against a weakened but still powerful *ancien régime*. These goals were achieved at an early stage in the American Revolution, even though it took many further struggles, including a civil war, to realise the noble sentiments in the constitution. There was, however, a protracted struggle in Europe to establish modern democracies in the face of many set backs and counter-revolutions. It is sobering to think that the democracies we enjoy today, in which ordinary men and women can vote, were established relatively recently.

Women over the age of thirty won the vote in England in 1918, the fruition of campaigns that began in the late nineteenth century (American women were enfranchised in 1920). These were successful mainly due to the economic and social effect of the First World War, which led to many women taking up work in recognised male occupations for the first time and strengthened the feminist case. However, the movement also employed both non-violent and violent forms of protest (Barnett 1998, pp. 41–3). There were a series of arson attacks on public buildings, and one protestor committed suicide by throwing herself in front of the King's horse on Derby Day 1913 (which could also have resulted in the deaths of jockeys and horses). The women's movement, at the time, was viewed by the press as the work of dangerous cranks. There are some similarities to the Animal Liberation Front in our own times, in that some activists resort to violence because there is little hope of law reform.

Winning the vote followed a successful campaign to secure legal protection for women after divorce. For most of the nineteenth century, women were not entitled to a property settlement after a marriage breakdown or custody of the children. Barbara Leigh Smith Bodichon (1854) noted in a feminist pamphlet that 'a man and his wife are one person in law; the wife loses all her rights as a single woman, and her existence is entirely absorbed to that of her husband'. Even after getting engaged, it was not possible for a woman to enter into a property or financial transaction without her fiancée's permission. Although the 1882 Married Women's Property Act gave women equal rights in marriage, this was the result of campaigns, and reluctant reform, over many decades. To give an example, judicial divorce was allowed in 1857, partly because of Bodichon's campaign. This Act allowed men to sue on the grounds of adultery, protecting them from having to support an illegitimate child. Women, however, could only obtain divorce on the grounds of adultery if they could also prove an aggravating circumstance such as cruelty or involuntary desertion.

The struggle for equal treatment in law has continued in the twentieth century. The most significant gains have taken place relatively recently. A father's automatic custody of his legitimate children was only removed in England by the 1989 Children's Act. There have been numerous European laws that have attempted to establish an equal relationship in employment markets and provide protection against sex discrimination. In America, the Equal Rights Amendment has been blocked (Mansbridge 1986), but many states have passsed laws with a similar intent. There have also been successful campaigns to give women the right to terminate pregnancies, against the opposition of religious groups. There have been laws that prevent clubs and associations or universities refusing entry to women. There has also been a tougher legislative response, and greater seriousness of purpose by law enforcement agencies, against sexual assaults on women. In each case, feminists have complained that the laws either do not go far enough, or are ineffective given the social and economic power of men. However, many would accept that formal equality has largely been achieved, after 200 years of political work against male power.

Economic and cultural objectives

The feminist movement has not simply sought to achieve legal rights for women, but to improve their economic position, and change the persistent view held by many women as well as men that they are biologically inferior, or best suited to child-rearing and giving emotional support to a male bread-winner. Even progressive thinkers such as Jean-Jacques Rousseau, or the founder of sociology Auguste Comte, believed that women were creatures ruled by emotions and incapable of rational thought. Early feminists, such as the English writer Mary Wollstonecraft (1975), argued that these flaws did not result from biology but because women were denied a proper education, and even the opportunity to exercise. In the next hundred years, a series of feminist campaigners, aided by social philanthropists, sought to create opportunities for women to be educated to a higher standard. Wollstonecraft also argued that, once educated, it would benefit society, and marriages, if women could do part-time work. She imagined that it might be possible, alongside raising children, for women to become nurses, or even doctors, to study politics and to run businesses.

During the nineteenth century, there were few opportunities for women to obtain well-paid responsible jobs. However, there has been a transformation of the economy in the twentieth century. This should, arguably, not be attributed to feminism as a political movement but to changes in the occupational structure, and in particular to the rise in clerical, administrative and professional work. Despite these changes, and formal legal equality, feminists can demonstrate that women are generally paid less than men, over-represented in low-paid occupations and in the lower ranks of the professions. The underlying obstacle is partly the persistence of nineteenth century assumptions about the nature of women. They are still sometimes seen as being emotional and lacking stamina and aggression in the male workplace. From this perspective, the formal legal position of women has been easiest to change: promoting different attitudes, and changes in the economic relationship between the sexes may only have just begun. As stated earlier, some of these advances at a cultural level are already being challenged, since the mass media and political establishment do not see this as a serious problem. They, of course, can point to many successful individuals who demonstrate there is no discrimination.

Feminism and jurisprudence

Feminism has generated a rich body of thought that cuts across, and in some respects transcends, different academic disciplines. In law schools this is usually encountered as one among a number of perspectives taught on compulsory courses in legal theory. There is also often the opportunity to study feminist thought and its implications for legal philosophy, and different areas of law, during the law degree. To give an example of what the subject covers, see Hilaire Barnett's (1998) text contrasting the schools of liberal, Marxist, radical and postmodern feminism. She looks at feminist debates and critques of laws relating to medical areas such as abortion and reproduction, violence against women, pornography and prostitution.

From a sociological perspective, the debate between liberals and radicals has some similarities to that between the consensus and conflict traditions. Liberals view society as held together by shared values, and favour reforms aimed to provide greater equality while preserving established institutions such as the family. Radicals believe there is a fundamental conflict between the interests and cultural values of men and women. In critiquing law, many commentators draw on each of these perspectives while recognising the tensions between them. They support or promote reforms while seeking to problematise law, and make us aware that changes in attitudes and economic power are required to make these effective.

Liberal feminism

The legal system in Western democratic societies still rests on the political philosophy known as liberalism which was advanced by nineteenth-century thinkers such as Jeremy Bentham and John Stuart Mill. At its heart is the idea that society consists of individuals with equal capacities and abilities who act rationally, and so can be persuaded by scientific evidence as to what is in their best interests collectively. They should be free to live their lives in any way they choose unless this harms other individuals. Influenced by his wife Harriet, John Stuart Mill (1989) made a case for allowing women to be educated and to work that has many similarities to the arguments advanced by Wollstonecraft 50 years previously. Mill advanced these progressive ideas as part of a broader case for liberalism, and over time these have become part of our taken-for-granted assumptions and aspirations in a democratic society. Like Wollstonecraft, he believed that women would always have the primary role of wives and mothers because this was their biological nature. However, they should have the right to be educated and to work in most occupations.

Although academic texts tend to present liberal feminism as a philosophical position, it perhaps makes more sense to see it as a practical or pragmatic political movement. In recent times, this has succeeded in improving the position of American women through asking courts to act against discrimination following the existing provisions of the Constitution, without even needing to lobby for new laws. A good example of a modern feminist thinker with this approach to law is Betty Friedan (1974). She became a campaigner in the 1960s for equal rights, and influenced a generation of feminist lawyers who took up Mill's agenda and opposed all forms of discrimination in employment and family law. Like Wollstonecraft, Friedan complained that the middle-class women she knew led shallow lives and were not realising their potential, but did not believe that women should abandon their children to pursue careers. Instead, she argued that 'the assumption of your own identity, equality and even political power does not mean you stop needing to love, and be loved by, a man, or that you stop caring for your own kids' (Friedan 1974, p. 380). Optimistically, Friedan believed that men would help women achieve their goals, by taking on a greater share of housework and raising children. Like Wollstonecraft, she argued that this more equal relationship would benefit men as much as women.

Radical perspectives

The dominant critical tradition in the human sciences during the 1960s and 1970s was Marxism which offered a comprehensive way of theorising different inequalities. It was, therefore, natural that many feminists were also Marxists or socialist-feminists: they did not see themselves as concerned only with women, but as promoting the interests of everyone affected by capitalism. Some varieties of Marxism were already friendly towards the feminist cause. Engels had supported the rights of women to work in male occupations. He had even advocated socialised child-care as a means of helping women, so they would not have to rely on the generosity of their partners in sharing household tasks (Adams and Sydie 2002, p. 138). He also believed that gender inequality, and the institution of the family, had arisen during industrialisation and would disappear after a working-class revolution (Engels 1972). The obvious problem with this prediction is that gender inequality, along with other kinds of discrimination, has remained in countries such as Russia and China after a socialist revolution. As Marxism declined in influence (see Chapter 4), those critical of liberalism advanced a different political programme based on recognising the formidable, entrenched nature of male power in human institutions.

Although there are different traditions in radical feminist thought, an underlying theme and argument against liberals is that women and men really are different. Difference theorists such as the pyschoanalyst Nancy Chodorow (1978) and the psychologist Carol Gilligan (1982) have argued that there is a scientific basis to women having a greater capacity to care for others and work collaboratively than men. This type of claim had an unfortunate effect in one American legal case in that the court accepted the view that women preferred less demanding work. It does, however, have some radical political implications. Andrea Dworkin (1987) argued that, instead of trying to become like men, feminists should instead seek to feminise male institutions.

The best-known radical feminist in legal studies is Harvard academic Catherine MacKinnon (1989). She has uncompromisingly argued that anti-discrimination laws will not be effective until men give up their economic and social power. Like other radicals, she is most interested in sexual violence against women (to some extent neglected by those seeking equal rights in the workplace). Along with Andrea Dworkin, she went further than many feminists in seeking to problematise pornography (Box 5.1). In arguing that women should have a civil remedy, she deliberately and directly invited opposition from liberal feminists who believed that women should be free to display their bodies provided that it caused no harm to others.

Box 5.1 Catherine MacKinnon and Andrea Dworkin's pornography ordinance

In 1984, Catherine MacKinnon and Andrea Dworkin succeeded in changing the law in Minnesota through a Civil Rights Ordinance giving women the right to claim damages for harm suffered as a result of pornography. This was defined as images where women were portrayed as 'dehumanised sexual objects' but also where they were pictured in a subordinate role to men.

MacKinnon sees pornography as a central means through which men exercise control over women, and as widespread in society:

> Under the law of obscenity, pornography is supposed to be against the law. In the real world of everyday life, it is effectively legal because it is pervasively there, available without fear of sanction. This is what a dead-letter law looks like. The combination of pornography being putatively forbidden but totally available … intrudes the law deeply into women's everyday lives…
>
> All the sexual abuses of women's everyday lives that are not recognised by the law are there in the pornography: the humiliation, the objectification, the forced access, the torture, the use of children, the sexualised racial hatred, the misogyny.
>
> (MacKinnon 1995a, p. 115)

The ordinance was quickly over-turned by the legal challenge that it restricted freedom of speech under the First Amendment of the American Constitution. Opponents also argued that it was difficult to demonstrate that pornography caused harm. MacKinnon was also criticised by both liberal and radical feminists. Liberals objected to the view that ordinary images portraying family life or romantic love could be considered pornographic (Dworkin and MacKinnon probably intended to provoke this reaction). Other feminists objected to the assumption that masochistic lesbian sex (to give one example) was necessarily coercive. This issue, perhaps more than any other, demonstrates the difficulties that radical feminists have faced in changing attitudes. Outside the Christian religious groups who supported the ordinance in a strange alliance with radical feminists, most people do not see pornography, when it does not involve children, as harmful.

More generally, she argued that male dominance starts in the family with male control over women's bodies which even extends to their ability to define and construct female sexuality. Law reform in itself would not address or remedy this problem.

Drawing on Marx's critique of bourgeois jurisprudence, MacKinnon believes that feminists should not rely on law since it represents male interests:

> To most women, the law is a foreign country with an unintelligible tongue, alien mores, secret traps, uncontrollable and unresponsive

dynamics, obscure but rigid dogmas, barbaric and draconian rituals, and consequences as scary as they are incomprehensible.

Actually this is true for most men as well. The difference is that those who can and do make law work for them, those who designed it so it would work for them, as if they were the whole world, are men – specifically, white upper-class men.

(MacKinnon 1995a, pp. 109–10)

MacKinnon also believes that feminists cannot work with men and sees the harm done to women as encompassing far more than economic discrimination. What is perhaps most disturbing to the non-feminist is her claim that the threat of rape is central to how men exercise control over women, and ever-present in their everyday experience. In some papers on pornography, she conflates sado-masochistic pornography (some of which, as critics have pointed out, is consensual) and child abuse with the experiences of all women:

You grow up with your father holding you down and covering your mouth so another man can make a horrible searing pain between your legs. When you are older, your husband ties you to a bed and drips hot wax on your nipples and brings in other men to watch and makes you suck his penis.... In this thousand years of silence, the camera is invented and pictures are made of you while these things are being done.

(MacKinnon 1995b, p. 115)

Although academic feminist writers often draw on radical arguments, they usually fall short of making this claim, which also seems to suggest separatism as the only strategy possible to achieve liberation.

The feminist critique of law

Before looking at some sociological studies, it is important to acknowledge that there is a large feminist literature in jurisprudence on different areas of law. This usually takes the form of examining the effects or implications of case law or statutes for women. Some laws directly discriminate against women, such as the English common law doctrine, only overturned by a judgement of the House of Lords in the early 1990s, that marriage is a defence to rape. In other cases, the difference between the sexes is not acknowledged by law. In other cases, the law prevents or restricts women from obtaining medical procedures, such as terminations or fertility treatment. There is also a large jurisprudential literature that applies different feminist theories, including postmodernist theory (see Chapter 7) in interpreting or deconstructing legal texts.

There is, to some extent, a blurred boundary between feminist scholarship in jurisprudence and sociology, given that sociologists can also use legal texts as their principal form of data. Carol Smart's *Feminism and the Power of Law* (1989) is an example. This examines how different bodies of law exclude or 'disqualify' the perspective of women, including the areas of pornography, rape and reproduction (see Box 5.2). In each case, she examines the difficulties of using law to achieve change, given the persistence of attitudes and institutions that support male dominance. Smart also demonstrates

---

Box 5.2 Fertility treatment as a feminist issue

Medical advances have made it easier for women who have had difficulties in conceiving to have children. Artificial insemination by donor (AID) is a procedure where a woman bears a child where the sperm has been provided by another man. In vitro fertilisation is a procedure in which conception takes place outside the woman's body, and the fertilised egg is implanted. Surrogacy is where a woman bears a child for a couple. All these procedures create ethical problems, and have sometimes resulted in legal cases. An example is the 1997 British case of Diane Blood who was refused permission to use the sperm of her dead husband to have a child since she fell outside the criteria determined by the 1984 Warnock Committee:

> To judge from the evidence, many believe that the interests of the child dictate that it should be born into a home where there is a loving, stable heterosexual relationship and that, therefore, the deliberate creation of a child for a woman who is not a partner in such a relationship is morally wrong ... we believe that as a general rule it is better for children to be born into a two-parent family, with both father and mother, although we recognise that it is impossible to predict with any certainty how lasting such a relationship will be.
>
> (Barnett 1998, p. 228)

From a feminist perspective, this raises a number of issues. First, it seems clear that governments and the medical profession tend to promote traditional gender roles in this new area of medical science. Second, the law itself requires women to undergo psychological counselling, and so have to accept the authority of experts who are often male. Third, the assumption informing the legislation is that women should have children: there seems to be the implication that anyone choosing to be childless is viewed as having a medical problem. Carol Smart (1989, p. 112) notes that:

> Although infertility procecures may directly touch relatively few people, the public debate about IVF, AID and surrogacy provides an opportunity for the symbolic reaffirmation of family life. The process of 'normalisation' may fall heaviest on the infertile, but no one escapes the power of the renewed medico-legal discourse on normal family life.

how it is possible to draw on radical feminist arguments, without denouncing all males as potential abusers or rapists. Instead, she concludes that 'while some law reforms may indeed benefit some women, it is certain that all law reforms empower law' (Smart 1989, p. 161).

Empirical studies of legal practice

Sociologists differ from jurisprudential writers in conducting empirical research in order to identify how people are affected by law or how laws are used in practice (Smart 1984). They have employed a wide variety of empirical methods, including statistical analysis, ethnography and discourse analysis, each of which can be used in investigating the impact of law on women. There is also a large body of writing concerned with developing a specifically feminist method of research that is influenced by radical feminism. The feminist philsopher, Sandra Harding (1986) makes a distinction between 'feminist empiricists' and 'standpoint theorists'. This section will start by looking at literature that could be described as feminist empiricism. Not all of this research was conducted by women but it identifies unequal treatment and understands this in terms of unequal power relations. It then looks at study about the experiences of Indigenous battered women which is informed by the ideas of Dorothy Smith (1987, 2005), a 'standpoint' theorist who has advanced a distinctive feminist understanding of method.

How women experience divorce

A good example of an 'empiricist' feminist study about the experiences of women in the legal system is Austin Sarat and Bill Felstiner's (1996) *Divorce Lawyers and Their Clients*. They were able to follow through one side of forty divorce cases in several law firms in Massachusetts and California in which the lawyer represented men and women. Unusually, they obtained permission to make audio-recordings of a large number of lawyer–client conferences. These demonstrate that the main task of the lawyer was to persuade 'a somewhat reluctant client to reach a negotiated settlement' (Sarat and Felstiner 1986, p. 96). Women often wanted to talk about their feelings about the divorce, but their lawyers tried to encourage them to focus on reaching a settlement.

Although men as well as women were dissatisfied with their experiences of the legal process, they found perhaps not surprisingly that women were in a weaker position, and had to make concessions. They also argue that in many cases matrimonial law benefits men. However, everyone coming to law is in a vulnerable and unequal relationship to the legal profession, since the main task of lawyers is to force reluctant parties to settle. This example also illustrates the complexity of sociology, since there are different ways of understanding this issue. Conflict traditions, particularly those influenced by Weber, often present the legal profession in a bad light, and see law as representing powerful groups in society. The consensus tradition, reviewed in Chapter 3, takes a different view. Talcott Parsons (1954) believed that it was necessary for law to exclude emotional issues and for lawyers to persuade clients to settle.

The experiences of indigenous battered women

Feminists in sociology have developed their own literature on method. An important theorist is the Canadian sociologist Dorothy Smith (Box 5.3). She asks researchers to look closely at the everyday experiences of women using ethnographic methods and show how they are shaped by what she

---

Box 5.3 Feminism as method

Feminist standpoint theorists, such as Sandra Harding (1986), have advanced the view that feminism offers a distinctive epistemology (a philosophical term meaning how we acquire knowledge of the world) that can be distinguished from that used by male researchers and theorists. There is also the suggestion that women have a distinctive ontology (a philosophical term meaning the nature of the world) in the sense that they experience and relate to the world differently from men. The sociologist who has done most to put this into practice is Dorothy Smith (1987, 2005) through proposing that feminists should seek to address women's everyday experiences.

Smith sees society as dominated by the 'relations of ruling' which rule through translating everyday human lived experience into texts. Like other sociologists who have written critically about the modern world, including Max Weber and Michel Foucault, she is concerned about the power of professions, and large organisations, over individuals. However, she develops this into a distinctive feminist argument by suggesting that women are excluded from the relations of ruling. As a subordinate group, they are more in touch with the everyday world. They have the capacity to care for others, to work collectively and to respect other people. In the terminology of standpoint theory, they have a distinctive epistemology and ontology superior to that of men.

To give the argument even more bite, she argues that sociology as a discipline concerned with producing statistics and grand theory, and dominated by men, is part of the relations of ruling. A feminist sociology would have to proceed in an entirely different way. This would first involve addressing the experiences of women using ethnographic methods, drawing on interpretive traditions such as symbolic interactionism and ethnomethodology (see Chapter 6) that are still viewed as marginal to the discipline by structural sociologists. The researcher would then seek to show how these individuals' lives are shaped and constrained by the relations of ruling. The focus throughout would, however, be on the experiences of actual women rather than, as often happens in sociology, their translation and incorporation into some abstract theory. This has become a popular research programme, particularly in North America, known as 'institutional ethnography'.

calls the 'relations of ruling'. This research programme lends itself to studying law, but in a different way to studying how statutes and case law have developed. Instead, Smith (2005) asks us to look at how law, often in the form of government regulations, is encountered in everyday life and at the workings of different agencies. Although her students rarely look at legal proceedings, or what happens in courtrooms, they are interested in how ordinary people experience different agencies which are established by law. A good example is a study by an indigenous group called Mending the Sacred Hoop about how battered women experience the legal process in Minnesota (Wilson and Pence 2006).

The central complaint made by this indigenous community about the criminal justice system is that it does not address the problems of domestic abuse holistically, as has traditionally happened in North American Indigenous cultures, and with a recognition of how cultural and economic dispossession contributes to the problems. Indigenous peoples, like women and other subordinate groups, are presented as being more in touch with nature, and better equipped to help and reintegrate offenders into the community. The American criminal justice system by contrast is presented as an alien force, remote from local communities, run by professionals employing their own specialist language that fails to help the victims of abuse.

Guided by Smith, this research group used ethnographic methods to map the workings of the criminal justice system and other agencies. They started by describing the everyday experiences of women coming into contact with the legal system and the professionals helping them. They were interested, among other things, in how ordinary experiences were translated into official categories, in such a way that harm was not recognised or help was not provided quickly:

> Procedures for gathering information for a form or report were a significant point where women's stories got lost. Forms are integral to the institutional process and to the organising sequences of institutional action ... In all the forms we reviewed we saw only vague attempts to document an account of events and interpretation of the situation from the woman's perspective. Police report formats, bail-setting interviews, pretrial consultation formats, and presentence investigation processes all treated women as data points eliciting very specific information and rarely calling on the practitioner to flesh out women's accounts. Even when a form did allow a practitioner to draw out a woman's account of events, we found practitioners almost universally failed to use it that way.
>
> (Wilson and Pence 2006, p. 215)

The problem, according to these researchers, was not the attitude of individual practitioners but the 'institutional ways of thinking about cases embedded in forms, rules, regulations, matrices and so forth that provide the overarching method and structure for managing cases' (Wilson and Pence 2006, p. 214). This institutional worldview was created and shaped by texts, ranging from law books to manuals in measuring domestic abuse. However, following a line of reasoning that has similarities with Weber and Foucault, as well as Smith, they argue that this has no obvious centre. It is not created by particular judges or legislatures but in the very 'processes and structures of the legal system' (Wilson and Pence 2006, p. 207). This complex of practices in the 'relations of ruling' is contrasted with the more effective community methods used to address violence against women in pre-modern societies. In this Indigenous community, there is an aspiration to preserve and recreate a community based on honouring place, family and one's ancestors that, it is claimed, both empowers women and addresses the underlying problem of social and cultural disintegration that causes domestic violence.

Women in the legal profession

Perhaps the most forceful way of making a feminist case in relation to law is to consider the legal profession itself. Those readers doing undergraduate or postgraduate programmes in law will know that there are roughly equal numbers of men and women hoping to pursue a legal career. There are also roughly equal numbers that enter the profession and qualify as lawyers. Thereafter, there is a gendered experience. A much greater proportion of men reach partnership than women. A disproportionate number of women either leave the law altogether, work part-time and specialise in low status areas such as property and matrimonial law. There are different explanations for this in sociology, and also different political views on whether the different career paths of women result from free choice or coercion into a subordinate gender role. This section will provide an introduction to this literature. It will look at three studies by Hilary Sommerlad and Peter Sanderson (1998), Margaret Thornton (1996) and Jennifer Pierce (1995), conducted respectively in Britain, Australia and the USA. The studies show how it is possible to use a range of theoretical resources and methods in studying the same topic, while working in the feminist tradition.

A two-tier occupation

The extraordinary changes that have taken place in the legal profession in recent times can be best appreciated through considering what has happened in one country. In England and Wales during the period 1980–2007, there was a fourfold increase in the percentage of women entering the legal profession. Hilary Sommerlad and Peter Sanderson have argued that this should be understood in the context of wider changes. These included:

> a period of expansion in the demand for legal services ... resulting in an overall growth in the number of solicitors with practising certificates;

the transformation of the profession into one which was predominately graduate ...; structural changes brought about by a greater involvement in services provided by the State ... and the transformation of the organisational structure of the profession, with the development of what has come to be called 'mega-lawyering' ... corporate firms with a smaller ratio of equity partners to assistant solicitors.

(Sommerlad and Sanderson 1998, p. 104)

By the 1980s, it was apparent that women's careers were not developing in the same way as men. Sommerlad and Sanderson report the findings of a Career Structure Survey conducted by the Law Society in 1988. This indicated that 44 per cent of women who had qualified in 1977 were working part-time, and a further 18 per cent not working. The Law Society's annual report for 1996 showed that there were still significant differences. A higher percentage of women than men did not have Practising Certificates, 13.3 per cent of respondents on an exit questionnaire identified sexism, and 22 per cent reported that it was difficult to obtain adequate child-care.

Sommerlad and Sanderson own contribution to this empirical literature was a survey of women admitted before 1990. The aim of the survey was to investigate the views and experiences of different groups: the senior partners in law firms who make decisions on employing women; and different categories of women such as 'Women out of practice' and 'Women who had returned to practice after a career break'. There was also the objective of examining how views and experiences changed over time through a follow up survey in 1994. There were numerous practical problems to overcome and some inevitable methodological flaws. One arose because the 1990 survey employed questionnaires targeted at different groups, whereas the questions were amalgamated for the 1994 survey. Another is that there was a disproportionate response from different sub-groups. There were, for example, more responses from women planning to return to practice than those who had abandoned a legal career. The relatively low number in the overall sample of those surveyed (about 400 women) was too low for the research team to employ statistical tests, although this was an ambitious study by British standards.

It is worth giving a taste of these methodological issues because they arise in any form of empirical research. If one takes the findings at face value, the 1994 survey appears to indicate a greater gender divide than national statistics for that year. The Law Society identified that 59 per cent of men had achieved an equity or salaried partnership (the survey question did not differentiate between the two) as against 26 per cent of women. Sommerlad and Sanderson survey found that 32.3 per cent of women respondents were partners. However, several people commented that 'the post of salaried partner was not only gendered, but had virtually been "invented" to accommodate women, and that the position was purely "token"' (Sommerlad and

Sanderson 1998, p. 112). Women did tend to work in specialisms like family law, and a significant number had left private practice for an academic career.

This study provides an example of how a relatively straightforward survey can provide ammunition for political arguments, even though one can always ask critical questions about the representativeness or completeness of the data obtained. There were also some surprising findings. The career histories obtained appeared to disprove the assumption that career breaks lead to losing the ability to practise as a lawyer (or that the job necessarily involves a high level of skill that has to be maintained by constant practice); 37 per cent of respondents in the 1990 sample had returned after breaks of five years or more, and in some cases after ten years.

Experiences of sexism

Qualitative studies usually receive more criticism that quantitative research when they are used to make a political argument. They are often seen as being simply 'anecdotal', the stories of a few respondents rather than resulting in solid or reliable findings. Feminists such as Sandra Harding (1986) and Dorothy Smith (2005) have, in turn, criticised quantitative analysis for not adequately addressing the everyday experiences of women. This is an example of how methodological debates between positivists and interpretivists (see Chapter 6) can become politicised: standpoint theorists see the survey, a research method used by Sommerlad and Sanderson in making a feminist case, as itself supporting or reflecting male dominance.

A good example of a partisan study that addresses the experience of women lawyers in some depth is Margaret Thornton's (1996) *Dissonance and Distrust*. This was based on interviewing a relatively small number of female lawyers in Australia, with the overt aim of critiquing sexism. There is a clear bias in that Thornton apparently found no women who were content with their position. It does, however, contain vivid examples that make one think about the mechanisms that produce statistical patterns. Consider, for example, the following extract in which a female lawyer is reflecting on the experience of a colleague:

> There was an example of a young woman who graduated with first class honours, known to be a real achiever in the office and who was classically beautiful looking, and it was common knowledge, to her as well, and she would say this, that she was taken on lunches, business lunches, for her beauty, and the fact that she could talk intelligently was another bonus sort of thing. At one client lunch, the men were talking to each other and then the client, a middle-aged sort of man, turned to her and said, 'And what do you do, dear?' – a complete wipe of her. She's a banking lawyer and she saw that the other males in the firm

were in suspense as to what she was going to do. I think that she was betrayed by them: it's their responsibility to bloody say something to the client, rather than have her being put in a junior position.

(Thornton 1996, pp. 136–7)

This not only indicates that women are not always valued for their abilities, but also illustrates the frustration of the interviewee at the reality of male power. It seems likely that these concerns were not raised in the workplace, because raising a political issue of this kind will not usually be welcomed, even by a sympathetic employer. There were other revealing reports of women who felt that they had to behave like men to advance their careers or even be taken seriously. In this extract, a lawyer complains that she finds it difficult to give orders to secretaries:

I tend to find myself drawing smiley faces on notes and saying, 'When you have a moment, could you do it?' rather than 'Do it now'. Whereas the men just throw the things at them and say, 'Do it now or whatever'. I find that very difficult ... I would rather socialise, I suppose, with the women that sit outside my office than the lawyers in the firm. But my work does not get done with the same speed as other people's work gets done.

(Thornton 1996, p. 33)

Pressure to adopt a male style or personality may explain why some female lawyers give up, or prefer non-adversarial forms of law. In commercial law firms, another problem was being expected to work long hours, which made it impossible to keep working while bringing up children:

We had time sheets that started at 4 o'clock in the morning and went to 9 o'clock at night. And I remember when they brought them into me that I just laughed. I thought that it was a joke. And they said, 'No, if you come in at 4 o'clock, you don't have to stay until 9 every night'.

(Thornton 1996, p. 150)

... you work very long hours and you sacrifice everything. You go in on Christmas Day if you have to go in on Christmas Day, and you go in for the kill if you have to go in for the kill, and all you care about is making money. All those things, I guess, I associate as being male qualities – good or bad – and I just never felt comfortable.

(Thornton 1996, p. 150)

These interview extracts may do no more than represent the view of a small group of women who have had unhappy experiences. Thornton, however, as a feminist, argues that all women have, and can recognise similar experiences. They suggest not simply that women are in a lower tier of the legal profession, but also why this happens. In simple terms, she argues that institutionalised sexism keeps capable women from senior positions, and from working in the largest and most prestigious firms.

An ethnographic study

Perhaps the most vivid, and disturbing, account of gender roles in law firms is Jennifer Pierce's (1995) ethnography about her observations while working as a paralegal in an American law firm. Pierce worked in the litigation department of a private law firm for six months, and for the in-house litigation department of a company for nine months. In addition, she worked in an organisation training litigators. What is interesting methodologically, and would make the study difficult if not impossible to pursue today, is that Pierce concealed her objectives from the two legal departments. To be more precise, she revealed after working there for some time that she was doing a dissertation about legal practice, but not that it concerned gender relations. She defends what some might see as unethical practice on ethical grounds:

> What is more worthwhile? To do a study that raises important questions about the sources of stress in the workplace and run the risk of offending the sensibilities of some of its participants, or, in the interests of offending no one, consider dropping socially important questions, or at the extreme, suspending study altogether? Although I strongly believe in protecting the confidentiality of subjects and in treating them with respect, I realise that not all people I study – particularly those in power – will like my presentation of their work world. However, sociology as public philosophy is not intended to please the people we study but rather to address the social and political conditions of their lives. In this way, sociology seeks to enhance the lives of those we study by bringing issues and questions to public attention and calling for social change.
>
> (Pierce 1995, p. 214)

The study itself offers a stark contrast between two work cultures, both maintained by law firms and the institution of law. The first is the gendered expectation that litigators should be 'tough, aggressive and intimidating' (Pierce 1995, p. 2). Pierce documents how novice lawyers are taught to be aggressive on training courses, and how one woman found this difficult:

> Laura's violation of these norms ... serves to highlight the implicitly masculine practices utilised in cross-examination. The repeated phrase, 'keeping complete control of the witness,' clearly signals the importance

of dominating other women and men. Further, the language used to describe obtaining submission – 'blasting the witness,' 'destroying his credibility', 'pushing him to back down' – is quite violent. In addition, the successful control of the witness often takes on the character of a sexual conquest. One brutal phrase used repeatedly in this way is 'raping the witness.' Within this discursive field, men who 'control,' 'destroy,' or 'rape' the witnesses are seen as 'manly,' while those who lose control are feminized as 'sissies' and 'wimps' ... .

(Pierce 1995, p. 63)

The paralegals, by contrast, were expected to be 'supporting and nurturing mothers' (p. 2) to male lawyers. Pierce argues that there is an emotional side of women's work which is not acknowledged in job descriptions. Paralegals had to be pleasant at all times, in a similar way to the airline stewardesses studied by Arlie Hochschild (1983). They had to defer to their bosses, and were not allowed to criticise or to demonstrate legal expertise. They also had to give emotional support to attorneys:

Reassurance focuses on alleviating the anxiety that ... professional work entails. For example, Jenna spent most of an afternoon doing what she called 'handholding.' By this she meant repeatedly reassuring John that he would make his five o'clock filing deadline. Similarly, Debbie spent much of her time acting as Michael's 'therapist.' She patiently listened to all his work related anxieties and concerns, gently asked questions, and offered reassurance.... And Cindy, another legal assistant, was constantly called upon to 'massage the ego' of her boss. 'I don't know which is worse, when he wins or when he loses – either way I spend lots of time massaging his ego'.

(Pierce 1995, p. 99)

According to Pierce, it is these 'emotional exchanges' that maintain 'the hierarchical structure of gendered relations'. It was very difficult, if not impossible, for a female litigator to avoid becoming like a man, or dropping out of this area of law. This is because they faced a 'constant double-bind': if they were not sufficiently aggressive, they were seen as failing, but if they followed the advice of instructors they were perceived as too aggressive for a female attorney. Similarly, male paralegals were treated with more respect, and 'considered more intelligent simply because they are men' (Pierce 1995, p. 177). And at the root of the problem lay the ability of men to molest and make sexual remarks about women, and the powerlessness of the recipients. They accepted this treatment without complaint, or through viewing the men like difficult children. This has some similarity to how liberal and radical feminists have portrayed submissive wives. Pierce has, however, more in common with the radicals in that she proposes alternative career paths and institutions as a solution, rather than believing that men and women can work things out.

Some critical issues

Like any other sociological tradition, feminism invites and deserves critical discussion. There is no reason to accept its central assumptions as part of the conflict or critical tradition, just as there is no reason to accept those informing the consensus traditions reviewed in Chapter 3. This chapter will conclude by considering, hopefully in a sympathetic light, the assumptions about gender difference advanced by radical feminists such as Catherine MacKinnon and Dorothy Smith and their implications for law and sociology. It will also look at possible reasons for the backlash, some of which relate to the difficulties faced by feminists in recognising differences between women.

A different way of doing law

In the liberal feminist tradition, law is seen almost as the saviour of women. Through the modern, democratic state women are given rights, and with men can achieve a more equal relationship, while continuing with the primary role of wives and mothers. In the radical feminist tradition, men as a group exercise power over women, through the threat of rape and excluding women from male institutions. There is also the claim that men and women have different values, and that social institutions maintain the dominance of male values. This is why radical feminists are not simply asking for more generous maternity benefits or equal divorce laws, but a transformation of male social institutions.

Although there are feminist literatures in each area, it is not immediately clear what would change if medicine, science or the media were informed by female values. Dorothy Smith seems to suggest that different varieties of professional knowledge, and the state itself, represent male values, but she does not indicate whether there is a realistic or desirable alternative. Many critical legal scholars have been persuaded by Chodorow and Gilligan's writings on the psychological differences between men and women. Gilligan (1978) asked 11-year-old children to solve an ethical dilemma, and concluded from this experiment that they had different understandings of law. In this view, women are better at caring and relationships, and men at solving logical problems. This kind of assumption has led scholars such as Margaret Thornton and Jennifer Pierce to see litigation as representing male values. Against this, there are many female lawyers who succeed as litigators, not to mention tough female politicians such as Margaret Thatcher or Hillary Clinton. As in other areas of sociology, there is considerable room for argument and debate.

Understanding the backlash

In many sociological traditions, the most difficult criticisms have been generated internally. In feminism, there have been fierce internal criticisms, first from working-class women, and then from 'women of colour' that the movement only addressed the experiences of white, middle-class women in the developed world. Postmodern feminists would also argue against those feminists who understand men and women as distinct groups with their own biologically determined cultures. Once one starts to question whether there really are separate genders (for example, Butler 1990), it becomes difficult to see what feminism can achieve as a political movement.

Most of the backlash against feminism has arisen, predictably, from institutions such as the media that are run mainly by men. One common tactic is simply to ignore the problem, and present radicals as a shrill minority out of touch with ordinary women. Even when there is no backlash, there remains tremendous complacency in the legal profession about the under-representation of women at senior levels. In part this is because major advances have been achieved in the last 30 years. Some believe that feminism has run out of steam as a political movement, and reached the limits of what can be achieved. Others would argue that this is simply a hiatus before the same concerns are advanced globally by a new generation of scholars and activists.

Questions

1 How do feminists see law as maintaining the power of men over women?
2 How can one conduct empirical studies about law that address the experiences of women?
3 Critically discuss ONE of the following studies about discrimination

   The Ties that Bind (Carol Smart)
   Divorce Lawyers and their Clients (Austin Sarat and Bill Felstiner)
   Gender Trials (Jennifer Pierce)

4 Why do so few women become partners in law firms?
5 'Feminists have not been successful in recognising differences between women'. Discuss in relation to campaigns for law reform.

Further reading

Given the large and theoretically diverse literature on feminism, it is worth starting with an overview, such as Walters' *Feminism: A Very Short Introduction* (Oxford University Press, Oxford 2006). Tong's *Feminist Thought* (Routledge, London 1989) offers critical discussion of a range of traditions. Humm's *Modern Feminisms* (Columbia University Press, New York 1992) offers a taste of the original writers and theorists.

Introductions to feminism and law include Barnett's *An Introduction to Feminist Jurisprudence* (Cavendish, London 1998) and her *Sourcebook on Feminist*

Jurisprudence (Cavendish, London 1997). Texts that critique different areas of law include Ngaire Naffine and Rosemary Owens' *Sexing the Subject of Law* (Sweet and Maxwell, London 1997), and Anne Bottomley's *Feminist Perspectives on the Foundational Subjects of Law* (Cavendish, London 2002). Influential texts include Catherine MacKinnon's *Toward a Feminist Theory of the State* (Harvard University Press, Cambridge 1989), and Carol Smart's *Feminism and the Power of Law* (Routledge, London 1989).

For a feminist perspective in sociology, see Smith's 'A Sociology for Women' published in her *The Everyday World as Problematic* (University of Toronto Press, Toronto 1987). Smith's collection *Institutional Ethnography as Practice* (Rowman and Littlefield, Lanham 2006) contains the paper on the experiences of indigenous battered women discussed in this chapter.

For different critical views on women in the legal profession, see Sommerlad and Peter Sanderson's *Gender, Choice and Commitment* (Ashgate, Aldershot 1998), Thornton's *Dissenting Women* (Oxford University Press, Oxford 1996), and Pierce's *Gender Trials* (University of California Press, Berkeley 1995).

Chapter 6

The interpretive tradition

Interpretivism as a theoretical perspective		115
'Macro' and 'micro' traditions		115
Researching action and meaning		117
Symbolic interactionism and law		117
Assumptions, questions and methods		118
Studies of legal practice		121
The labelling tradition		123
Ethnomethodology, conversation analysis and law		125
Practical reasoning as a sociological topic		126
Meaning as a local accomplishment: the case of a firm of 'radical lawyers'		128
Inside legal practice		129
Investigating language		130
Assessing the interpretive tradition		135
Critical researchers and the 'micro'-level		136
A distinctive sociological agenda		136
Questions		137
Further reading		137
Boxes	6.1 Everett Hughes on what makes a profession	120
	6.2 A study of a jury deliberation	127
	6.3 How a mediator stopped an argument	132

Before reading this chapter, it would be worth observing some hearings at a local criminal court. When you sit in the public gallery, you can see defence and prosecution lawyers getting through their practical tasks, and magistrates or judges making decisions. If you are intrigued or curious about how courts work, then you should find something of interest in the sociological traditions reviewed in this chapter. They employ qualitative research methods, such as observing hearings or interviewing practitioners about their work, to investigate what happens inside courtrooms or legal agencies at some level of detail.

Before going any further, it seems important to acknowledge that many law and society researchers, and particularly critical anthropologists in North America, have also employed qualitative methods to describe what happens inside law courts and other legal agencies (Conley and O'Barr 2005). The last section in this chapter will discuss the difference in approach adopted by critical anthropological and socio-linguistic studies, which are influenced by the structural theories reviewed in Chapters 4 and 5, to the interpretive tradition in sociology. The main purpose will be to explain the theoretical assumptions of interpretivism as a philosophy of social science, and show how empirical researchers in the traditions of symbolic interactionism, ethnomethodology and conversation analysis have investigated law.

Interpretivism as a theoretical perspective

Sociology is an unusual scientific discipline in that it is divided into theoretical traditions that have radically different ontological assumptions about the nature of human societies, and also different epistemological assumptions about how one can obtain knowledge about the social world. Two of the most influential positions, positivism and interpretivism, were set out respectively by Durkheim and Weber in their writings on sociological method. Durkheim argued that sociology should become a science, like natural science, and crucially that in doing so it could not rely on common-sense knowledge. Weber, by contrast, argued that sociology had to address the meaningful character of human group life. Which position one adopts has implications for the methods employed in conducting social research, and for the kind of social phenomena that interest sociologists in the two traditions.

'Macro' and 'micro' traditions

Structural sociologists, influenced by Durkheim, study the 'macro' level of society: the relationship between large, complex institutions such as the legal system or the political system and how they shape the actions of individuals. In *The Rules of Sociological Method* (1966), Durkheim argued that sociologists should be concerned with studying 'social facts' that are greater than individual human beings and constrain their actions in a similar way to objects in the natural world. An example would be a criminal statute or body of judge-made law that creates a criminal offence. It is easy to see the black-letter of the law as something outside ourselves, that can have real, physically constraining, consequences for any individual who commits an offence. In Durkheim's terms, it is a social fact *sui generis* ('of its own nature'). It may last as a social institution over many lifetimes as a structural feature of society, in the same way as a mountain is a structural feature of the landscape. From this sociological perspective, what individuals are doing in any particular social setting is less important than these 'macro' social structures which arise and develop over a long period of time.

Interpretive sociologists, by contrast, study the 'micro' level of society: for example, how lawyers represent their clients charged with an offence created by a statute in court. They are influenced by Max Weber (1978) who argued that society ultimately consists of individuals and groups pursuing different actitivies in local settings. When we talk of society as a whole, institutions such as the legal system, or collective groups such as classes or women, we are really talking about a complex collection of interacting individuals. The same observation can be made about a body of law which was created by judges, or through the legislative process, and maintained by people using the law in actual situations. From this perspective, the assumption that law is a constraining force like a physical object, does not tell the whole story. As many studies have shown, criminal laws have to be enforced by agencies like the police, and this involves the exercise of judgement and discretion. Moreover, not all members of society recognise or respect the law. To understand law as a social phenomenon, therefore, requires investigating the 'micro'-level of society: how individuals think about, or make use of, law in particular situations.

Another way of distinguishing between the two traditions is that sociologists influenced by Durkheim see themselves as scientists studying the groups and organisations that constitute society from the outside, identifying patterns and trying to explain these using scientific methods. The interpretive sociologist, by contrast, is more interested in the view from within society: how individuals and groups understand their own actions, including the relationship between what they are doing in any situation and 'macro' institutions such as law. Weber argued that sociology required a special method, not available to natural science, known as 'verstehen' (understanding). This is the natural ability we all have as human beings to get inside the heads of other people and see the world through their eyes. Interpretive sociologists try to pursue this interest in meaning systematically, as a scientific enterprise. There are, for example, large literatures that discuss how best to conduct interview studies or ethnographic research, and how to analyse qualitative data.

Researching action and meaning

Although Weber did not specify how one should conduct empirical research, he would have approved of the methods developed by anthropologists during his lifetime, and by American sociologists associated with Robert Park in the University of Chicago during the 1920s. They pioneered the interview as a method of collecting data, along with ethnographic fieldwork where the researcher spends time observing the activities of a particular social group. Later in the twentieth century, the invention of the portable tape-recorder made it possible to investigate the 'micro' level of society even more closely, through tape-recording conversations and studying language.

All these methods can be employed in researching action and meaning in legal settings. If you have the opportunity to observe a courtroom, consider what you might be able to learn about what is taking place by interviewing practitioners about their work. It would be possible to learn even more by conducting ethnographic fieldwork, which involves observing as well as interviewing practitioners over a long period, with the aim of understanding their work in more depth. There have been several informative and revealing studies by sociologists who observed work in legal firms or agencies (for example, Flood 1983 Frohman 1991, Travers 1997 and Emmelman 2003). Finally, some researchers have obtained permission to tape-record courtroom hearings, which offers a means of addressing what takes place in fine detail. In America, video-recordings of many criminal cases, including celebrity trials such as the O.J. Simpson case, are available from Court TV.

There are all kinds of qualitative methods one can use, and many ways in which one can analyse this data. The rest of this chapter introduces the main interpretive traditions that have employed these methods. It starts by introducing their theoretical assumptions, which in the interpretive tradition has to do with how they understand action and meaning. It then summarises some ethnographic and discourse analytic studies about the work of lawyers in different occupational settings.

Symbolic interactionism and law

Interactionism is the sociological tradition associated with the ideas of the social psychologist George Herbert Mead (1934) and sociologists at the University of Chicago, although it has diversified into many different sub-traditions (for a review, see Travers 2002). Key sociologists include Robert Park, who conducted a programme of urban ethnography in Chicago during the 1920s (the first Chicago School), Herbert Blumer and Everett Hughes who continued and developed the tradition during the 1940s and 1950s (the second Chicago School), and their students who include Anselm Strauss, Howard Becker and Erving Goffman.

Interactionism is still immensely influential in sociology, even though it tends to be subsumed or incorporated into other traditions. This is because any sociological tradition will ultimately want to address both the 'macro' and 'micro' levels of society, and interactionism supplies a set of concepts and methods that are useful both in studying what happens inside organisations, and relating these to wider social processes and structures.

The courses in qualitative methods taught in social science programmes also owe a great deal to the interactionist tradition. Many of these teach students grounded theory, which involves coding interview transcripts into analytic themes, and employing procedures designed to produce objective or verifiable findings. This tradition of qualitative research was originally developed by Barney Glaser and Anselm Strauss (1967) in the 1960s, with the aim of making qualitative research respectable at a time when many believed that sociology should model itself on natural science. There are, however, other traditions within interactionism, such as postmodern ethnography, that seek to challenge the concept of objectivity (Gubrium and Holstein 2003). One thriving field of work today in North America is autoethnography in which researchers write about their own lives, celebrating the problematic nature of representation or advancing a political viewpoint.

Assumptions, questions and methods

The central assumption informing symbolic interactionism, like other interpretive traditions, is that human beings live in a meaningful social world, which can be investigated systematically using qualitative methods. The world is meaningful in that we communicate through interpreting symbols, unlike animals which Mead believed responded in an automatic or instinctual way to external stimuli. In our everyday lives, or in specialist interpretive communities such as the legal profession, we are constantly using or updating the knowledge acquired about different cultural objects. The world is social in the sense that how we understand objects or people, or even our individual selves, is influenced by other people. Mead noted that socialisation occurs through an active process of 'taking the role of the other', so that individuals have some degree of choice over how they develop as a person, or behave in any social setting. Later theorists have developed these ideas through showing how individuals are influenced by reference groups (an example would be a professional community) or by a 'significant other', who might be a real person but could be an historical or fictional role model. In this way, symbolic interactionism offers one solution to the central sociological problem of understanding the individual in relation to society: individuals are constrained and shaped by other people and social groups, but also exercise agency to a greater extent than is recognised in many sociological theories.

Although Mead was not interested in conducting empirical research, this theoretical framework lends itself to studying these processes using observational methods. Writing in the 1950s, Herbert Blumer (1969) argued that to address meaning adequately, the sociologist should develop an intimate familiarity with different social worlds:

> a military elite, the clergy of a church, modern city prostitutes, a peasant revolutionary body, professional politicians, slum dwellers, the directing management of a large industrial corporation, a gambling syndicate, a university faculty and so on endlessly.
>
> (Blumer 1969, pp. 38–9.)

Taking their research questions from Mead, symbolic interactionists have often been interested in the nature of different perspectives within these social worlds. They are particularly interested in how identities are formed and changed through interaction with other people in the course of occupational careers. More generally, however, interactionism as a theoretical tradition encourages researchers to describe what happens in different social worlds, with the aim of addressing 'lived experience' (Prus 1996). This can be contrasted with the approach pursued by quantitative sociologists in measuring variables, and seeking to find causal relationships. Blumer, like other interpretive sociologists, including Weber, has argued that the natural science model is inappropriate for studying human beings. Although variable analysis is valuable in studying some topics, it does not allow one to address the 'process of interpretation' that lies 'at the heart of human group life'. From an interactionist perspective, this is the central question and challenge, and it can only be addressed through conducting inductive ethnographic research inside different social worlds.

Another member of the sociology department at Chicago during the 1940s and 1950s, Everett Hughes, encouraged students to study a range of occupations using ethnographic methods. Although none of Hughes' students looked specifically at lawyers, his essays offer a distinctive approach towards the professions. Many sociologists at the time wrote about professional work in idealised, positive terms, in many respects taking the claims made by professional associations at face value. Hughes was one of the first sociologists to examine the nature of the professional–client relationship, and the inevitable problems that can arise from the difference in perspective between those giving and receiving a service that often deals with sensitive, personal information (Box 6.1). He was also one of the first sociologists to recognise that there are many sub-groups and different occupational perspectives within the professions.

Hughes and Blumer recognised that the sociologist could employ a variety of methods, including biography and documentary analysis in researching different social worlds. However, interactionism as a tradition is best known for using the methods of in-depth interviewing and ethnographic fieldwork. Sociologists in the first and second Chicago Schools used interviewing

---

Box 6.1 Everett Hughes on what makes a profession

While teaching at the University of Chicago in the 1940s and 1950s, the anthropologist Everett Hughes encouraged students to study different occupational groups. Here are some of his observations about the special character of the professions:

> The lawyer, the policeman, the physician, the reporter, the scientist, the scholar, the diplomat, the private secretary, all of them must have license to get – and, in some degree, to keep secret – some order of guilty knowledge. It may be guilty in that it is knowledge that a layman would be obliged to reveal, or in that the withholding of it from the public or from the authorities compromises the integrity of the man who so withholds it, as in the case of the policeman who keeps connections with the underworld or the diplomat who has useful friends abroad....
>
> The prototype of all guilty knowledge is, however, a different, potentially shocking, way of looking at things. Every occupation must look relatively at some order of events, objects or ideas. These things must be classified and seen in a comparative light; their behaviour must be analysed and, if possible, predicted. A suitable technical language must be developed in which one may talk to his colleagues about them. This technical, therefore relative, attitude must be adopted toward the very people one serves; no profession can operate without the license to talk in shocking terms behind the backs of its clients...
>
> License of all these kinds may lie at the root of that modicum of aggressive suspicion which most laymen feel toward professionals, and of that raging and fanatical fear which burns chronically in some people and which at times becomes popular reaction.
>
> (Hughes 1994, pp. 26–7)

---

extensively during the 1920s and 1930s, and this has become the most popular method in qualitative research. It places fewer demands on the individuals and organisations being researched than ethnographic fieldwork, and is a cheap and flexible method of collecting data. Howard Becker's (1951) study of teachers provides one model of how to pursue this type of research. He interviewed fifty high school teachers in Chicago about their work and careers. Like other interactionist studies, this revealed that teaching is not a unified occupation, and there was a big difference between working in a public school serving working-class and ethnic minority children and the private sector.

Interactionism is best known for the fieldwork tradition in which researchers spend time as observers or participant observers within some organisation or social group. This has advantages over ethnography in that the researcher can see what people do, in addition to hearing their own views or recollections expressed in interviews. Becker et al.'s (1961) *Boys in*

White showed what could be achieved in using this method by spending three years in a medical school accompanying students to classes, and describing the difficulties they encountered during their professional training. Erving Goffman (1989) has noted, in relation to fieldwork, that it is time-consuming and imposes much greater emotional demands than other research methods. Nevertheless, he argued that the justification is that it allows you to share and experience the problems of some work group, and see their routine activities over a long period.

Studies of legal practice

Researchers influenced by the interactionist tradition have published some valuable studies of legal institutions. These include John Flood's (1983) ethnography of barristers' clerks, Alan Paterson's (1982) study of the Law Lords who decide appeals cases in the United Kingdom, and Jerome Carlin's (1962) study of sole-practitioners in Chicago (which are summarised in Travers 2002). These studies were, however, conducted some years ago, and never developed into a large programme of empirical enquiry. There are much larger literatures based on observation and interviewing in schools and hospitals, and more recently in scientific laboratories, than about courts or legal agencies.

One reason is that it is often difficult obtaining permission to interview lawyers or judges, or observe lawyer–client interviews, although researchers have benefited from being able to study public legal hearings. Another is that few sociologists are employed in law schools, and the curriculum still mainly consists of black-letter subjects. By contrast, reflective practitioners in education, medicine and nursing are encouraged to conduct empirical research as part of their professional training, drawing on their access to schools and hospitals. The following studies illustrate what can be achieved through interviewing lawyers or conducting ethnographic fieldwork in a legal agency.

Flood on corporate lawyers

John Flood became interested in the interactionist tradition while teaching law during the 1970s in the United Kingdom, and went on to do a doctorate in America where he was co-supervised by Howard Becker. His more recent work (discussed in Flood 2002) is based on interviewing commercial lawyers about their work and changes in this sector of the legal profession.

Flood pursued these studies by immersing himself in the section of the legal press that covers corporate law, and attempting to gain an understanding of what mattered to insiders:

> Since 1988, I have been engaged on a rolling process of interviewing corporate lawyers and accountants for research projects. For this specific

project I interviewed between 30 and 40 professionals. They included lawyers, accountants, judges, officials of professional associations and trade press journalists. Where I was able, I would speak with the most senior person in the organisation, be they senior partner, head of department, editor, etc. The interviews themselves lasted between a half an hour, the shortest, to up to three hours. Typically, they took an hour to one and a half hours, mostly in the form of an extended conversation about the firm, its work and its philosophy. This last point was important in dealing with the cultural aspects of legal globalisation. I used a list of topics as a platform, not as an interview schedule, to pursue these points ...

(Flood 2002, p. 171)

Flood's wife is a corporate lawyer, so this may partly explain why he has been able to gain access to those working in a specialist area of law as a relative outsider. The study itself documents how corporate firms are responding to the needs of a world where business transactions increasingly take place across international boundaries. This means that large law firms need a presence in other countries, and an expertise in law in different jurisdictions. Since clients often have a choice over which law should govern a transaction, law firms are also engaged in promoting their own 'product'. However, it was also possible in some fields, such as international arbitration, to create a 'type of law not specifically attached to a particular state' (Flood 2002, p. 192). Globalisation also raised the issue of how commercial lawyers should respond to competition from accountants who already operate internationally. Although one can argue that this study falls short of a systematic account of how different law firms respond to change, or what is involved in practising international commercial law, it does convey how particular lawyers understand the challenges of globalisation.

Emmelman on public defenders

A very different type of legal work is described in Debra Emmelman's (2003) ethnography *Justice for the Poor*. Emmelman was interested in the work of organisations providing free legal services to defendants in a criminal court. She obtained access as a participant observer to a 'defense corporation' through a student intern programme, and adopted a systematic approach to documenting and analysing its routine work:

As a student intern and a law clerk, I was permitted to observe virtually every aspect of the Defender's behavior – including that which occurred in such behind the scenes places as the attorney's offices, judges' chambers and jail. These attorneys also accepted me as an 'insider' to the extent that some extended invitations to attend parties or other get-togethers ...

Throughout the observation period, field notes were recorded and then later analyzed through a grounded theory methodology. Specifically, field notes were coded and then examined for underlying patterns. Each pattern was then described in a memo, and all the memos were then compared and contrasted ... In order to clarify and refine these preliminary research findings, in-depth interviews were then conducted toward the end of the study.

(Emmelman 2003, pp. 7–8)

Some well-known studies have presented an uncomplimentary view of public defenders, suggesting that most of their work involves persuading clients to accept plea-bargains, or that they have a low opinion of their clients, and believe that most are guilty (Sudnow 1965). Emmelman, by contrast, argues that the defence lawyers she observed are doing their best for clients. Instead of presuming guilt, they 'guage the strength of evidence (and thereby the probability of conviction for a crime through trial) and then compare the likely sentences after trial and through plea-bargaining' (Emmelman 2003, p. 67). In addition to interviews with lawyers, the study contains descriptions of the work involved in particular cases. The reader obtains a thorough and sympathetic account of what is involved in representing working-class defendants.

The labelling tradition

This summary of interactionism might give the impression that it is solely concerned with producing rich descriptions, based on interviewing and ethnographic fieldwork, about how people in different social settings understand their own lives. This is certainly an important and distinctive feature of interactionism, and distinguishes it from structural traditions in sociology where there is less concern with how people understand their own lives or the detail of their day-to-day activities. However, interactionism also provides a distinctive theoretical framework for studying social institutions that still has considerable political bite. A central assumption, which follows from Mead's interest in symbolic communication, is that the meaning of any object one encounters in the world arises through a social process of interpretation and definition. This informs a tradition known as labelling theory, advanced by Howard Becker's (1966) *Outsiders*, which offers a distinctive, if controversial, means of understanding criminal law. The same approach can be used to make sense of how social problems are identified and recognised. This can be illustrated by looking at recent debates about euthanasia.

Becker's outsiders

It is still often assumed that criminals have some psychological or biological defect, and that laws are required to control this deviant behaviour. From an interactionist perspective, however, the criminal nature of the act only arises through an interpretive process of definition and labelling. As Becker observed:

> ... social groups create deviance by making the rules whose infraction constitutes deviance, and by applying those rules to particular people and labelling them as outsiders. From this point of view, deviance is not a quality of the act the person commits, but rather a consequence of the application by others of rules and sanctions to an 'offender'. The deviant is one to whom that label has been successfully been applied; deviant behavior is behavior that people so label.
>
> (Becker 1966, p. 9)

Becker was particularly interested in the criminalisation of drugs, and shows how this happened through a process of political lobbying by 'moral entrepreneurs' who secured the enactment of the 1937 Marijuana Tax Act. He also argues that sociologists should look carefully at how laws are enforced, how the label of being an offender is applied in particular circumstances. This influenced a large number of interactionist and ethnomethodological studies about the police. Jerome Skolnick (1975) showed, for example, that the police exercise considerable discretion in arresting and charging suspects. They would, for example, be criticised if they sent too many 'trivial' cases to the courts. Becker even suggested that not everyone convicted of drugs offences may have actually committed a criminal offence: implying that the police may not always act properly, especially towards ethnic minority or working-class youths. In many countries, this remains a political issue, and there are debates over whether drug-taking should be legalised (in which case, a large group of deviants would disappear). However, from a sociological perspective, the main value of labelling theory is that it directs attention towards how laws are made and enforced. Much writing on law takes what happens in the political process, or organisations like the police and courts largely for granted. For interactionists, how laws are made and enforced is a complex process subject to many organisational and political contingencies.

The social problems tradition

Although labelling theory is usually applied to the criminal justice process, it can also be employed in understanding other areas of law. In the modern state, there are numerous agencies concerned with administering and enforcing different areas of law, ranging from taxation to the environment. Although they do not always explicitly discuss theory, many socio-legal researchers have adopted a broadly interactionist approach in writing about regulation, and have often employed ethnographic methods. In America, the social problems tradition has examined campaigns seeking to regulate different activities (Best 1989).

During the 1960s, interactionists like Howard Becker have often aligned themselves with minority groups, such as drug-users, and campaigned for changes in the law to reflect their own progressive, political views. Other sociologists in this tradition have been reluctant to take sides, arguing that the objective is to understand the political process through which laws are made. Typically, in a pluralist society there will be a number of groups each seeking to promote or advance their view of reality often in the face of determined opposition from those who stand to lose out if they are successful. A good example of a pressure group that has succeeded, after years of trying, are those who believe that smoking is harmful. Forty years ago smoking was generally viewed as beneficial, and campaigners as harmless cranks. Today, however, the weight of scientific evidence and moral opinion, supports the reformers.

There are, however, other areas of law and regulation where there is either no consensus on the scientific evidence or where moral opinion is divided. On these issues, the media tends to be divided or offers no guidance. Laws may differ significantly between countries, and there are always political and moral debates around enforcing the law. A good example is the law relating to euthanasia (Griffith et al. 1998). Pressure groups are campaigning for the right for relatives to 'terminate' someone suffering from a terminal illness in some circumstances, for example if they have made a 'living will'. Other pressure groups oppose this on moral or religious grounds. From an interactionist perspective, this offers an interesting site for investigation, irrespective of one's own moral beliefs. It allows one to study how any group persuades others through the media and political process to accept its view of law.

Ethnomethodology, conversation analysis and law

Ethnomethodology is another interpretive tradition in sociology that was developed by Harold Garfinkel during his doctorate at Harvard during the late 1940s, and subsequently in California where he was employed on a number of applied research projects before obtaining a lectureship at the UCLA sociology department. Among his associates was Harvey Sacks who founded what has become known as the discipline of conversation analysis. These research traditions share a commitment with symbolic interactionism to employing observational methods in investigating social activities, but go further in looking at the methods and procedures used in making meaning. Many of the early studies were conducted in legal settings, and ethnomethodologists have always taken advantage of the public character of courtrooms, so there is quite a rich body of research about the work of legal professionals and the language employed in courts and other legal settings.

Practical reasoning as a sociological topic

Garfinkel developed ethnomethodology as a theoretical perspective through thinking about the problem of meaning which had been posed by Weber and considered by the phenomenological philosopher Alfred Schutz (1962). He was also interested in the problems rasied by Parsons' theory of action. Parsons had set himself the difficult task of explaining how social order is possible without coercion and arrived at the idea that individuals are socialised with the norms and values required for society to work smoothly. He argued, like many sociologists subsequently, that human beings learn or internalise a shared culture that maintains and reproduces itself through social institutions. Garfinkel, however, believed that this was an idealised picture that did not fully address how people co-ordinated and made sense of each others' actions in any particular situation. In what became known as the 'breaching experiments', Garfinkel tried to reveal and investigate the interpretive methods that made possible social order. These included the documentary method of interpretation through which we make sense of people's actions prospectively in terms of an underlying pattern and then revise this retrospectively in the light of fresh events.

Although these methods are used in any social setting, Garfinkel and his first cohort of graduate students and associates happened to be employed on research projects concerned with legal processes and institutions. Garfinkel came up with the term 'ethnomethodology' while working on a project in which an inter-disciplinary team of researchers were given access to the tape-recordings of jury deliberations (see Box 6.2). The data was never published but proved stimulating to Garfinkel in showing how a group of people having a conversation in real-time reached a verdict on damages in a civil trial. From watching fictional dramas such as the film *Twelve Angry Men*, it is possible to imagine all kinds of things taking place inside the jury room relating to group dynamics. Garfinkel (1984) was, however, making the more fundamental point that, both in assessing evidence and reaching a verdict, the jurors mostly employed everyday knowledge and skills that everyone shares as competent members of society (they were 95 per cent jurors before entering the jury room). Part of their practical task lay in making sense of the evidence, and to do this they acquired bits and pieces of knowledge they had acquired through their own driving experiences or their knowledge of particular roads and intersections. They were also, however, trying to understand and follow the instructions of the judge, for

---

Box 6.2 A study of a jury deliberation

Harold Garfinkel (1984) coined the term ethomethodology while listening to audio-tapes of jury deliberations, and considering the interpretive methods they employed in reaching decisions. This was an unusual research project in that the research team obtained permission from the court, but there were subsequently political objections, since there are good reasons why jury rooms should remain private. However, some years later a jury deliberation was video-taped for an American television programme. This allowed Doug Maynard and John Manzo (1997) to analyse how a decision was made, but also to publish extracts from the transcript.

The defendant in this case was charged with the illegal possession of a fire-arm, and the judge instructed the jurors that, on the law and admitted facts, they should find the defendant guilty. Nevertheless they acquitted the defendant. Maynard and Manzo found that reaching a consensus was a messy business in that one juror held out against the majority view, changed his mind but then expressed doubts over the verdict. This is an example of what Garfinkel called 'reaching the outcome before making a decision', in that jurors continued to discuss reasons after they had reached a not-guilty verdict. It also seems likely that, if interviewed after the event, they would have been dissatisfied with how the decision was made. The different stages are documented in some detail in this study, so we can see the tension between lay and professional views of justice being discussed and worked through in a jury room.

---

example, in applying the burden of proof or using the right criteria in assessing damages. Moreover, he noticed that instead of putting forward rational arguments and agreeing on a verdict, what often happened was that a decision somehow got made and then jurors searched for reasons through re-interpreting the evidence in justifying the decision to an interviewer (the verdict came before the decision).

It is possible to see Garfinkel's study about jurors as a criticism of everyday common-sense knowledge and decision-making, and to believe that lawyers and judges, because of their professional training, always make better or more reliable decisions. One would hope that this is usually the case, but Garfinkel also argues that those engaged in professional work also necessarily employ practical reasoning, and their technical expertise rests on common-sense skills and knowledge. He demonstrates this in his (1997) ethnographic study of the work of investigators in the Los Angeles Coroner's Office. Their practical task was often to decide whether someone had died of natural causes or had committed suicide. To do so, they obtained evidence from the scene, such as whether there was a suicide note, and also interviewed friends and relatives about the deceased's state of mind. Garfinkel notes, however, that they did not have indefinite time and resources and had to arrive at a decision that was 'adequate for all practicable purposes'. It was always possible for a decision to be challenged and revised later, but a good decision was one reached with the time and resources available. There are, in fact, many similarities with the work of jurors, in that coroners also draw on our shared common-sense knowledge about people and situations, and jurors know that they cannot deliberate indefinitely.

As we will see in Chapter 7 on postmodernism, there are a number of traditions that adopt a broadly constructionist approach to how lawyers and judicial officers determine facts. Ethnomethodology is, however, distinctive in not treating the potential revisability of facts as a philosophical problem, and not seeking to challenge the legitimacy of law on the grounds that judges can disagree both on the facts and the application of legal rules. Instead, it views practical reasoning as something that can be investigated using ethnographic methods. It is also committed to respecting what Schutz (1962) calls 'the natural attitude'. An important insight in the coroner's study is that everyone knew about the practical circumstances of the work: this allowed them to make objective findings even though they knew that, in certain circumstances, they could be challenged.

Meaning as a local accomplishment: the case of a firm of 'radical lawyers'

Through its focus on the interpretive methods employed in making sense, ethnomethodology offers a distinctive way of approaching meaning. This can be explained through considering how ethnographers normally describe the people or organisations they study. The objective of the ethnographer is normally to arrive at general characterisations about people or institutions, through spending time in a social setting, most of which will match or draw on the views of people working there. Studies about courtroom communities have, for example, discovered that there are 'hard' and 'soft' judges. Similarly, comparative studies often result in typologies of different organisations: for example, McConville et al. (1994), in a study about British solicitors, found that there were three types of firm: traditional firms; factory firms; and political firms.

From an ethnomethodological perspective, what is interesting is how these characterisations are produced from within the setting. My own ethnography of a form of radical lawyers shows how this happens (Travers 1997). In some respects, Gregsons was no different from any other legal aid firm. However, the lawyers there presented themselves as being different. They would, for example, often complain that other local firms were just in the law to make money whereas they had a more caring attitude to the client. They also sometimes spoke and acted differently to other lawyers. The owner, Jane Gregson, for example, often adopted a more aggressive, adversarial approach to the court and prosecutors. One lawyer in the firm was reprimanded for scowling at the magistrates, and members of the firm sometimes referred to the police as 'pigs' when advising their clients. This ethnography also shows that the same phenomenon can be interpreted in different ways. Gregson had admirers who viewed her as a person of great integrity and champion of the poor. However, critics including members of the local police saw her either as a fraud or someone who was too close to criminal elements in society. Although it was possible to characterise Gregsons in general terms as a firm of 'radical' lawyers, this does not fully address how this radical character was recognised or produced.

Inside legal practice

There have been few ethnomethodological studies that investigate the nature of practical reasoning in legal work in much detail, partly because of the difficulties in obtaining access. The best is still arguably David Sudnow's (1965) paper, based on spending six months as a participant observer in a Public Defender Office. This describes the reasoning behind decisions on whether to offer a defendant the opportunity to plead guilty in return for being charged with a less serious offence. Sudnow argues that being a competent Public Defender required knowing how to recognise a 'normal crime':

> I shall call normal crimes those occurrences whose typical features, eg., the ways they usually occur and the characteristics of persons who commit them (as well as the typical victims and typical scenes), are known and attended to by the P.D. For any of a series of offense types the P.D. can provide some form of proverbial characterisation. For example, burglary is seen as involving regular violators, no weapons, low-priced items, little property damage, lower class establishments, largely Negro defendants, independent operators, and a non-professional orientation to crime.
>
> (Sudnow 1965, p. 260)

Like Garfinkel's study of coroners, this study suggests that legal work often involves drawing on common-sense knowledge, rather than technical knowledge of legal rules. There was nothing in the California Penal Code that determined how plea-bargaining decisions should be made. Instead, Public Defenders had to learn to recognise cases where a guilty plea to a lesser charge was appropriate, and would not be challenged by a judge or District Attorney. It would be a mistake professionally to offer a plea-bargain in a burglary case that involved violence.

Investigating language

At the same time as Garfinkel was investigating the interpretive procedures involved in making meaning, his associate Harvey Sacks (1992) was developing a research programme based on the study of tape-recorded talk that has become known as conversation analysis. Although to some extent distinct, they share the same commitment to studying the taken-for-granted methods and procedures used by competent members of society in getting through their ordinary activities. Sacks founded the discipline of conversation analysis that looks at the communicative methods used in everyday conversation, and subsequent researchers have employed this approach in studying interaction in legal settings. He also investigated the cultural properties of language in what has become known as membership categorisation analysis. Both these discourse analytic methods allow one to study what happens in legal settings at greater detail, and with more scientific rigour, than in a purely ethnographic study through paying close attention to language. This can be illustrated by looking at two conversation analytic studies about mediation hearings and cross-examination in a rape trial.

Mediation hearings

Since the 1960s, there have been attempts in America and other countries to find cheaper alternatives than the traditional court process to resolving civil disputes. There is a large socio-legal literature about Alternative Dispute Resolution. Supporters see it as fair and effective, and point to the fact that disputants are generally satisfied with outcomes, and settlements last at least as long as those obtained in ordinary courts. Critics, on the other hand, have argued that it is a second-class form of justice, and that disputants are pressured to reach an agreement that may not be in their best interests, even though they are satisfied with the outcome. This debate has been particularly heated in the USA where low income litigants have been required to use mediators. It is also relevant to family breakdown since governments in many countries require couples to try mediation as part of the pre-trial process.

Despite the current faith placed by governments in evidence-based policy, people with strong political views are seldom persuaded by empirical research. Nevertheless, studies by conversation analysts are useful in demonstrating the benefits of mediation hearings. Angela Garcia (1991) has identified a number of features of mediation hearings that explain why they are likely to result in agreement. In ordinary conversation, people take turns at talk, and usually start speaking immediately. Utterances are also organised into pairs so that if someone makes a complaint or accusation, a response is normally required. These conventions or tacit rules make conversation possible. However, they also make it possible for people to have arguments in which there is an escalation of disagreement. Garcia provides a piece of data that shows what a domestic argument looks like:

```
1    Stan:     I don't want to talk to you ( )=
2    Karen:    =I DI:DN'T: (.3) HAVE ANY
3              THING, =
4    Stan:     =YOU HAD (RIGHT) TO DO
5              WITH=IT!
6    Stan:     [(YOU ARE ALWAYS)]
7    Karen:    [YOU KNOW THAT IS]
8              BULL I DIDN'T
9    Stan:     [YOU ALLOWED IT]
10   Karen:    [( see it )]=I DIDN'T EVEN DO
11             THAT CRAP I DIDN'T SEE
12             THAT.
```

Transcription conventions: = no gap between utterances; ( ) indistinct; capitals – increased volume; [ ] simultaneous speech; _ stress or emphasis (Garcia 1991, p. 820).

This kind of heated argument does not usually happen in mediation hearings which are intended to bring parties together to resolve differences. One way of understanding this from a sociological perspective is that there are normative pressures and expectations that result in people behaving differently in mediation hearings. Garcia shows how this works in more detail through focusing on four ways in which the 'speech-exchange system' differs from ordinary conversation.

In the first place, the presence of the mediator prevents an immediate response to an accusation or complaint. This is because the parties are telling their stories to the mediator and not directly addressing each other. They can respond but only when it is their turn to speak and it is difficult to escalate an argument after a delay. In the second place, because the parties are addressing the mediator, it is difficult to make direct accusations. Many accusations in the hearings analysed by Garcia were in the third person: which allows the other party to save face. A third feature of this speech exchange system is that parties had time to think before responding to various complaints and this meant that there was no response to many issues raised. This can be contrasted with arguments that take place in everyday settings where every accusation generates an immediate response. Finally, Garcia shows that parties employed polite language in the hearings, and often talked about experiencing injuries in the third person, rather than directly blaming the other party. For these reasons, it is interactionally difficult to have a heated argument during a mediation hearing, although Box 6.3 gives an example of how a mediator sometimes had to struggle to prevent this.

Box 6.3 How a mediator stopped an argument

Angela Garcia (1991) found that those bringing disputes to mediation hearings usually talk politely through the mediator. There were some exceptions, however, where the mediator had to struggle to prevent an argument. In the following data extract, one party raises an emotive issue relating to the history of a divorce, and the other responds in kind. The over-lapping speech and immediate responses are characteristic of everyday arguments. Garcia only provides extracts from this hearing, so it is difficult to know if the mediator retained control or whether the parties reached a settlement.

1.	C:	YEA:H, I- (.) you=know?=I- I still don't feel
2.		good=about=it, because like this is my fle:sh
3.		and blood!, you=know?,=and (.2)
4.		you=know?, (.3) uh- I['m yeah-]
5.	R:	[But] you shouted abortion, for nine months:!
6.		[with Sharon]
7.	M:	[Listen, we] are no:t=
8.	C:	=Hey,=
9.	M:	=talking (a[bout)]
10.	C:	[WHO] had the abortion? (.1)
		Y[ou wanna get] SMA:RT?
11.		M: [Wait a minu:te!]
12.		(.1)
13.	C:	DIDN'T SH[E JUST] HA:VE? ONE?
14.	M:	[Hey wait!]
15.		(.2)
16.	M:	HO:LD IT!, (.3) WE'RE NOT IN HERE TO
17.		TALK ABOUT THAT. I DIDN'T TALK
18.		ABOUT MY: PROBLEMS, OR WHAT-
19.		EVER=WE'VE A:LL GOT A STORY. (.2)
20.		S.h That's no:one's business:!S

Transcription conventions: = no gap between utterances; ( ) indistinct; capitals – increased volume; [ ] simultaneous speech; _ stress or emphasis (Garcia 1991, p. 829).

Cross-examination in a rape trial

For another example of how conversation analysis can contribute to our understanding of the legal process, it is worth reading Paul Drew's (1997) study of the methods used by the witnesses and attorneys in a rape trial. Atkinson and Drew (1979) had already in an important study described the pre-allocated turn-taking system that constitutes the courtroom. In common with other conversation analytic studies, this started by describing obvious features of interaction in this setting that one does not find in everyday conversation, such as the fact that only lawyers are permitted to ask questions, and there is an audience that includes the judge and jury. In this study, Drew went further in looking at the communicative resources available to witnesses and lawyers in an attempt to persuade the jury to accept their version of events. To do this, he examined a 47 line exchange between a witness and defence lawyer in the tape-recording of a rape trial. In this summary, I will start by presenting part of this data, describe the methods employed by the witness in responding to a hostile line of questionning, and consider the interactional advantage enjoyed by the lawyer:

```
16   A:    Well yuh had some uh (p) (.) uh fairly lengthy
17         conversations with thu defendant uh: did'n you?
18         (0.7)
19   A:    On that evening uv February fourteenth?
20         (1.0)
21   W:    We:ll we were all talkin.
22         (0.8)
23   A:    Well you kne:w. at that ti:me. that the
24         defendant was. in:terested (.) in you (.)
25         did'n you?
26         (1.3)
27   W:    He: asked me how I'(d) bin: en
28         (1.1)
29   W:    J-just stuff like that
30   A:    Just asked yuh how (0.5) yud bi:n (0.3) but
31         he kissed yuh goodnigh:t. (0.5) izzat righ:t.=
32   W:    =Yeah=he asked me if he could?
33         (1.4)
34   A     He asked if he could?
35         (0.4)
34   W:    Uh hmm=
35   A:    =Kiss you goodnigh:t
36         (1.0)
37   A:    An you said: (.) oh kay (0.6) izzat right? (Drew 1997, pp. 53–4).
```

These questions were intended to discredit the complainant in a rape trial by suggesting that she knew the defendant well and may have consented to sexual relations. The lawyer wants the witness to admit that she had 'some fairly lengthy conversations with the defendant' in a bar while she was out with friends, and that she knew that he was 'interested in her'. One feature of the exchange that interested Drew was why the defendant did not directly reject the version by, for example, saying, 'No we did not have any lengthy conversations'. Instead, the witness avoids having to directly contradict the lawyer, through giving a different version of events. In answer to the first question, she states that 'Well, we were all talking'. Drew argues that this was an effective response because we hear it as a 'maximal' description. Even though it would have been possible for there to have been a lengthy conversation while they were all talking, we hear it as saying that there was *only* a conversation between friends. Similarly, the response 'He asked me how I'd been' suggests both that she had not seen the witness for a while, and that they were not especially close. Drew notes that these answers demonstrate the subtle ways in which lay people can produce different versions that defend against potentially damaging inferences:

> Without necessarily directly rejecting and contradicting the attorney's versions, the witness nevertheless disputes these by designing her descriptions in such a way that they stand for a different characterisation of a scene than that proposed by the attorney. The witnesses' descriptions achieve their (implicitly) disputatious force, through a combination of their sequential placement, as being done as 'nexts' – and hence as alternatives to – the attorney's; of their being qualified versions, which do not endorse the attorney's prior versions; and of their maximal property.
>
> (Drew 1997, p. 72)

Lawyers are in a structurally advantageous position during cross-examination in that they ask the questions. This enabled the lawyer in this case to set up a contrast between what the witness says and what might have actually happened. At an earlier point in the cross-examination, the lawyer asked the witness to confirm that the defendant had kissed her goodnight. After asking a series of questions about what happened during the evening to which the witness gave defensive replies, the lawyer was able to return to this previous answer and make a potentially damaging contrast. According to the witness, the defendant had 'just asked you how you'd been', which makes it seem strange that later in the evening he kissed her goodnight. Drew argues that this kind of contrast does a lot of work in a criminal trial: without explicitly accusing the witness of lying, which would give her an opportunity to respond in her next turn at talk, it creates a puzzle for the jury to work out for themselves:

> The contrast achieved through this juxtaposition ... does not simply propose that if one is right (e.g. if the defendant did kiss her goodnight) then the other must be wrong (ie. it must have been a warmer greeting that she is admitting).... Instead the difference between them in terms of intimacy/non-intimacy generates a puzzle about how it could have come about that the witness and defendant ended the evening on much warmer or closer terms than it is claimed they began it.... The puzzle which the contrast poses implicitly is, therefore, what happened

between the greeting and the farewell which could account for the intimacy of the latter, when they had apparently begun on a non-intimate footing.

(Drew 1997, pp. 67–8)

The witness in this case heard this question as potentially discrediting and in her answer at line 32 attempts to reconcile the discrepancy by stating he asked permission to kiss her goodnight (suggesting that they were not especially intimate, or no formal permission would have been required). However, one can see that the lawyer is in a structurally advantageous position when it comes to making these contrasts during cross-examination, since the witness has little opportunity to present a different version of events without sounding defensive. Drew also observes that the pre-allocated turn-taking system allowed this lawyer to emphasise damaging points without appearing to do so, in the same way as the witness gave defensive answers without directly contradicting the lawyer. This is again because the lawyer asks the questions and can create pauses to enable the over-hearing audience to consider the puzzle.

Assessing the interpretive tradition

This chapter started by contrasting the assumptions of 'macro' traditions influenced by Durkheim that focus on whole societies and how they are changing, and interpretive traditions that study the interaction between individuals at the 'micro' level. This is a complex debate within sociological theory, and there are many ways of approaching the problem. The dominant view has been that the two levels can be combined, so it is possible to address both individual action and structural constraint. Anthony Giddens (1976), for example, views this as one dialectical process which he calls 'structuration'. Although they are associated with studying the micro-level of society, symbolic interactionists also recognise the importance of structural constraint. Through taking the role of individuals and groups towards themselves, individuals are shaped or socialised by society. Even ethnomethodologists in studying practical reasoning accept that individuals cannot do what they like: the coroners studied by Garfinkel were constrained by the resources and policies of the coroner's office.

All this might suggest that sociologists agree on the structure/agency issue, or meet in the middle. There is still, however, room for considerable debate and argument. Structural sociologists and sociolinguists have criticised interpretive studies about legal institutions for not adequately addressing the nature of society as a whole and its constraining effect on individuals (Conley and O'Barr 2005). Interpretivists have responded by arguing that critical sociolinguistic studies about law, even though they claim to address the micro-level of society, do not fully address action or meaning (Travers 2006).

Critical researchers and the 'micro'-level

Interpretive sociologists do not have a monopoly of conducting ethnographic or discourse analytic research, and there is a large literature about legal settings by critical traditions in anthropology and sociolinguistics. Critical studies include Sally Merry (1990) and Conley and O'Barr (1990) on small claims courts, Susan Philips (1998) on judicial work, Sarat and Felstiner (1996) on lawyer–client interviews, and Elizabeth Mertz (2007) on law school teaching. There is also a textbook, *Just Words* (Conley and O'Barr 2005), now in its second edition, that brings together these studies and advances a critical political viewpoint.

From a critical perspective, studies by interpretive researchers are interesting, but need to be supplemented by an understanding of wider relations of power. Conley and O'Barr (2005, p. 13) note that 'in conversation analysis in particular, researchers and theorists have frequently shied away from making a connection between conversational organisation and the dynamics of power'. These researchers are, for example, normally reluctant to use general terms like 'patriarchy' when describing the wider context.

A distinctive sociological agenda

From an interpretive perspective, these criticisms are misplaced. Conversation analysts would argue that, although the critical analyst might be comfortable with the term 'patriarchy', most women attending a mediation hearing or even rape victims do not use this concept when talking about their circumstances. The objective of interpretive inquiry is to understand how the participants in a legal hearing understand what is happening. The term 'patriarchy' also assumes that there is a set of core values in society that shape and influence the behaviour of groups and individuals at the 'micro'-level. It is, however, difficult to demonstrate this as a strong causal relationship. To give an example, Conley and O'Barr (2005) argue that the low conviction rate in rape trials must reflect or be caused by patriarchal values (see also Matoesian 1993). It is also possible that it illustrates the evidential difficulties faced by prosecutors in proving beyond reasonable doubt that there was no consent without normally having corroborative evidence.

The approaches reviewed in this chapter, therefore, represent in their pure forms a distinctive sociological agenda about law. They can be combined with, or absorbed into, other approaches that seek to transcend the 'micro'–'macro' divide, such as Niklas Luhmann's autopoesis theory or Bruno Latour's actor-network theory (Latour 2009). Thomas Scheffer (2005) combined a number of traditions, including autopoesis theory, actor-network theory and ethnomethodology in studying legal practice. However, these attempts at synthesis often fall short of examining what lawyers do and how they understand their own activities (the strength of the interpretive tradition). There are inevitably many areas of legal practice that have not so far been studied by any of these traditions since it is difficult to get access to closed institutions. Although sometimes criticised for being simply descriptive, the best studies raise challenging sociological questions about the nature of law. Interactionists demonstrate that law is constructed through the contingencies of the legislative process, and how it is enforced by different agencies. Ethnomethodologists show that legal practice draws on common-sense skills and knowledge, not least our ability to communicate, rather than being a separate realm of abstract knowledge. This has similarities to the view advanced by the legal realists against mainstream legal philosophy (Chapter 2), although it is more provocative because based on empirical research.

Questions

1 Obtain an evaluation report of some legal institution from a government website. Why would an interpretive sociologist feel that it does not fully address how people working there understand their own activities?
2 How can ethnographic research contribute to our understanding of the law-making process?
3 'Ethnomethodologists focus on how lawyers make decisions in real-time'. Explain and discuss.
4 What can conversation analysts contribute to understanding the skills used in cross-examination or mediation?
5 How do interpretive sociologists respond to the charge that they are not addressing the wider social context?

Further reading

Symbolic interactionism and ethnomethodology are introduced in most sociological textbooks, for example, Cuff, Sharrock and Francis' *Perspectives in Sociology* (Routledge, London 2006) or Ritzer's *Sociological Theory* (McGraw-Hill, New York 2007). See also the chapters by Travers and Dingwall in Banakar and Travers' *An Introduction to Law and Social Theory* (Hart, Oxford 2002). Specialist introductions to symbolic interactionist include Charon's *Symbolic Interactionism: An Introduction, An Interpretation* (Prentice-Hall, New York 2006) and Prus's *Symbolic Interaction and Ethnographic Research* (State University of New York Press, New York 1996). Blumer's essay 'What is Symbolic Interactionism' is an influential methodological statement in his *Symbolic Interactionism: Perspective and Method* (University of California Press, California 1969). See also Hester and Eglin's *A Sociology of Crime* (Routledge, London 1992) which reviews a number of interactionist studies about criminal justice.
Recent introductions to ethnomethodology and conversation analysis include Francis and Hester's *An Invitation to Ethnomethodology* (Sage, London 2004), and Ten Have's *Doing Conversation Analysis* (Sage, London 1999). The radicalism of the

approach comes across most strongly in early texts, such as Livingston's *Ethnomethodology* (Routledge, London 1987) and in Heritage's *Garfinkel and Ethnomethodology* (Polity Press, Cambridge 1984). See also Travers and Manzo's *Law in Action* (Ashgate, Aldershot 1997) and Burns' *Ethnographies of Law and Social Control* (Elsevier, Amsterdam 2005) for empirical studies.

Chapter 7

Postmodernism and difference

The postmodern movement and law		142
A new age in human history?		143
Questioning the idea of truth		146
Derrida, law and sociology		148
Deconstructing legal texts		149
Deconstruction in sociology		150
Foucault and law		151
Foucault's criticisms of the Enlightenment		152
Cutting the head off the king		153
Governmentality as a research agenda		153
The politics of identity and difference		155
Postmodern feminism		156
Queer theory		157
Multiculturalism and law		158
Assessing postmodernism		160
The problem of relativism		160
Postmodernism and empirical research		162
Questions		162
Further reading		162
Boxes 7.1	Lyotard on the postmodern condition	145
7.2	Derrida on justice	149
7.3	The Islamic headscarf debate in Europe	159

There are all kinds of divisions and debates between the sociological traditions reviewed up to this point in this text. Some traditions generally approve of the way society is organised, whereas others deeply distrust established institutions, including the legal system, for benefiting economically powerful groups. Some believe that sociologists should focus on how people like lawyers and their clients understand what is happening within particular social settings without claiming that the researcher has superior views of society as a whole. Others argue that the whole purpose should be to challenge common-sense knowledge, and advance a political viewpoint. Nevertheless, despite these differences, sociologists in all these traditions share some important assumptions.

The first is that the social world can be investigated using empirical methods. Although this book has not introduced these in much detail, it will be apparent that sociology as an academic discipline is concerned with conducting empirical research, whether this is by administering surveys, doing documentary analysis or employing qualitative methods such as interviewing or ethnography. The second is that, although there are often fierce debates between traditions with different epistemological assumptions about how to obtain knowledge, in the main sociologists seek to produce objective findings. There is a certain paradox here in that researchers with opposed political viewpoints often see the world differently: but in making sense of these studies we usually accept that they reflect these different viewpoints, rather than being led to question our fundamental beliefs about the possibility of objective knowledge.

At its most radical, in the writings of French thinkers such as Jean-Jacques Lyotard (1984), Jacques Derrida (1988), Michel Foucault (1977) and Jacques Lacan (1994), postmodernism as an intellectual movement has had considerable success during the last 40 years in questioning exactly this assumption. If one accepts this philosophical argument, there are significant implications for sociology and law as academic disciplines. In legal studies, it has led to the creation of postmodern jurisprudence as a sub-field of legal philosophy. There have also been some important influences on empirical sociology of law, particularly in the way Foucault's ideas have been taken up as an alternative to Marxism in theorising the relationship between law and society, and the emphasis placed on identities and difference, as opposed to social class, in researching social divisions. However, it would be fair to say that postmodernism mostly lends itself to abstract, and what critics would see as self-referential, theorising rather than investigating law using empirical methods. One can also add that many postmodernists are not seeking to make a better sociology by pointing out its philosophical errors, but are instead trying to make us question whether empirical sociology is worth doing.

This chapter will seek to explain the influence of postmodernism, both actual and potential, on sociology of law, although it will also necessarily have to summarise its influence on legal philosophy. It will start by introducing postmodernism as an intellectual movement that has generated two related literatures. There are, first, social theorists, such as Jean Baudrillard (1988) and Jean-Francois Lyotard (1984), who have argued that we now live in a new stage of human history after the modern world. There are also poststructuralist philosophers who are concerned with challenging the assumptions that had been successfully promoted by the eighteenth-century intellectual movement known as The Enlightenment, such as the belief that one can obtain objective truth through academic enquiry. The chapter will then summarise the ideas of two thinkers most associated with postmodernism in the human sciences, Derrida and Foucault, focusing on what is most radical in epistemological terms about their ideas, how they have influenced legal philosophy, and the potential implications for sociology of law.

The next section will consider how postmodernism has influenced, or might influence, sociology of law in a broader sense through encouraging empirical research about identities and difference. This will be contrasted with the kind of research and theorising about subordinate groups conducted by critical theorists and feminist researchers in Chapters 4 and 5. The chapter will conclude with an assessment of postmodernism. As one might expect, there has been much criticism not only in legal philosophy, but also in sociology of law and criminology. Despite these criticisms, postmodernism has been a highly successful intellectual movement since the 1980s, and the chapter will also try to explain the reasons for its continuing appeal to progressive intellectuals. Along the way, it will demonstrate that a number of terms and concepts that have become common currency in the human sciences, and are used in variety of ways, originate in postmodern philosophy. These include 'discourse' (Foucault), 'grand narrative' and 'performativity' (Lyotard), 'death of the social' (Baudrillard), 'will to power' (Nietzche), 'deconstruction' (Derrida) and 'the imaginary' and 'the other' (Lacan).

The postmodern movement and law

Postmodernism in law is principally associated with legal theory and philosophy, so the law student is most likely to come across this in a course on jurisprudence (provided, of course, this is taught by someone interested in critical approaches) rather than sociology of law. However, there are a number of traditions within postmodernism, which is a diverse intellectual movement, and some of these are concerned, in conventional sociological terms, in understanding the nature of society and how it is changing. It is important to remember here that sociology, as much as legal philosophy, is a subject concerned with debate rather than agreement, and to complicate matters there are also debates within debates. This section will consider the arguments of postmodernist thinkers who believe that we have entered, or are in the process of entering, a new stage of human history called post-modernity, which has implications for understanding law. It will then look at the ideas of Jacques Derrida and Michel Foucault. Although they are not strictly speaking postmodernists, these poststructuralist theorists and philosophers are seen as culturally characteristic of this new stage of history, and have influenced legal philosophy.

A new age in human history?

Postmodernist thinkers who believe that we have recently entered a new age of human history include Jean Baudrillard and Jean-Francois Lyotard, although the claims are also made more widely in sociology and have almost become common currency. Caution is advisable when assessing these claims since whatever aspect of our own times the postmodern theorist puts forward as distinctive, can also be demonstrated as having existed in the modern world. American sociologists and political commentators were interested in the 'death of class' in the 1940s. This was also a central theme in the writings of the Frankfurt School during the 1960s whose ideas were reviewed in Chapter 4. Similarly, novelists and sociologists were aware of the identity problems created by mass migration long before post-modern theorists in the 1980s. More generally, if postmodernism is identi-fied with globalisation or rapid change in a society driven by consumerism, market forces and technological advance, there was much discussion of all these developments during the nineteenth century, including by Karl Marx and Friedrich Engels in their (1967) *The Communist Manifesto*.

One way to resolve the problem is to see postmodernity as really the latest stage of capitalism, the economic and social system that developed in Europe from the second half of the eighteenth century and has spread round the world. This is why sociologists such as Anthony Giddens (1991) prefer the term 'late modernity'. On the other hand, one could also argue that these developments have reached a stage or taken forms that no one could have predicted in the nineteenth century, even if they correctly predicted the direc-tion in which an advanced, technological society was heading. Although there is much poverty in the world today, especially in countries not connected to the global market, there has still been amazing economic progress and an increase in living standards. Because of this one can argue that class divisions, in the sense of societies divided between a small elite and large working class no longer exist, or are not culturally significant. At the same time the level of individualisation in our society, and the variety of life-styles and identities one can pursue or create would have amazed most nineteenth-century theorists. There is also, arguably, a greater cultural mixing of the world's populations today although care should again be taken with these claim since there was more mass migration in the nineteenth century, including the millions of Europeans who emigrated to the melting pot of the New World.

If any cultural or political trend in the past 200 years can be claimed to be postmodern, it is not surprising that such claims have also been made for changes in the legal system, and particularly the growth of the state or international law (Stacy 2001). These arguments, however, face the problem that law today does not seem that different in its essentials from when Marx and Engels were writing in the 1840s: it is certainly hard to see any major shift in the work of judges or legislators, or the content of law, in the last 30 years at least when compared to the vast changes that took place at the start of the modern period. It is also striking that, whereas postmodern theorists have written a lot about changes in the economy, politics, identity, technology and the nature of organisations, they do not usually mention either law or regulation. This, however, may just mean that no one has set out to demonstrate how law has changed in recent times in a way that supports or reflects other aspects of postmodernity.

The most famous theorists associated with postmodernity are Jean-Francois Lyotard and Jean Baudrillard. Lyotard (1984) advances a view of society in which knowledge has become simply a commodity, or where different spheres of life have become separated and over-rationalised in a similar way to Marx and Weber. There is no discussion of law in this text, and put in these terms one could equally well describe Luhmann (Chapter 3) or Habermas (Chapter 4) as postmodern theorists. What distinguishes Lyotard from these modern theorists is that he believes that one cannot any longer place hope in knowledge as a means of producing a better society (see Box 7.1). One might argue that Weber and Luhmann come fairly close to this position, and in the process say more about the nature of law. However, Lyotard's argument that we can no longer rely on 'grand narratives' such as Marxism or science given the fragmentation of society remains a powerful and distinctive commentary on our times. Although there has always been disenchantment with science, intellectuals seem particularly disillusioned with grand explanatory theories in our own times, including those relating to law.

Baudrillard's ideas are, in some respects, similar to the Frankfurt School considered in Chapter 4 as part of the cultural turn in Marxism. Like Marcuse and Adorno, he was fascinated and horrified by the rapid growth of an affluent, consumer society based on the production of goods and services that in his view were not needed, and resulted in a shallow form of consciousness (shallow that is when contrasted with how we could ideally live in a simpler society). If anything, Baudrillard was even more pessimistic about the prospects for change, arguing that in a media-saturated society it is no longer even possible to determine what is real (the concept of 'hyperreality'). Again, it is unclear what, if anything, this has to do with law where judges or litigants are not troubled with philosophical worries of this kind, but it is relevant for those who have the modern belief that law can address social problems. Baudrillard believes, in a similar way to other social theorists going back to De Tocqueville in the early nineteenth century, that the

---

Box 7.1 Lyotard on the postmodern condition

Jean-Francois Lyotard (1984) wrote one of the most influential texts announcing the arrival of postmodernism. It argues that, because we are in a society based on information, the scientific theories of the past no longer have authority or meaning. Instead, we need to recognise that society is made up of numerous narratives or language games.

> The object of this study is the condition of knowledge in the most highly developed societies. I have decided to use the word *postmodern* to describe that condition. The word is in current use on the American continent among sociologists and critics; it designates the state of our culture following the transformations which, since the end of the nineteenth century, have altered the game rules for science, literature and the arts ....
>
> Simplifying to the extreme, I define *postmodern* as incredulity towards metanarratives ... To the obsolescence of the metanarrative ... corresponds, most notably, the crisis of metaphysical philosophy and of the university institution which in the past relied on it. The narrative function is losing ... its great hero, its great dangers, its great voyages, its great goal. It is being dispersed in clouds of narrative language elements.... Each of us lives at the inter-section of many of these. However, we do not necessarily establish stable language combinations, and the properties of the ones we do establish are not necessarily communicable.
>
> (Lyotard 1984, pp. 1–2)

Although he makes this case in general terms, it would apply equally to legal philosophy and sociology of law as to any other discipline concerned with producing knowledge. Like other poststructuralists, Lyotard argues that language no longer has a fixed meaning, and since culture is constituted by language, there is also no longer a stable morality. The last sentence seems to suggest that, in a highly complex society, it is no longer possible even to understand one another, so there is no point in trying to construct a science of society.

---

masses have lost their capacity for critical judgement in an affluent, consumer society (this is what he calls 'the death of the social'). This presumably means that they accept law and the legal system, and the professionals who administer this sphere of social life, along with the other institutions that constitute society. It also means, however, that the issues that concern lawyers and judges are largely irrelevant for the critical theorist who takes this cultural path. There is no longer a need to analyse law as an ideological force in the postmodern world, since the masses are controlled and kept in place through the advertising industry, computer games and television.

Questioning the idea of truth

Perhaps the most persuasive argument advanced by those suggesting there has been a decisive break from modernity is the fact that in the postmodern age we have lost our belief in science and the pursuit of truth. This is a nicely circular argument in that the intellectual ascendancy of postmodernism itself is seen as evidence of a new emerging period in human history. There can be no doubt, however, that poststructuralism as a movement in philosophy has been successful at challenging received ideas, and this has also influenced popular culture. One can argue that great art has always tried to challenge the idea of one truth (so again there is nothing new about postmodernism). On the other hand, many American television drama series (perhaps most notably in recent years *Lost*) play imaginatively with different perspectives, or mix different styles or genres to a greater degree than in previous decades. One could argue that a concern with the representational character of language that started with French structuralist theorists in the 1940s, such as Claude Levi-Strauss (1963) and Roland Barthes (1982), and was subsequently radicalised by the poststructuralists, has played a part in producing this postmodern outlook, not least because writers and artists have been exposed to these ideas on humanities courses. Alternatively, one could see them as part of the affluent, knowledge society identified as the latest stage of human history by Lyotard and Baudrillard.

The idea that it is possible to arrive at the truth through the exercise of human reason is a central assumption of the eighteenth-century intellectual movement known as The Enlightenment. It can best be appreciated by considering that before this period, it was believed that only the Church or divinely ordained monarchs had access to truth. When Descartes argued in the seventeenth century that human beings were reasoning beings, this was at the time a subversive and radical statement. It implied, for example, that the new experimental methods used in natural science, that had already challenged religious beliefs, could be used to produce a better world. From this optimistic intellectual movement developed much of what we take for granted in the modern world. It underpins, for example, our assumption that individuals are important, and should have rights in a democratic society based on the rule of law. It also provides the rationale for academic disciplines, such as law and sociology, that have employed scientific methods in creating and managing a good society based on these principles.

The most influential critic of the scientific assumption of Enlightenment thinkers was Friedrich Nietzche (1968) who celebrated in his philosophical writings the imaginative qualities suppressed by an over-rationalised, industrial civilisation. These ideas influenced Max Weber who expressed doubts whether science could produce a better world, if reliance on scientific rationality was part of the problem. They have also influenced poststructuralism which emerged in France during the 1960s and 1970s as an intellectual movement critical towards a previous generation of structuralists, including

Althusser (Chapter 4) who believed that a science of society was possible. The main target of this movement was not so much the complacency of bourgeois, industrial society but the philosophical ideas underpinning modernity. These include the idea that the exercise of Reason (in the case of sociology the use of scientific procedures) can produce Truth.

This is arguably what is most radical about Lyotard's (1984) analysis of the postmodern condition. He is not simply observing that we have become disillusioned about science, but making the epistemological argument that we should no longer trust grand narratives because there are many equally valid ways of explaining reality. Foucault's analysis of human history in terms of discourses is similarly subversive in philosophical terms. Enlightenment thinkers believed in the idea that human societies would progress through stages towards perfection guided by science. Foucault, by contrast, sees change as happening through chance and contingency, and not necessarily resulting in a better world. Then there are other thinkers who argue against the Enlightenment assumption that it is possible to represent reality objectively. Derrida's method of deconstruction is perhaps the most extreme and well-thought-out exercise of this kind.

Another poststructuralist who has been influential in law and the humanities (but not in sociology) is the psychoanalyst Jacques Lacan (1994). This discipline grows out of the ideas of Sigmund Freud who developed a theory of the mind in the late nineteenth century, based on the idea that beneath our conscious mind there is an unconscious which can be studied using scientific methods. Like modernist thinkers in sociology, Freud believed that it was possible to use scientific theory to produce a better world.

Lacan differs from Freud in arguing that the human individual is produced culturally through language, and recognition by 'the other'. As a poststructuralist, he also advances a morally, relativistic view of society in a similar way to Foucault or Derrida that makes us question the 'symbolic realm' (established values and institutions) without suggesting there are alternatives. In its more extreme formulations, there is no longer such a thing as either the individual or society. They are simply part of the 'imaginary', our illusory experience of the world as 'whole' and 'complete' which arises from separation from the mother:

> These intellectual and emotional perceptions of coherence and wholeness are a misperception because we are each 'really' nothing more than a fragmented collection of drives and body .... For Lacan, the infant experiences 'castration' from the moment it realises that the mother wants something beyond the child. Thereafter, the subject spends life desperately trying to stabilise her identity so as to re-claim the illusory state of connection with the mother.
>
> (Stacy 2001, p. 108)

Although the next part of this chapter will focus on Derrida and Foucault, Lacan's ideas could equally well be used to analyse legal texts, or for that matter empirical studies by sociologists. What should be apparent, however, is that the critique starts, and almost always remains, at a philosophical level. One can, for example, accept everything Lacan says about law as an imaginary institution, while still knowing that, if we drive carelessly, there will be legal consequences. Derrida also offers a philosophical critique of law. Foucault, on the other hand, has more of interest to say to sociologists: he offers a means of understanding the nature of law in modern societies.

Derrida, law and sociology

Jacques Derrida has done more than any poststructuralist philosopher in challenging received ideas about representation. It is, for example, easy to assume when reading a literary text that, to uncover its meaning, we need to recreate the intention of the author. Derrida has, however, argued that the meaning of a text comes from how it is used and interpreted. He once famously observed 'there is nothing beyond the text'. This can itself be interpreted in a variety of ways, but one is that everything we do, whether speech, action or its representation in a text has no fixed meaning. This is partly because texts are connected to other texts: meaning is always deferred or postponed till the next text become available (the concept of 'differance'). The meaning of any text can also be deconstructed since oppositions or dualisms that constitute our language cannot be sustained under philosophical scrutiny. Cuff et al.(2006) summarise this in the following terms:

> The operation of deconstruction works in the opposite way to conventional attempts to identify a coherently structured text, unified under its title and the name of the author. The conventional direction seeks out as much internal consistency as possible, trying to bring all aspects of the text within the scheme. Its obverse, deconstruction, cultivates incongruities and paradoxes, highlighting the ways texts are internally divided within themselves, showing how one part of the text counteracts the effect ostensibly sought in another, and revealing especially where aspects of the text resist, confound and unravel the order which seeks to impose itself upon the text.
>
> (Cuff et al. 2006, p. 285)

Derrida employed this philosophical technique, primarily in relation to philosophical writings themselves, for example in his (1986) *Glas* which contrasts and deconstructs writings by the philosopher G.W.F. Hegel and Jean Genet, a French novelist and playwright associated with deviant or transgressive behaviour. One can see how similar techniques could be applied to legal or even sociological texts, although deconstruction in these fields usually means advancing relativist arguments against the truth claims of texts, rather than identifying internal contradictions or interpretive problems through close textual analysis.

Deconstructing legal texts

Derrida himself did not consider legal texts when writing about deconstructionism, and his best-known essay about legal philosophy defends the concept of justice, demonstrating that poststructuralist philosophers often retreat from or qualify what initially appear to be relativist positions when they are asked to comment on political issues (Box 7.2). What is perhaps initially surprising is that postmodern jurists, influenced by his ideas, have

---

Box 7.2 Derrida on justice

One infuriating quality of poststucturalist thought is that it recognises no rules or consistency, so this makes it possible to shift from questioning the concept of truth and arguing there are no moral standards, to apparently endorsing these, admittedly in a complex, qualified fashion in other writings or interviews. When giving an address at Cordozo law school, Derrida surprised his audience by making a distinction between law as a constructed institution, and justice which had a universal character and could not be deconstructed. There are many interpretations of this lecture, but one is that he seems to be arguing for the possibility of achieving justice through doing deconstructionist work:

> ... law *(droit)* is esentially deconstructible, whether because it is founded, constructed on interpretable and transformable textual strata ... or because its ultimate foundation is by definition unfounded. The fact that law is deconstructible is not bad news. We may even see in this a stroke of luck for politics, for all historical progress. But the paradox that I'd like to submit for discussion is the following: it is this deconstructible structure of law *(droit)* or if you prefer of justice as *droit*, that also insures the possibility of deconstruction. Justice in itself, if such as thing exists, outside or beyond law, is not deconstructible. No more than deconstruction itself, if such a thing exists. Deconstruction is justice ... deconstruction takes place in the interval that separates the undeconstructibility of justice from the deconstructibility of *droit*...
>
> (Derrida 1992, pp. 14–15)

This passage provides a good illustration of how philosophers are concerned with philosophical questions rather than the ordinary arguments that take place in politics, such as whether law benefits particular groups. Philosophers are less interested in achieving justice and more in determining whether justice is *possible* as a philosophical concept. Derrida discusses this with reference to several philosophers and the literary critic Walter Benjamin in the rest of the talk, rather than giving his views on contemporary politics.

also not generally written about particular legal texts or bodies of law at any level of detail. Perhaps the best example of this kind of critique is Duncan Kennedy's (1979) *Blackstone Commentaries*, one of the founding texts of Critical Legal Studies, a movement of philosophers and legal theorists who were influential as a leftist, oppositional force within American and later British law schools in the 1970s and 1980s. This cannot, however, be described as postmodern or deconstructionist since it criticises positivist or formalist jurisprudence from a Marxist perspective.

Postmodern jurisprudence emerged out of Critical Legal Studies. In America, a key text is Peter Gabel and Duncan Kennedy's 'Roll over Beethoven' (1984), a conversation about the possibility of critique and the importance of representing the world in its interpretive complexity. In America, the terminology of deconstructionism has supplemented critiques of formalist positions in jurisprudence by constructionist and critical jurists such as Stanley Fish (1989) or Druscilla Cornell (1991). This is a very old argument between those who believe that judges discover or make the law, or whether there are underlying principles informing the piecemeal development of case law.

In Britain and Australia, a group of legal philosophers, including Sean McVeigh (2002) and Costas Douzinas (Douzinas et al. 1994), have drawn on poststructuralist theory in a more thoroughgoing manner. Usually, the target is the claims of positivist legal philosophers that it is possible, at least in principle, to find truth and certainty in the law. Sometimes, as in the case of Peter Goodrich's (1995) writings, there is extensive discussion of philosophical claims made by Lacan in relation to characters in Sophocles' play *Antigone*. Sometimes, there is an attempt to identify contradictions in legal texts, in a similar way to the 'trashing' of law by Critical Legal Studies theorists, although with a relativising intent. Although this literature sometimes sees itself as continuing the tradition of legal realism, and having affinities with sociology of law, it demonstrates that there is often little real dialogue or even a point of contact between them. Legal philosophers argue about foundational questions concerning the nature of law or justice, and have little interest in what lawyers and judges actually do, the nature of social institutions or how societies are changing.

Deconstruction in sociology

Although deconstructionist philosophy has had little or no impact on legal practice or on the discipline of black-letter law, it has changed the way in which some sociologists conduct and understand empirical research. Here it is important to make it clear that postmodernism as a philosophical critique has influenced only a relatively small group of researchers. Most sociological work proceeds without anyone raising doubts, even at a philosophical level, over whether it is possible to produce objective findings. However, there are anthropologists and qualitative sociologists who have set out to critique realist ethnographic texts, by showing that there are different versions within the text, or they can be interpreted in different ways (Clifford and Marcus 1986). There are also new forms of ethnographic writing such as dialogic texts, autoethnographies or performance ethnographies which seek to challenge conventional ways of representing reality. There have also been researchers in the sociology of science who have written experimental reflexive texts challenging the concept of truth or the possibility of representation which are close in spirit to Derrida's deconstructionist programme in philosophy.

While these experiments are interesting, one can argue that they often fall back into the critical tradition, and have had only a limited impact on sociology which remains a scientific discipline concerned with producing objective, empirical findings. They have so far been confined to a relatively small group of ethnographers who are mainly concerned with understanding social groups or emotional experiences, and have not looked at work in professional settings. There are no dialogic texts, autoethnographies or performance ethnographies about legal settings; but there have also been no experimental, poststructuralist texts challenging representation in schools or hospitals.

Foucault and law

The poststucturalist theorist who has had most influence on sociology of law is Michel Foucault (1926–84). He has also been a popular theorist in mainstream sociology since the 1980s, partly because he makes it possible to advance a progressive or leftist view of society that seems more suited to our own times than Marxism. Marxism generated a rich empirical literature about law, including both historical studies and ethnographies. Foucault has also informed or influenced a variety of studies, but it would be fair to say that, with a few exceptions (for example, Merry 1990) he is mainly the subject of theoretical discussion in sociology of law and legal theory (for example, Golder and Fitzpatrick 2009). This is perhaps understandable because whereas Marx had little to say about law, Foucault explicitly argued that law had been given too much attention by social theorists. This has led to attempts to make his ideas palatable to a law and society audience by showing that he was interested in law despite making statements to the contrary, or by identifying this neglect or omission as a problem.

To understand what is at issue in these debates, it is necessary to know more about Foucault's intellectual project as a poststructuralist. He was first and foremost a critic of the Enlightenment, and of Enlightenment thinkers, including Marx. This led to a distinctive way of conceptualising power, and his ideas on bio-power and governmentality have also influenced research by sociologists and political scientists about how the state governs that involves more than studying law.

Foucault's criticisms of the Enlightenment

In a series of books published in the 1960s, Foucault investigated the birth of the modern world during the eighteenth century. Whereas Marx had focused on underlying economic processes, Foucault, like Weber, concentrated on changes in culture and thought. *Madness and Civilisation* (1967) looked at changes in how society recognised and treated madness: from being part of society and culture, the insane were confined in asylums and treated by the new science that became psychiatry. The *Birth of the Clinic* (1973) looked at the development of medicine as an institution, and *The Order of Things* (1970) at more profound changes in how the human sciences thought about the subject and representation. These historical studies are all implicitly critical of celebratory accounts about how modern civilisation developed from the Middle Ages, including Marx's writing on the origins of capitalism. However, it is *Discipline and Punish* (1977), in which Foucault discusses law, where he advances this critique most forcefully, in a way that makes us reflect on our received assumptions about what makes a good society.

Discipline and Punish starts with a lengthy and graphic account of someone being tortured for committing a criminal offence in the Middle Ages. The rest of the book is about the rise of a more civilised way of dealing with criminal behaviour that was promoted by enlightened thinkers, and was then taken up by governments, following the French Revolution. This involved developing a science concerned with the causes of crime (which has become criminology) and also with humane methods of punishment. While it is easy for us to feel superior to the pre-moderns, Foucault also wants us to appreciate that execution as normal and beneficial at the time, as the healthy expression of public anger. This might be contrasted with the scientific procedures used by the American government to describe practices such as water-boarding and sleep deprivation today, and how this is euphemistically called intensive interrogation (Bagaric 2008), as if we could not possibly engage in torture as a civilised modern society.

However, Foucault was also making a much broader critique of modernity in the same way as Weber or Nietzche. He was particularly interested in the ideas of Jeremy Bentham, a penal reformer who designed prisons so that inmates could be observed in their cells from a central tower (the Panopticon). The rise of the modern administrative state, that employs professionals such as police officers, prison guards, but also psychologists and social workers, to monitor and improve the health and moral well-being of the population, may seem a great advance on arbitrary torture and executions. However, Foucault argues that scientific rationality allows the state to control whole populations that was not possible during the Middle Ages. In many senses, we are living in a gigantic prison, in that our actions are observed by numerous government agencies, and all kinds of professional groups shape and influence our conduct from early childhood.

Cutting the head off the king

Foucault has created problems for legal thinkers who are otherwise attracted by his ideas by explicitly stating that he has little interest in the legal system or the sovereign law-making state (Wickham 2002). Instead, he argued that it was important to 'cut the head off the king' and look beyond the traditional institutions and agencies that are usually viewed as exercising power. He has also criticised traditional understandings of power, suggesting that this should be seen as widely dispersed through society, rather than exercised through legislation that seeks to enforce the will of the sovereign. It has been suggested by some legal sociologists that Foucault cannot possibly mean this since there are many references to law in his various studies about the modern world, or that he displays some failing for not acknowledging the protections afforded by law.

Although there are always many ways of interpreting any theorist, it makes sense to take Foucault's 'expulsion' of law (Hunt 1992) at face value, as an attempt to direct social theorists away from the view that governments can be overthrown or justice achieved through the creation of rights, and instead ask them to recognise how we are in the grip of ideas and practices that extend considerably beyond law. To give a few examples, our conduct and how we understand our own actions are shaped and regulated by professional groups such as psychiatrists, accountants and management consultants, but also fitness experts, sexual therapists and cosmetic surgeons. Although some of these professionals are licensed by the state, this is not the source of their power over human populations. There is also no simple way of resisting this power, since it will remain even if we overthrow the government, or change the law. Viewed in this light, Foucault's comments on the need to look beyond sovereignty seem to be making a similar point to nineteenth century theorists like Weber concerned about the rise of the state. One might also add that Foucault is not the only theorist suspicious of law and its claims to provide a good society through guaranteeing rights. Marx can also be read, particularly in his (1975) essay about the limitations of rights, as expressing scepticism and distrust towards liberal jurisprudence.

Governmentality as a research agenda

The Foucauldian framework is often used loosely within law and society studies as an alternative way of talking about subordinate groups to Marxism or feminism. Sally Merry's (1990) ethnography, *Getting Justice and Getting*

Even, describes law in Foucauldian terms as a set of discourses that influence how people settle disputes. Joe Hermer's (2008) study looks at the practices of local councils in promoting an acceptable form of begging. These studies can be read as advancing a political programme for establishing a more humane or egalitarian society. However, it is important to remember that Foucault himself was not interested in ideology critique. He supported minority or deviant groups, but without seeing them as a potential revolutionary force.

Arguably the most productive agenda influenced by Foucault is not about law but the regulatory state. This came about when a group of mainly British political theorists engaged with Foucault's writing about bio-power and governmentality. Bio-power refers to the various ways in which the state is concerned with producing a healthy and economically productive population. It can be seen as a larger version of the Panopticon and encompasses the work of numerous professionals concerned with monitoring and measuring human populations. Governmentality has to do with the knowledge and practices concerned with regulation and governance:

> Knowledge ... does not simply mean 'ideas' but refers to the vast assemblage of persons, theories, projects, experiments and techniques that has become such a central component of government. Theories from philosophy to medicine. Schemes from town-planning to social insurance. Techniques from double entry book-keeping to compulsory medical inspection of school-children. Knowledgeable persons from generals to architects and accountants. Our concern, that is to say, is with the 'know how' that has promised to make government possible.
> (Rose and Miller 1992, p. 178)

Although Foucault himself wrote about the rise of the state during the past 300 years, the Foucauldian governmentality tradition has been mostly concerned with changes that have taken place in recent times. Rose and Miller, for example, have been particularly interested in the shift between 'welfarism' and 'neoliberalism' as forms of governance in the last 40 years. The assumption in social democratic or welfare societies was that the state should secure full employment through borrowing. In recent years, governments have followed quite different principles concerned with encouraging economic competition, although there has been a dramatic reversal of policy following the 2007–8 financial crisis. Neo-liberalism has resulted in changes to the nature of public sector work, such as the greater emphasis placed on auditing and internal markets. An example of a technology of government that should be familiar to readers in higher education is the feedback form administered at the end of each course. This is intended to change the relationship between teacher and student, but also to introduce competition within and between universities through measuring the quality of teaching.

Feedback forms cannot directly be seen as the exercise of power by a sovereign state through making legislation, although the university does obtain many of its internal regulatory powers from the state. Instead, this system of regulation has grown up as managers and administrators have discovered a new form of knowledge, which they exercise in the name of students as consumers. Unlike Marxists, governmentality theorists do not see these processes as driven by the needs of the capitalist class to make profits. Nor do they even necessarily disapprove of developments such as auditing and quality assurance regulation. They are not, for example, interested in defending professionals against managerialism (Rose, 1996, p. 353). Instead, like Foucault, they have a broader project in problematising expert knowledge and the regulatory state.

The politics of identity and difference

Lyotard explained the success of poststructuralism in modernist terms as the response of intellectuals to real social, economic and political changes that have taken place in Western societies since the Second World War. One of these has been the gradual weakening, and then the collapse of Marxism as a political project. It was weakened during the 1950s and 1960s as French intellectuals gradually recognised that Stalin, previously seen as hero of the left, was a dictator and mass murderer. It collapsed dramatically at the end of the 1980s with the end of the Soviet Union, not through external military or economic pressure, although this played a part, but from mass popular unrest and the ideological triumph of free market capitalism and democracy (Fukuyama 1992). Meanwhile in Western countries, there were significant changes in socio-economic structure associated with de-industrialisation. Whereas in the 1940s, there was a sizeable working class employed by manufacturing industry, today the majority of the population in America and Western Europe have managerial and administrative jobs, or work in the service sector, including financial institutions. Many sociologists argue that class still exists in the sense that it allows one to predict life-chances. However, it has become increasingly difficult to identify classes as cultural groups whose members dress, speak or vote distinctively. There are no longer class-based, political parties with distinctive programmes.

The past few decades have also seen the rise to prominence of social movements concerned with the discrimination experienced by different minorities. The most successful has been the feminist movement, but there have also been campaigns for rights to fair treatment by homosexuals and ethnic groups. However, in each case, the political leadership has faced criticism for purporting to represent every member of the category while not addressing or acknowledging their special needs and interests. This has developed into a recognition that there are, in fact, numerous ways of being female, homosexual or belonging to an ethnic group. Some prominent sociologists had recognised and written about identity and difference well before postmodernism, including Weber who realised during the 1900s that class divisions could undercut the effectiveness of a status group as a political movement. However, it only became a question of major interest in the social sciences and humanities, including critical jurisprudence, in the 1970s and 1980s. This section will illustrate how poststructuralist ideas have been employed to theorise the experiences of women, homosexuals and ethnic minorities.

Postmodern feminism

Feminists have made an important contribution in the sociology of law and critical jurisprudence by showing how women face discrimination in the legal profession and that in many areas of statute and case law the body of statutes favour men as a social group. They have also campaigned as a political movement for remedies, such as tougher laws to protect women. Postmodern feminists do not normally oppose these initiatives, but they do argue that presenting women as a universal group is misleading and the wrong strategy to achieve progressive social change.

The most influential theorist who has promoted these ideas, although without specifically referring to law, is Judith Butler (1990). Drawing on Foucault, she has argued that gender should be considered a discursive or linguistic construct, something that is performed through our speech and actions rather than having any real or objective basis. Whereas radical feminists had recognised the existence of biological sex, Butler argues that this, as much as gender, is constructed in an age where sex-change operations have become commonplace. This has considerable implications for feminism as a theoretical project and form of political action. This passage from Hilaire Barnett (1998) identifies some of the problems:

> From a legal-theoretical perspective, the postmodernist rejects the grand concepts of traditional theory: rights, equality, rationality must be re-thought and reunderstood from a critical standpoint which dismantles the perceived false certainties and reveals the realities of life. As noted above, fragmentation, contingency and diversity must replace coherence, uncertainty displace certainty. The implications of the postmodern critique for feminist jurisprudence are profound. If 'grand theory' is no longer sufficient to explain women's condition, concepts such as patriarchy and gender ... lose their explanatory force, and throw doubt on the potential for a convincing coherent theoretical understanding of women's live and conditions. In place of grand theory, there must be developed critiques that concentrate on the reality of the diversity of individual women's lives and conditions, critiques which reject the

universalist, foundationalist, philosophical and political understandings offered by modernism. With the 'age of innocence' lost, in its place there exists diversity, plurality, competing rationalities, competing perspectives and uncertainty as to the potentiality of theory.

(Barnett 1998, p. 180)

For empirical sociology of law, this seems to suggest that the researcher can only describe the problems of particular women, rather than linking them to campaigns of 'grand narratives' by feminists as an international movement. It also suggests that the concept of rights has to be abandoned, not because women do not benefit from employment laws or street lighting, but because this supports traditional categories of thought.

Queer theory

Sociologists of law and critical legal thinkers influenced by poststructuralism have made similar arguments about homosexual identity. In arguing for de-criminalisation of consensual sex or same-sex marriage, critical theorists tended to present homosexuals as a unified or homogeneous group. In fact, outside the academy there were always tensions and debates between male homosexuals and lesbians, those who favoured a public or private identity, and between groups with different sexual practices. Queer theorists have, however, gone even further by arguing, in a similar way to postmodern feminists, that all sexual behaviour is socially constructed. One suggestion is that everyone has heterosexual and homosexual desires, and it just happens that one form of sexuality is dominant or approved in our culture.

Carl Stychin (1995) demonstrates how it is possible to question or undermine assumptions about sexual identity through examining cases brought against soldiers in the US army seeking to disqualify them from serving on the grounds of homosexuality. The relevant statute was directed against soldiers who had committed the homosexual act of sodomy. However, a soldier was told to leave the army on the grounds of having confessed to being a homosexual, without having committed any homosexual acts, and a court upheld this as sufficient evidence. Stychin agrees that the outcome of this case about a 'celibate homosexual' was important for the individual involved, but he is more interested in drawing out the implications for how we understand sexual identity. The courts in this case seemed themselves to adopt a performative conception of sexuality:

In separating act from identity within legal discourse, sexual identity becomes individuated, as the object of knowledge is allowed to intervene within the discourse. That, in turn, creates the possibility of the problematisation and proliferation of categories, such that the overdetermined category 'homosexual' is evacuated of any essential meaning.

(Stychin 1995, p. 194)

In this case, the court determined someone as having a homosexual identity that had not previously been recognised by the statute. The implication is that sexuality is far more diverse and fluid than usually recognised in our culture, and constructed through language.

Multiculturalism and law

The issue that dominates international politics today, and has resulted in restrictions on taken-for-granted freedoms in Western countries, is the threat posed by Al-Qaeda, the fundamentalist Islamic sect that declared war on secular, democratic societies when it flew hi-jacked planes into the World Trade Centre on 11 September 2001. This has resulted in legislation to combat the potential threat from ethnic groups, with different cultures and values, who live in Western, multi-cultural societies.

Migration has been a feature of human societies since our early history, so there is nothing new about attempts to control movement, or debates on how to treat newcomers. Forced migration has included the slave trade between Africa and the New World, and the refugees displaced from war zones today. Voluntary migration includes the mass movement from Eastern and Southern Europe to America in the late nineteenth century. In Britain, there was immigration from its ex-colonies in the Caribbean and the Indian subcontinent following the Second World War, which has resulted in substantial communities of Muslims from Pakistan and Bangladesh.

Many different sociological traditions have analysed the mixing of the world's populations. Everett Stonequist (1937), a student of Robert Park, published a book about identity problems facing migrants to America in the 1930s. More recently, poststructuralists have addressed the cultural and psychological problems arising from culture contact. One influential text is Edward Said's *Orientalism* (1979). This drew on Foucault's ideas and methods to examine how Western writers and government officials represented countries in the East during the colonial period. Said showed that those from a different culture were often portrayed in stereotypical terms as members of a homogeneous group, which did not do justice to their cultures. Orientalism has generated the field of post-colonial studies which is equally concerned with showing how commentators in the colonial world developed their own stereotypes about Western countries.

Although not written from a poststructuralist perspective, Dominic McGoldrick's (1996) study of debates surrounding the 2004 ban placed on wearing Islamic headscarfs and other religious symbols in France illustrates how difference and identity create a problem for law-makers. A growing proportion of young people from Islamic communities is choosing to wear the headscarf or hijab. This has become a contested symbol both within these religious groups (Box 7.3) but also in general society where it is viewed by some as representing freedom of expression and belief, central to

---

Box 7.3 The Islamic headscarf debate in Europe

A decision by the French government outlawing religious dress in school has resulted in legal challenges on the grounds that it infringes human rights. However, these cases also illustrate the difficulties that arise in trying to understand a different culture in monolithic terms. The postcolonial feminist, Lena Abu Odeh identifies a variety of ways in which Muslim women in different countries relate to wearing the veil:

[There are those who] wear make up with the veil. They are more creative and fashion conscious in public, so that they constantly attempt to subvert the blandness of the veil. They invent a million ways to tie a colourful scarf on their heads, supplanting the more standard white. The loose dress of the veil suddenly becomes slightly tighter, more colourful, and daring in emulating western fashions, even if it doesn't explicitly reveal more parts of the female body. One also notices them on the streets conversing and strolling with men, subverting the segregation that the veil imposes on the sexes.

There are also those who wear the veil but retain a fiercely ambivalent relationship with it; wearing it is a decision that is made almost every day. It is not uncommon to find them wearing it on some days and taking it off on others ...

And, then there are those who use their bodies and dress as a statement of opposition. They differentiate themselves from others in their environment by wearing the veil, using it as a statement about female subordination in the non-fundamentalist ... Arab households in which they find themselves....

Of course, a veiled woman is not necessarily 'this' or 'that'. She might shift from one position to the another. At times colourful, other times bland, seductive and prudish, publicly and privately. A veiled woman's subjectivity appears to be much more complicated than any meaning the word 'veil' could possibly convey.

(Odeh 1993, pp. 34–5)

---

a liberal democracy, and by others as indicating the potential breakdown of society through unassimilated minorities. The 2004 law in France prohibited 'the wearing of signs or dress by which pupils overtly manifest a religious affiliation'; examples given, in explanatory regulations, included muslim headscarves, Jewish skull-caps (kipot) and large Christian crosses. This inevitably created intractable interpretive problems. Schools and the courts had to decide, for example, whether a bandana constituted a headscarf even though it did not cover the whole face and neck. Then there was the issue as to whether a symbol was worn with religious intent:

What if a non-Muslim child wears a headscarf-hijab as a fashion statement .... What if a male pupil wears a beard for religious purposes?

Could this be interpreted as wearing a sign? What if the pupil wears a beard but not for a religious purpose? How does the school know the difference?

(McGoldrick 1996, p. 94)

Interpretive problems of this kind were resolved by the French courts on a case-by-case basis and have also been raised by appeals under human rights Conventions protecting the right to freedom of religion. However, whether or not they can be resolved, a poststructuralist would argue that this again shows the difficulties of establishing boundaries. As in the case of gender and sexuality, it no longer makes sense to see identities as fixed, or to believe that there are simple solutions in campaigning for rights. Instead there are multiple identities within shifting over-lapping discourses, and identity has a constructed or performative character. The target of this kind of theorising is not only laws that discriminate against subordinate groups, but the comforting illusion maintained and promoted by law that there are fixed identities.

Assessing postmodernism

Our objective in this chapter has been to show how poststructuralist ideas are significantly different to the theorising conducted by those working within either the consensus or critical traditions. Instead of seeing society as a whole that can be described or categorised within some explanatory framework, poststructuralists see it in Foucauldian terms as the site of competing discourses or in Derridean terms as a text subject to endless interpretation. Instead of seeing social groups engaged in a contest for resources and status, poststructuralists prefer to problematise identity and meaning itself. Perhaps more than most theoretical frameworks, it invites and has generated numerous critical responses. These include the charge of relativism from critical legal theorists, and the complaint from sociologists that poststructuralism makes it impossible to conduct empirical research.

The problem of relativism

Critical legal theorists often have an interesting ambivalent relationship with poststructuralism. They are drawn to poststructuralism as a means of overcoming the inability of Marxism to address changes in the social structure of advanced, industrial societies, and its apparent failure as a political project, but at the same time they are concerned that it leads to relativism and the inability to engage in politics beyond the local level.

These ideas are discussed by Alan Hunt (1990) in an article written shortly before the collapse of the Soviet Union. In a revealing passage, he described the growing realisation of failure among progessive thinkers, and the recognition that new ideas were needed in the following terms:

> The closing years of the twentieth century are proving to be an epoch fraught with difficulties for progressive intellectuals. Contemporary Western societies seem further than ever away from the major structural transformations necessary for the dismantling of the hierarchies of class, gender and race and the achievement of social justice. It no longer seems relevant to repeat the old battlecries of the variant forms of the socialist movement. Despite the exciting chinks becoming visible in the monolith of the communist East. ... Marxist socialism is simply too encrusted with its history to provide contemporary inspiration. But neither has the social democratic tradition been able to transcend its own bureaucratic and paternalist legacy. ... Despite the commitment of progressive intellectuals to the quest for links between theory and practice, meaningful engagement with 'where people are at' in relatively affluent, consumerist societies is more difficult than ever to achieve. The manifestations of resistance and the glimmers of possible alternatives appear as a bewildering plurality. Few would retain the hope that the working class (or any other unitary subject) has the capacity to bring the fragments together.
>
> (Hunt 1990, pp. 510–11)

Poststucturalist ideas have been taken up in various ways by progressive theorists as a means of addressing diversity and difference, but also as a means of challenging received views and introducing marginalised or subversive voices into legal studies. However, once one employs or engages with these ideas at more than a superficial level, they make it difficult either to engage in political struggles, at least beyond the local level, and even worse they make it difficult to hold any political or moral viewpoint with any certainty. This is what Hunt calls the 'Big Fear' created by postmodernism for critical legal scholarship:

> It generates anxiety because it seems to deny the existence of any firm ground in which knowledge can be rooted and seems to leave us, fully aware of our frailties, in an ever changing and variable existence in which access to reality, truth or objectivity is forever denied. It is, in particular, moral relativism which generates the greatest anxiety since its espousal seems forever to prohibit us from settling any argument about what's right or wrong. We seem incapable of getting beyond personal preference or culturally given consensus.
>
> (Hunt 1990, p. 529)

In attempting to find a way out of this problem, Hunt argues that the critical theorist should recognise difference and diversity, while rejecting 'radical relativism' (Hunt 1990, p. 537). What this actually means in relation to engaging in political activity, beyond expressing sympathy for 'deviant' or minority groups remains unclear. The most productive body of scholarship in the law school has been mainly philosophical in character and has taken the form of debates with other positions in critical legal thought or mainstream jurisprudence.

Postmodernism and empirical research

One question that may have occurred to the reader is whether postmodernist thought has much bearing or relevance to empirical research. One reading of what has happened is that there has been a divergence in law schools, and the field of sociology of law, in recent years between three groupings, each of which have a different institutional base. On the one hand, there are those doing increasingly quantitative, empirical research for government agencies informed by positivist assumptions that one can obtain the truth and represent reality objectively. Their institutional base is often in law schools, where there is a tradition of teaching policy-oriented law in context and methods courses. Then there are the critical legal theorists who have worked through debates between Marxism and postmodernism for a number of years. These are also based in law schools and teach courses in jurisprudence. The third group are sociologists of law. They are mainly based in social science departments and include traditions such as Marxist and feminist sociology of law, autopoesis theory, interactionism, ethnomethodology and legal pluralism (based in anthropology departments) reviewed in this book. Postmodernists have attempted to challenge and subvert each of these fields by raising philosophical questions about truth and representation. They have only really had an impact on the critical tradition in jurisprudence. Foucault's ideas have, however, been influential in mainstream sociology and resulted in a distinctive empirical research agenda on law.

Questions

1 What do you understand by the term 'postmodernity'? How is this relevant to studying law?
2 How does Foucault challenge how we understand law and the state?
3 What do you understand by the term 'deconstructionism'? How can this be used in studying legal texts?
4 Why are poststructuralists interested in identities and difference?
5 'Although poststructuralism has influenced legal philosophy, it has only had a limited impact on empirical sociology of law'. Explain and discuss.

Further reading

For some clear introductions to postmodernism and poststructuralism as intellectual movements, see Cuff, Sharrock and Francis' *Perspectives in Sociology* (Routledge,

London, 2006), and Best and Kellner's *Postmodern Theory* (Macmillan, Basingstoke, 2001). For two good introductions to law and postmodernism, see Stacy's *Postmodernism and Law: Justice in a Fragmenting World* (Ashgate, Aldershot, 2001) and Edgeworth's *Law, Modernity, Postmodernity* (Ashgate, Aldershot, 2003).

Influential texts for legal studies include Foucault's *Discipline and Punish* (Tavistock, London, 1977) and Derrida's lecture, 'Force of Law' in a collection on *Deconstruction and the Possibility of Justice* edited by Cornell, Rosenfeld and Carlson (Routledge, New York, 1992). Examples of postmodern jurisprudence include the articles in Patterson's *Postmodernism and Law* (New York University Press, New York, 1994) and Douzinas, Goodrich and Hachamovitch's *Politics, Postmodernity and Critical Legal Studies* (Routledge, London, 1994).

For critical discussion of the significance of Foucault for law, see Hunt and Wickham's *Foucault and Law* (Pluto Press, London, 1994). Hunt's article 'The Big Fear' (*McGill Law Journal* 1990, Vol. 35, No. 3, pp. 507–40) considers the implications of postmodernism for critical legal thought. Judith Butler's *Gender Trouble: Feminism and the Subversion of Identity* (Routledge, New York, 1990) employs poststructuralist ideas to problematise identity in feminism and post-colonial studies

Chapter 8

Legal pluralism and globalisation

The problem of legal pluralism   168
  Indigenous, community and state law   169
  Weak and strong versions   171
  Pluralism and the classical tradition   172

Globalisation and law   173
  Debates about globalisation   175
  The field of international arbitration   178
  The global law firm   180
  Implementing human rights   182

Thinking globally   184
  Comparative legal research   185
  International regulation   186

Questions   187

Further reading   187

Boxes 8.1 The Cheyenne Way   170
     8.2 Towards a new legal commonsense 174
     8.3 Three failures of globalisation 177
     8.4 Doing a global study   185

This book has been published by a multi-national company, which has offices or representatives in several countries, with the aim of reaching a potential international readership. In theory, courses on sociology of law, socio-legal studies or law and society could be taught in any university around the world. In practice, the largest markets for books of this kind are Britain and the United States – English-speaking countries which have developed university systems. They also have long-established democracies, and a tradition in civil society of reflection and debate about social issues which has generated academic subjects such as sociology, social policy and political science. The largest and most theoretically developed research literatures about law and society have been produced in the developed world. It has been natural to use examples from these countries, rather than from Africa, Latin America, India, the Pacific Islands, China or Japan. This is simply because many of the best resourced and theoretically developed studies are by American law and society researchers. Nevertheless, because it deliberately does not present much detail about particular legal systems, some readers may find this book too international for their tastes. Academic publishing seems to demonstrate that very few textbooks sell well outside a national readership. If this is true, to what extent can one really say that we are living in a globalised world?

This chapter reviews three over-lapping academic literatures that take globalisation, and the fact that legal systems differ across the world, seriously. The first has resulted from a group of mainly American anthropologists who have become interested in legal pluralism, defined as the existence of different legal systems in the same territory. The second is an international, multi-disciplinary literature that has been concerned with exploring how law has been changed by globalisation. This can be defined in simple terms as the claim (contested in some quarters) that the world has recently become a smaller place, often associated with the normative view that we need a world government or should embrace cosmopolitan identities. The third is a programme of research in law and society studies concerned with comparing legal systems in different countries. The chapter will also consider possible topics that one could study related to globalisation, and the practical and methodological challenges.

The focus of this book has been on theoretical traditions, and debates between and within traditions, rather than substantive topics. For this reason, a caveat is needed before this chapter. It is common to assume, having spent time trying to understand different theories and the relationship between them, that they are no longer needed or relevant when looking at substantive topics, such as the legal profession, women's rights, mediation or, in this chapter, globalisation. In fact, as should be clear from previous chapters, any aspect of the legal system, and any method for studying it, can be approached and debated from a range of positions.

To give one example, Talcott Parsons promoted globalisation during the 1940s and 1950s as a consensus theorist. We looked at his ideas on the development of American society in Chapter 3, but he also believed that a broader process was happening globally. Researchers influenced by his ideas developed an approach to understanding development known as modernisation theory. In simple terms, this advanced the normative view that developing countries should become more like America. They should industrialise and become democratic secular societies, based on individualistic values. Conflict or critical theorists countered with their own version of globalisation, known as dependency theory (Frank 1967). This portrayed America, and Western countries generally, as exploiting the Third World through imperialism and neo-colonialism. Contact with the West had not always helped these societies and there were alternative political and social models for development. Those celebrating the achievement of globalisation today (for example, Fukuyama 1992) often ignore these older debates, or see dependency theory as simplistic given that countries such as India and China have industrialised. Critical theorists today, such as Michael Hardt and Antonio Negri (2000), argue that what has really happened is the triumph of liberal capitalism against the alternative offered by the Soviet Union during the 1960s. Those proclaiming the end of theory are promoting Western values, such as individualism and consumerism, for the developing world in a similar way to modernisation theory.

To give a second example, those writing about globalisation often describe institutional change at the 'macro'-level such as the rise of human rights in international law. However, any topic can also be approached at the 'micro'-level through examining what happens inside international agencies using ethnographic methods (the 'macro'–'micro' distinction is introduced more critically in Chapter 6). To give a third example, the debates that take place between sociologists about whether one should employ quantitative or qualitative methods (not really discussed in this text) are relevant to the field of comparative legal research. There is a big difference between trying to understand a culture from within, and identifying variables with the aim of finding causes (Travers 2008). One should not, therefore, assume that debates about theory and method disappear once one starts researching a substantive topic, even though they might be concealed or not given much emphasis in these academic literatures.

The problem of legal pluralism

Legal pluralism is a sub-field of anthropology, the academic discipline that arose within Western industrialised countries during the late nineteenth century that has been concerned with studying societies in the developing world (Griffiths 2002). Anthropologists since Malinowski (1926) have been interested in the legal systems that have arisen to punish deviance or resolve disputes. Because many countries in the developing world have been colonised by Western powers, the first anthropologists became interested in the relationship between Indigenous and imperial legal systems. Decolonisation during the twentieth century resulted in the formation of states exercising sovereignty over diverse ethnic groups with their own customary laws.

Anthropologists have pursued many empirical studies describing the interaction between these legal systems. It was not, however, until the 1990s that the field of legal pluralism became influential in law and society studies. This was partly because American anthropologists turned their attention to different legal orders in their own society. The field also became more theoretical, as different schools with their own understandings of law and pluralism emerged, and there was some interest from legal theorists.

Indigenous, community and state law

The history of empires usually shows how a weak colonial government is nominally in control of a vast territory, but in reality relies on the administrative agencies that existed before colonisation. The British, for example, brought their law to India and Africa, but most people entered into marriages, made business contracts, punished criminal offences and settled disputes employing traditional or customary laws. This remains the case in settler societies, such as the USA, Canada and Australia in that, while everyone is subject to the same legal system, in practice Indigenous peoples have their own systems of law. This phenomenon has been extensively studied by anthropologists (see Box 8.1). They have found that, in some societies, Indigenous law has given ground in some areas to state law. In other societies, customary practice is incorporated into the Western legal system, in the same way as traditional religious practices have been absorbed into the churches established by Christian missionaries.

Different legal systems also exist within Western, industrialised societies. During the nineteenth century, Ehrlich and other sociological jurists argued that ethnic minorities, religious groups and traditional associations should be protected against state regulation. Even those progressives, like Pound, who supported greater state intervention in the economy, felt that law could only be effective if it understood and addressed community sentiments. This suggests that, even today, there may be local practices that exist alongside, or within, official legal institutions. Anthropologists studying courts in the USA have, for example, argued that practices such as plea-bargaining, or the pre-trial settlement of neighbourhood disputes, draw on community notions of justice outside the formal legal system (Merry 1990; Yngvesson 1988). They have also shown how, when settling disputes, people in many areas of social life rarely use the legal system and regard it as disruptive and unhelpful (Harrington 1985). Stewart Macauley (1963) demonstrated this in an influential study about how businessmen make agreements drawing on relations of trust, without formal contracts.

Box 8.1 The Cheyenne way

Based on two summers of fieldwork in a Reservation in Montana, Karl Llewellyn and E. Adamson Hoebel's (1941) study vividly conveys how legal decisions were made by this tribe of American Indians through examining cases from an 80 year period. This is an example of legal pluralism in that the Cheyenne retained their own law, even though they could have made use of the American legal system in settling disputes or punishing criminal behaviour. What makes the study particularly interesting, however, is that Llewellyn and Hoebel suggest that the methods used by these 'primitives' in resolving debates on a case by case basis were similar to those in the American courts.

During the 1930s, there were pressures on judges to adopt more formal procedures in the interests of producing certainty for litigants. Llewellyn believed that these changes were unnecessary and potentially harmful. An effective legal system required judges to make decisions creatively, responding to the circumstances, rather than being tied by precedent or procedure:

> The suspicion must be, no less, that neither ritualization of procedure nor fixed wording of legal rules is needed to produce much of predictability. It may well be that a very large degree of the regularity and predictability which we ourselves now enjoy in things of law is actually due not to the rules of law to which we have long been ascribing it, but to underlying legal institutions of our own which are as inarticulate, but which in their own way are as effective as those which one can observe at work in the Cheyenne cases.
>
> (Llewelyn and Hoebel 1941, p. 334)

Aside from the issue of pluralism, *The Cheyenne Way* is also sociologically interesting because it attempts to describe the content of law, through documenting cases, and considering how judges make decisions (see Chapter 1). Through describing cases, Llewellyn and Hoebel seek to convey a sense of when law was working well, or when it was 'off target'. They offer this account of how they recognised consistency, which also reveals the difficulties involved in understanding another culture:

> [We understood this] from the direct impact of the cases, which is the impact of sure variation around a sure core; there is a sureness of 'feel' about the action taken in most of the individual cases. The trouble is that both core and variation were lived too subtly for us to give form to them. We felt their presence too late to reach their substance. But the confusion in [this] picture of Cheyenne divorce law may well be our confusion, not that of the Cheyennes.
>
> (Llewellyn and Hoebel 1941, p. 324)

Weak and strong versions

There are different ways of understanding legal pluralism, and a lively theoretical literature has been generated around the empirical studies. Anne Griffiths (2002) distinguishes between weak and strong versions. Weak pluralism characterises early studies that sided with the colonial state against what were seen as backward or lawless societies. From this perspective, the growth of a legal system with a 'relative autonomy' from the state and society, and which exercised authority through interpreting legal rules was necessary for economic and social development:

> While associated with government, law was at the same time able to develop relative autonomy both from the state and from society through the existence of its own institutions, which dealt exclusively with legal matters. Legal activity became set apart from other forms of social and religious activity, not just in terms of institutions, but also through the language that accompanied this development, which reinforced the need for specialist personnel. In this way law became established as a self-validating system, a system whose validity, authority and legitimacy rely no longer on any external source such as morality or religion, but rather on internal sources which are self-referential for its regulation and perpetuation.
>
> (Griffiths 2002, p. 292)

Critics of this model (essentially a version of structural-functionalism reviewed in Chapter 3) have argued that it does not adequately acknowledge the sophistication of Indigenous legal systems, which existed outside or in parallel with state institutions. Others have argued that the boundaries are blurred, in that Indigenous law makes use of state systems, and state law incorporates Indigenous concepts or procedures. From this perspective, the state should not be privileged, and some anthropologists side with Indigenous peoples, although without always making clear whether there are alternatives to the state as a means of maintaining order in the multiethnic societies created after decolonisation. Strong or 'deep' pluralists have gone further and sought to apply this critical view of law to Western societies. Sally Falk Moore (1973) has, for example, argued that any social institution or area of social life can be conceptualised as a 'semi-autonomous social field' (although she does not describe herself as a legal pluralist). She developed this concept through comparing customary practices in the Chagga of Tanzania and those working in the garment industry in New York. The garment factory, like many workplaces, was governed by a set of rules, but these were regularly broken for commercial reasons:

> The basic union contract ... specifies such things as wages and hours. However, the exigencies of the business are such that it would be

impossible to make a profit unless the precise terms of these contracts were regularly broken. For one thing, when the opportunity arises to do a lot of work it has to be done quickly or there is nothing to be gained. A design will sell at one particular moment, and not at any time thereafter. Hence when business is plentiful, workers and contractors must produce dresses in a hurry and put in many more hours than the union contract permit. On the other hand, when business is slack, workers must be paid even when they are not in fact working. The floor lady, for example, since she is the person in the most favored position in the contractor's shop, may be paid while she cruises around the world on vacation. It is simply understood between the union's business representative and the contractor that he will not enforce the contract to the letter.

(Moore 1973, p. 725)

These informal customs and practices exist alongside labour law, and it is possible for workers in the garment industry to 'mobilise' these outside forces. However, Moore argues that 'state-enforceable' law is only a small part of the 'complex' of informal rules that govern conduct:

This complex, the operation of the social field, is to a significant extent self-regulating, self-enforcing, and self-propelling within a certain legal, political, economic, and social environment. Some of the rules about rights and obligations that govern it emanate from that environment, the government, the marketplace, the relations between the various ethnic groups that work in the industry, and so on. But many other rules are produced within the field of action itself.

(Moore 1973, p. 728)

Strong pluralists, therefore, see the informal rules that govern different areas of life as independent from the state legal system, and in many respects more important and consequential for ordinary members of society. They have aligned themselves with Indigenous groups in post-colonial societies, but also more generally with critical jurisprudence, in challenging the authority of state law.

Pluralism and the classical tradition

There are some similarities between legal pluralism and the questions raised by sociological jurists, such as Erhlich and Pound, on the relationship between law and society. It will be remembered from Chapter 2 that these theorists were also concerned about the rise of state law and its effect on existing social relationships. Ehrlich's concept of the 'living law' seems similar to Moore's 'semi-autonomous social field'. There are also, however, significant differences. Erhlich was a social conservative seeking to defend local interests and associations from intervention by the state. Pound supported law as a means of improving social life but felt that it had to proceed cautiously and respect local customs and mores. Strong pluralists, by contrast, tend to draw on the critical tradition in social theory. From this perspective, community or local 'forms of ordering' (Griffiths 2002, p. 302) are suppressed by dominant groups who control the formal legal system. The concepts of 'power' and 'ideology' remain central within this anthropological literature, even though it is not always clear what political programme is being advanced either in relation to the developing world or the USA.

This again demonstrates the distinction between identifying some phenomenon and seeking to explain this within different theoretical or political frameworks. No one would deny that there is a distinction between the rules constituting different areas of social life, or how disputes are informally managed and the legal system. Both the sociological jurists and the legal pluralists defend custom and tradition against state law, but with different political objectives. Like any other area of sociological investigation, it is also hard to avoid being drawn into questions raised by legal philosophers about the nature of law. Brian Tamanaha (1993), for example, has argued that if pushed too far, pluralism leads to the view that there is no distinction between law and society.

Globalisation and law

Globalisation is the view that the world is becoming a smaller place, which is evident from our everyday experience. We are, for example, connected by the media into what Marshall McLuhan (1962) termed the 'global village'. We are brought up-to-date with what is happening on the other side of the world through watching the evening news or reading the local daily newspaper. Through these channels, most people already know about the international institutions and agencies that are increasingly important alongside nation states. As I am writing this chapter in Australia, the local newspapers are covering the world financial crisis, and the response of the International Monetary Fund and World Bank. There is discussion in the editorial pages about the effects of the 'credit-crunch' that originated in the USA on Europe, and how a possible economic slow-down in China will affect the Australian economy. There are also daily news reports about a civil war in the Congo that has created a refugee crisis. In addition to the diplomatic efforts of African states and regional organisations, the United Nations has sent a special envoy to attempt to avert a civil war.

Although there is an extensive literature on economic and cultural globalisation by sociologists and political scientists, few seem interested in the detail of either international law or regulation. Those legal theorists who write about globalisation usually ask philosophical questions rather than drawing on empirical studies (for example, Twining 2000). An exception is

Bonaventura de Sousa Santos (2002) who developed an interest in globalisation through conducting fieldwork in a shanty town in Brazil. However, he seems most interested in discussing the moral and political implications of globalisation for legal theory (Box 8.2). This section will start at a general level by giving a taste of the debates that take place about globalisation in social theory. It will then look at what is actually involved in the development of international law and a global legal profession, and at how one aspect of human rights law has been imperfectly implemented in Britain.

Box 8.2 Towards a new legal commonsense

One of the most ambitious contributions to legal theory in recent years has come from the Brazilian legal scholar and sociologist Bonaventura de Sousa Santos. In his *Toward a New Legal Common Sense* (2002), he develops a critical approach to law that is concerned with the tensions between regulation and emancipation. Law forms the basis of the modern state, but de Sousa Santos also asks whether it can fulfil the hopes of Enlightenment thinkers in creating a perfect or utopian society. Like many thinkers in classical jurisprudence and the legal pluralists reviewed in this chapter, he also makes much of the distinction between state law and other ways of ordering human behaviour.

In addition to reviewing works by legal philsophers and considering law in general terms, de Sousa Santos also draws on sociological research. He conducted a participant observation study based on spending time in a squatter camp or favela, given the anonymised name Pasagarda, in Rio de Janeiro. He describes how disputes were settled there by the presidente, a local shopkeeper, without recourse to state law, and without using professional lawyers. One advantage was that law was cheap and quick:

> Pasagarda law is accessible both in terms of its cost in money and time, and in terms of the general pattern of social interaction. Pasagarda residents do not pay lawyers' fees or court costs, though they may be asked to join the RA [Residents' Association] if they are not already members and to pay a membership fee. They do not have to pay for transportation or lose a day's salary, as they would if they had to consult a lawyer or attend the court in Rio.
>
> (de Sousa Santos 2002, p. 159)

de Sousa Santos approves of communities running their own affairs. However, he also recognises the importance of globalisation, and how the decisions made by multinational corporations affect poor people in Brazil. The book, therefore, moves from this local level to the international struggle for human rights and multiculturalism. As is common with critical thinkers influenced by Marx, there is an ambivalence towards law: it often acts in the interests of capital against labour, but it also protects the under-privileged and dispossessed.

Debates about globalisation

Many contemporary social theorists see the growing inter-connectedness of the world as something new and significant, and that we have recently entered a new epoch in human history (Robertson 1992; Giddens 1999). From this perspective, disciplines that confine themselves to looking at what happens inside nation states, are living in the past: the future lies in recognising and celebrating the new global age (Albrow 1996). Others have argued that the claims made for either a global economy, culture or political system have been exaggerated, or represent nothing new (for a review of debates, see Held and McGrew 2003). One could, for example, have read about global events in newspapers published in the nineteenth century during the period of European empires. There was migration on a scale greater than today, for example the millions of Europeans who settled in America. From this perspective, there is nothing new about globalisation, and in some respects there were closer international ties during the nineteenth century.

Hirst and Thompson (2003, p. 100) have shown how there were higher levels of trade and investment between different regions of the world: 'during the Pax Britannica system from the mid-nineteenth century to 1914' than in the 1980s. Contrary to what one might believe, most international trade today takes place in a few regional economic blocks. These globalising sceptics believe that the breaking down of barriers associated with neo-liberalism is something of a myth. This might also lead one to question the extent to which migration is on a greater scale than during the nineteenth century, or the extent to which global cultures influence how people think and live in particular places. It is true that we buy produce in the supermarket that comes from all over the world. One can, however, enjoy drinking coffee without needing to know where it was grown: this rather nicely shows the distinction between understanding globalisation from a 'macro'-perspective as a social scientist, and how people understand the phenomenon subjectively in their own lives. Most of the population in Western societies do not travel abroad, and in fact rarely leave their own local area. The most advanced country, the USA, is arguably also the most local in that many Americans know very little about what happens outside their own state.

These debates about the extent of globalisation are also relevant to law. One can argue that we have moved beyond the age of the nation state, or see this as premature given that we are very far, in practice, from having a world government or international law that is enforceable. What is most interesting, and also most sociological about this literature, is that it demonstrates how one cannot resolve what is ultimately a normative debate about how we should live by empirical enquiry. Even the greatest sceptic would accept that, in many respects, the world is getting smaller. It is hard to argue against this in relation to the global financial markets or their effect on particular economies. The sceptic would, however, disagree with the optimistic hyper-globaliser over whether this is a good thing, and where it might be heading. Here it is interesting to consider what the classical sociologists thought about globalisation. In the following passage from their (1967) *The Communist Manifesto*, Marx and Engels predicted the emergence of a global culture, and also identified its causes in the dynamic and expansionary character of Western capitalism:

> The bourgeiosie has through its exploitation of the world market given a cosmopolitan character to production and consumption in every country.... In place of the old local and national seclusion and self-sufficiency, we have intercourse in every direction, universal inter-dependence of nations. And as in the material, so also in intellectual production. The intellectual creations of individual nations become common property. National one-sidedness and narrow-mindedness become more and more impossible, and from the numerous national and local literatures, there arises a world literature.
>
> (Marx and Engels 1967, pp. 83–4)

Marx and Engels saw globalisation as an inevitable process that would result in a world economy divided between the forces of capital and labour. They believed that there would ultimately be a working-class revolution leading to a better society, once capitalism had spread across the world. One can see globalisation in these terms today, since one development is that workers in Western countries are losing their jobs as manufacturing and increasingly high value jobs in knowledge industries are being exported overseas.

From this perspective, the multinational corporation represents the concentration of capital in the way Marx predicted: an organisation that has no loyalty to local workforces or even to nation states, and which is driven by the pursuit of profit, whatever the human or environmental consequences (see Box 8.3). Alternatively, one can welcome the triumph of capitalism and democracy as the best possible way of guaranteeing individual freedom and prosperity. This has, after all, happened in individual countries in which the state redistributes income produced by industries competing in the market place. Most people have benefited from almost continuous economic growth, and are protected during periodic recessions. Many social theorists today welcome the liberalisation of trade, and believe that international organisations can provide the same protections internationally (for example, Braithwaite and Drahos 2000).

Finally, it is worth remembering that Max Weber (1978) took a darker view of globalisation as the spread of Western rational ways of organising economic and social life around the world. He saw our fate as having to live in a prosperous, managed world in which we have lost our freedom to make our own choices in the way that was promised at the start of the modern period. From this perspective, the prospect of a world government that promises to solve the problems of the world through relying on scientific

Box 8.3 Three failures of globalisation

This summary by Chris Brown (2003) of the ideas of the leftist political economist Susan Strange identifies three failures of globalisation. In each case, optimists believe that international law and regulation will ultimately offer solutions along with scientific advances. They would dispute the claim, made by Strange, that global inequality is increasing, and indeed argue that millions in countries such as India and China are living more affluent lives because of economic globalisation. On the other side of this political debate, critical theorists influenced by Marx have argued that only radical economic, social and political change can improve human welfare in the twenty-first century. The prediction in the first paragraph seems prescient in view of the global financial crisis that began in 2007:

... the global financial system is now beyond the control of any government and of the institutions that governments have created to attempt monetary management. Strange sees the creation and regulation of credit as the central international economic task. In the last resort, trade will look after itself – the giant corporations which dominate global production have an interest in world trade, and the efforts of such bodies as the WTO to regulate and control trade are of secondary importance to the motivations of these companies, who are well able to look after their own interests – but international monetary relations require supervision that a system of territorially based sovereign states can no longer supply. The destruction of Barings Bank in 1995 and the Asian collapse of 1997 are simply straws in the wind, indicators of what may be to come ...

The inability of sovereign states to cope with the consequences of environmental degradation is the second such failure. Global economic growth has taken place without reference to environmental consequences such as global warming. ... and the international system has proved unable to prevent the situation from getting worse in many areas, much less actually reverse these harmful consequences. The reason for this inability is clear: the system of sovereign states allows, even encourages, individual states to act selfishly ...

Even more directly contrary to general human welfare ... on the one hand, the present economic order works to increase global inequality, with the least advantaged left ever further behind to face a future of malnutrition, poverty and, probably, increasingly violent civil strife, while on the other, inequalities within 'successful' states grow worse, as the possibility that domestic welfare states can protect their peoples from the restructurings forced on them by global capitalism recedes. Whatever possibility there might have once been that the state could act as an agent for social justice is being undermined by the logic of an economic system that is out of human control and serving no general interest.

(Brown 2003, pp. 565–6)

experts (Saint-Simon 1975), is disturbing rather than liberating. There is also, however, something soul-destroying about the spread of standardised products, such as the McDonald's hamburger (Ritzer 1995) and Starbucks Coffee, across the world. The modern university itself can be criticised from this perspective: as encouraging, and institutionalising, a shallow form of education that suits the credentialising needs of a mass society, rather than actually promoting learning. Although this might seem a little elitist in suggesting there is something wrong with ordinary people enjoying hamburgers or attending universities, it strikes a chord in suggesting that the modern world (what contemporary theorists really mean when using the term globalisation) has costs and benefits.

There is, therefore, no agreement in these literatures either on the extent of globalisation, or whether it benefits human beings. One can also note that all these theorists, and even those sceptics who have investigated the history of world trade and investment, tend to write about globalisation at a general level. The following empirical studies can be understood as correctives to general statements about globalisation (one way in which sociologists can contribute to these debates).

The field of international arbitration

It is not easy studying the international legal system. It requires making contacts with researchers who have similar interests in different countries, or obtaining funding to support visits to research sites. Yves Dezalay and Bryant Garth's (1996) study of international commercial arbitration provides an example of what can be achieved given generous funding. This employed a theoretical framework derived from the French sociologist Pierre Bourdieu (1987), in looking at competition and conflict within this occupational field.

In Chapter 4, Bourdieu was introduced as a critical theorist who combined ideas from Marx and Weber, and was interested in how professional groups, such as the legal profession, compete for power and status. In this study, the leftist side of Bourdieu is down-played. While the subordination of developing countries in the international legal order is acknowledged, there is no political criticism of how multi-national corporations do business around the world. Instead, the authors are interested in how the field of international arbitration developed, and in the debates and conflicts that take place within this field.

Bourdieu, himself, argues in a preface that his own framework offers a means to advance beyond general or 'essayistic' understandings of globalisation:

> To speak of a global – or, better, international – legal field is immediately to escape the temptation to explain the processes of unification observed in very different domains of practice in one of two ways: either as a

quasi-mechanical effect of the intensification and acceleration of circulation and exchange, leading to an ecumenical reconciliation of all cultural traditions, or as an effect of imperialism exercised by a few industrial powers capable of exporting and imposing, on an universal scale, not only their products but also their style of life. The notion of field ... requires a position beyond the sophomoric alternatives of consensus and conflict, and thus permits us to understand and analyze the process of unification as a product of competition and conflict.

(Dezalay and Garth 1996, p. vii)

The field of international arbitration developed after the Second World War as a means of settling disputes between companies based in different countries without either party 'being forced to submit to the courts of another' (Dezalay and Garth 1996, p. 5). The demand for these services has grown substantially, especially after a series of high profile disputes about oil concessions and international construction contracts in the 1970s. The most important institution is the International Chamber of Commerce (ICC) in Paris. This started almost like a gentleman's club of mainly European eminent retired lawyers and academics who developed their own informal code and language for settling disputes: the lex mercatoria. Over time, this faced two related challenges to its dominance and authority in the field of arbitration. The first was a new generation of arbitrators who sought to introduce more formal and adversarial procedures, partly as a means of establishing their own identities and reputations. These arose, and obtained influence (what Bourdieu terms 'cultural capital') in the field, with the help of 'the grand old men who control access to and prominence in the field of arbitration' (Dezalay and Garth 1996, p. 57). To establish their own position, they turned against their patrons, promoting their 'technical sophistication' over the 'charisma' of grand old men.

The 'routinisation of charisma' is a theme in Max Weber's writings on how institutions develop. It has also influenced researchers associated with the 'new institutionalism', discussed in Chapter 3. Dezalay and Garth show how the challenge from this younger generation became possible when American law firms realised the potential of arbitration in settling international disputes. Over time, they infiltrated and gradually transformed the practice of arbitration so that it included the procedures employed in commercial litigation such as discovery and the cross-examination of witnesses. This is described in terms of the contact between two different legal cultures, but also as the imposition of American power, helped by a 'fifth column' of insiders. The result was an unequal struggle in which the older, gentlemanly tradition lost out:

... the reality of the relations of forces between this small club of learned artisans and these great conglomerates of legal experts was that, rather quickly, those who had opened the doors of their club to the Anglo-American practitioners became bothered by the transformation of approaches to arbitration under the influence of the 'American lobby'.... The 'Americans in Paris' may actually have fallen for the charm of arbitration in the Continental manner. But behind them was lined up an army of great law firms who, by simple fact of their mode of organization, could only throw into profound disorder a game of arbitration conceived essentially by and for the civilian academic.

(Dezalay and Garth 1996, p. 54)

As one might expect from a study influenced by Bourdieu, this approach to globalisation emphasises conflict and power relations, and there are references to the history of imperialism in which colonisation often took place through 'palace wars' rather than in actual gunboat diplomacy (Dezalay and Garth 1996, p. 53). The study does, however, demonstrate that more was involved than simply the imposition of American power. Instead, it shows how there were internal conflicts within the arbitration world, and also within American legal practice, that explain how the field became Americanised. It also suggests that American litigation was shaped and influenced, to some extent, by arbitration in that the litigators who spent time in Paris developed a greater respect for arbitration as a means of settling domestic disputes. One can agree with Bourdieu that globalisation should not be viewed as simply a site for political argument: it is possible to study how international institutions develop over time, in this case through interviewing arbitrators and lawyers in several countries about their work (see also Dezalay and Garth 2002).

The global law firm

The field of arbitration is an example of a specialist area of law that has arisen to settle international disputes. More generally, the growth of world trade, and markets of all kinds, have provided new areas of work for lawyers, and changed the nature of legal practice. This has been a theme in John Flood's (1996) interviews with practitioners in large law firms in the City of London (see also Chapter 5). In the first place, there have been more transactions between companies based in different countries:

Markets have become increasingly more globalised... Structuring transactions involves longer, more detailed negotiations – frequently including representatives of state organs, whose agendas might diverge from those of the contracting parties – during which the parties have to arrive at a common understanding of what their business is to be. For example, with parties engaged in a joint venture to produce automobiles in Indonesia, the relationship is one that will endure over many years...

And as both internal and external conditions change, the parties will probably want to alter some aspects of their agreement or possibly dissolve it.

(Flood 1996, p. 172)

New international work for lawyers has also been created by de-regulation and privatisation. Flood describes the emergence of a global securities market in the 1980s in which foreign companies bought stakes in utilities such as British Gas. In the last 10 years, there have been new markets in different types of securities and bonds, and in the complex products deriving from mortgage loans that were partly responsible for the 2007–8 financial crisis. There have also been increased levels of investment and take-overs across national borders.

It is apparent from Flood's paper that a great deal of the expansion of City law firms, following the so-called 'big bang' of financial de-regulation has concerned local commercial activity, such as private company sales and privatisations. However, the brochure of one law firm (one source of information for those researching the legal profession) suggests the importance of international work:

> In broad terms, our work can be seen as falling into three principal categories: corporate finance, banking (including restructuring and insolvency work) and international capital markets... Recent years have seen remarkable and exciting developments in the corporate finance area... We have been particularly pleased by the continued expansion of our mergers and acquisitions and new issue work and there has been dramatic growth in the demand for our special skills in relation to management and leveraged buy-outs, which have helped many complex transnational buy-outs ...
>
> (Flood 1996, p. 183)

As one might expect, there has been competition within the legal profession, and between the legal profession and other professions for this lucrative work. Within the legal profession, there have been mergers creating 'mega-law firms' (Galanter 1983). These have the resources to put together large teams to serve corporations quickly by, for example, taking over a failed bank over a weekend following a financial collapse (Flood 1996, p. 170). They can also establish overseas offices, and engage in lobbying government officials. Although this study, based on interviews, does not describe the work of corporate lawyers in detail, it would seem that it may involve social and political skills, as much as knowing legal rules. For this reason, large accountancy firms have taken a large proportion of the market, sometimes by setting up multi-disciplinary practices (MDPs). The British Law Society initially opposed this, in an attempt to maintain control over this market.

There has also been competition between British and American law firms for international business. Inevitably, when drafting contracts British lawyers tended to favour their own law, rather than being truly international. Flood notes that 'a proportion of the lawyers subscribe to [the] view that the rest of the world should use English law which, of course, would substantially benefit English lawyers' (Flood 1996, p. 191). American firms have set up offices within London, and poached existing teams by offering higher salaries. There are also many American law firms in Brussels. The British lawyers interviewed tended to look down on the abilities of these well-resourced competitors to establish relationships with government officials and retain clients. As one senior partner observed: 'Brussels produces a big culture clash between the American and British firms. Americans think of it as Washington DC so it can be lobbied in the same way. But it doesn't work that way' (Flood 1996, p. 194).

This paper provides only a taste of what one could discover through interviewing international lawyers about their work. The findings are interesting, in the context of discussions of globalisation, because one might assume that this would lead, if not to a level playing field, then to greater participation by lawyers in different countries. In fact, just as world economic activity mainly takes place within a few regions (Hirst and Thompson 2003), the market for international legal work is dominated by Anglo-Saxon law firms. There are also no truly global firms, the brand equivalent of Coca-Cola, because it makes sense to rely on local expertise.

Implementing human rights

The rise of international human rights protections is an aspect of globalisation which has captured the imagination of social theorists and legal philosophers. Many optimistic globalisers believe that these protections should be strengthened, and that it might eventually be possible to create a world government that could address global problems such as injustice, racial prejudice or poverty (Donnelly 2003). The first act of the United Nations formed after the Second World War was to issue a Declaration of Human Rights. Article 1, proclaimed that:

> All human beings are born free and equal. They are endowed with reason and conscience and should act towards one in a spirit of brotherhood.

The International Covenant on Civil and Political Rights, ratified in 1974, provides protection to anyone in the world who suffers from torture and arbitrary arrest. No one, of course, would disagree with these sentiments, which have been expressed by governments and international organisations at various times since the 1789 Declaration of the Rights of Man. Nevertheless, there is scope for considerable scepticism over what has been achieved.

The UN can take action against individual states for human rights abuses. This, however, requires passing a resolution in the General Assembly, and even then sanctions have to be authorised by the Security Commission. No action was taken by the United Nations against the alleged use of water-boarding as a means of interrogating terrorist suspects following the Second Iraq War since the United States exercised its veto. On this occasion, there was no agreement in the international community on what constitutes 'torture' when seeking to protect human rights (Bagaric 2008).

The sociologist can make a contribution to these political debates by examining how international laws are understood and implemented in practice. Although not intended to contribute to debates about globalisation at the time, my own study about decision-making by British Immigration Appeals Tribunals (Travers 1999) illustrates how any international agreement has to be enforced through local institutions, often without adequate levels of funding.

To give some background, the right to claim protection as a political refugee in a safe country was established by a 1951 UN Convention with the aim of assisting displaced people after the Second World War. The problem of implementing this right has arisen following the dramatic rise in asylum claims from the developing world during the 1980s. Britain was particularly affected as a country that had closed other routes to immigration in the late 1960s. It was perceived as an attractive and tolerant land of opportunity for migrants, and where there were already communities with family and cultural ties to many of its ex-colonies. The numbers of claimants rose from a few thousand each year in the 1980s to a peak of 100,000 in the 1990s. Immigration Appeals Tribunals refused a large number of these appeals, in many cases because the tribunal did not believe the appellant's account of being persecuted.

To understand the difficulties that faced the adjudicators who made these decisions, it is worth considering part of the following appeal made by a Kurd in December 1996 who claimed that he had been tortured, although there was no physical evidence (Travers 1999, Chapter 4). This appellant argued that he attracted the attention of the authorities through having distributed leaflets for the TKPMLH, a Kurdish militant group. He claimed to be suffering from post-traumatic stress disorder, and submitted evidence from psychologists. The Home Office had refused the application because, among other things, he had not convinced them that he really belonged to the TKPMLH.

One can get a sense of the practical and interpretive difficulties faced by Immigration Appeal Tribunals from these answers to questions from his representative during the hearing:

R: Can you tell us what the TKPH is?
W: They defend TKPMLH actions. They defend the rights of workers, the rights of arrested people, and their aim is to

R: stand by such oppressed people from whom their rights have
   been taken away.
R: And who founded the TKPMLH?
W: His name is Ibrahim Kaypakaya.
R: Can you spell his second name?
W: K A Y P A K A Y A
R: And if I said to you which concept of communism do the
   TKPMLH follow, what would you say?
W: There are no different concepts in communism.
R: So, what do you mean by that?
W: Communism is a world-wide system of labourers and peasants.

                  (Travers 1999, pp. 112–13)

The adjudicator in this asylum appeal had to decide, applying a low burden of proof, whether the appellant was a genuine refugee on the basis of
whether his account seemed credible. The ideal of giving protection to victims of political persecution was implemented through a system in which
civil servants and judicial officers routinely made these difficult decisions.

Thinking globally

The academic literature on globalisation often advances a normative position, as much as reporting and analysing what is happening in an increasingly inter-connected world. Although this chapter has offered a more
cautious or sceptical view about the extent of globalisation, or the value of
universal moral statements, it is hard to avoid a sense of excitement about
what has happened in a relatively short period of time. Because of the inter-
net, and cheap air travel, the world has become a smaller place, not least for
those working in universities in affluent Western societies. This qualification
seems important because, at present, those who attend international conferences, for example the four yearly meetings of the International Sociological
Association, come predominately from the USA and Western Europe.

If countries like China, India and Latin America continue to develop, it
seems likely that there will be a lot more intellectual activity in those countries (China already has several world-class universities). This still leaves
open questions about whether academics and thinkers from different parts
of the world, such as the African sub-continent, will participate in a truly
global conversation (Connell 2007), or whether it will still be dominated by
the views of Americans and Europeans. The next generation of social and
legal theorists may include those with different life experiences, and who
belong to a wider range of cultures, than in the past.

Thinking globally poses challenges for anyone, whether you live in the
developed or underdeveloped world (see Box 8.4). It is quite usual, and perhaps inevitable, that the curriculum should primarily address what happens

---

Box 8.4 Doing a global study

Yves Dezalay and Bryant Garth (1996) conducted an empirical study, based on interviewing 300 informants around the world, about the field of international arbitration. The following passage illustrates the resources, including time, required to conduct a project of this kind:

> After some three years of research, we have conducted almost three hundred interviews, in eleven countries, with the average interview running almost two hours (with both of us present in virtually all of them). The informants have come from twenty-five countries – mainly Europe, the United States, and the Middle East, but also Asia, Latin America, and North Africa. We have interviewed most of the leading members of the international arbitration community and the representatives of the leading institutions, attended two conferences, and scanned the massive literature on this subject. Most of our interviews have been concentrated in Europe and the United States – the places where international commercial arbitration is relatively well established; but we have also visited ... the places where arbitration is only beginning to gain acceptance, such as Africa and Latin America.
>
> This research began with an effort to learn the major names and institutions in international commercial arbitration. We first interviewed persons whom we had identified through their writing or reputations as experts in this field. We built up a list of names through the technique of snow-balling, starting from very different origins – large law firms in New York and Chicago, in-house counsel in New York, American Bar Association Committees, well-known Paris arbitrators, journalistic accounts of arbitration, editors of arbitration journals, and administrators of arbitration associations and institutions.
>
> (Dezalay and Garth 1996, p. 9)

---

in your own country. When teaching law and society studies in Britain or the USA, it can become easy to forget what happens elsewhere in the world. Outside the developed world, or in countries with smaller populations such as Australia, the difficulty lies in doing studies that address local issues, while drawing on the best international scholarship available, and contributing to a global conversation on where the world is heading. There are also increasing opportunities to pursue research outside or across national boundaries. Two research fields are worth mentioning: comparative legal research and the study of international regulation.

Comparative legal research

There is a long-standing tradition of comparative quantitative research in sociology and criminology influenced by Emile Durkheim (1951). In law and society studies, comparative research has mostly been pursued by anthropologists. Researchers in this discipline have traditionally spent an extended period of time in a different culture, and written about its culture and way of life for different audiences. Some legal scholars have pursued this route through spending time studying the legal systems of different countries. David Nelken (2002), a British researcher who lives in Italy, has written about the distinctiveness of Italian legal culture. His work demonstrates that spending a relatively short period of time elsewhere can produce interesting insights about our own legal cultures:

> Similarities and differences ... often come to life for an observer when they are exemplified by 'significant absences' such as the lack of any reference to 'community' in discourse about crime prevention in Germany. This obliges us to interrogate the way our own cultural assumptions shape the questions we ask and the answers we find convincing. Do we want to understand why Italy has apparently high rates of political corruption or why the UK has apparently low ones? Do we seek to explain why the Italian system of criminal justice has relatively more built-in leniency than the Anglo-American system or the opposite?
>
> (Nelken 2002, p. 337)

The fact that ordinary citizens have a different understanding of law and justice, and even the state, in different countries seems to provide more useful ammunition for sceptics in the globalisation debate. If such basic cultural differences exist, we should expect to find that they become relevant where ever members of different cultures meet including at the negotiations of international legal contracts or in the General Assembly of the United Nations.

A recent film that nicely conveys the experience of an American encountering Japanese society is *Lost in Translation* (Coppola 2003). Although this makes comparative observations about table manners and the advertising industry rather than the legal system, one can see how anyone having to live, and find their way around, a different culture will initially find this strange. It seems likely that, at least initially, globalisation may result in more cross-cultural misunderstanding, as against agreement on universal standards.

International regulation

Another way of doing global research, which also poses considerable challenges, is to examine the workings of international organisations. Globalisation has generated many trans-national agencies, ranging from the World Bank, to co-operative ventures between national police forces against terrorism, and the various Non-Governmental Organisations (NGOs) concerned with these issues. In the future, there are likely to be many new agencies concerned with combating environmental problems, including climate change.

There have already been some sociological and anthropological studies of these organisations (Riles 2000; Harper 2000; Hopgood 2006), although none that focus on legal processes or decision-making.

The practical and political problem facing researchers is perhaps no different to studying law enforcement or regulatory agencies within particular countries. How can one gain access to sensitive organisations without compromising the objective of publishing independent studies for a general audience? There is an additional problem for those of us not living in or near international centres such as New York or Brussels: to study an international agency involves conducting fieldwork, or at least multiple interviews, and this requires more time and resources than doing research locally. Nevertheless, this is likely to be an important and fruitful area for law and society research. There will undoubtedly be social and legal theorists who write about the problems of climate change, or international terrorism, and their implications for the modern world. It would also help to have empirical studies that examine how these global issues are understood and addressed as practical problems by international agencies working within a budget and legal mandate.

Questions

1 What do you understand by weak and strong legal pluralism?
2 How has globalisation changed the legal profession?
3 Why are theoretical debates between consensus and conflict traditions relevant to understanding globalisation?
4 What practical problems arise in implementing human rights legislation? Discuss in relation to the 1951 UN Convention on Refugees.
5 What conceptual difficulties arise when one compares law in societies with different cultures and values? What insights can be gained from conducting comparative research?

Further reading

For a good introduction to legal pluralism, see Griffiths in Banakar and Travers' *An Introduction to Law and Social Theory* (Hart, Oxford 2002 pp. 289–310). Reviews and statements include Merry's 'Legal Pluralism' (*Law and Society Review* 1988, Vol. 22, pp. 869–96), and Moore's 'Law and Social Change: The Semi-Autonomous Social Field as an Appropriate Subject of Study' (*Law and Society Review* 1973, Vol. 7, pp. 719–46). For a classic empirical study, see Llewellyn and Hoebel's *The Cheyenne Way* (University of Oklahoma Press, Oklahoma 1941), which is about the law of the Cheyenne Indians in America, or the section on squatter camps in de Sousa Santos' *Toward a New Legal Common Sense* (Butterworths, London 2002).

There are many theoretical statements on globalisation in sociology and political science. Held and McGrew's *The Global Transformations Reader* (Polity Press, Cambridge 2003) is an excellent collection. Albrow's *The Global Age*

(Polity Press, Cambridge 1996) and Giddens' *A Runaway World* (Profile Books, London 1999) are worth reading as optimistic statements. For discussion on the implications for legal theory, see Twining's *Law and Globalisation* (Butterworths, London 2000).

Nelken provides an introduction to comparative sociology of law in Banakar and Travers' *An Introduction to Law and Social Theory* (Hart, Oxford 2002, pp. 319–43). See also his collection *Contrasting Criminal Justice* (Ashgate, Aldershot 2000) for some empirical studies.

Chapter 9

Conclusion

A central question	191
Debates about inter-disciplinarity	193
The relationship between scientific and applied research	195
New topics and directions	197
Further reading	199

This text has covered a large number of theoretical traditions, each of which have different assumptions about the relationship between law and society, and how to study legal phenomena. For specialists, the summaries will hopefully be recognisable, even if they do not fully convey the range of approaches or debates within any tradition. The general reader is encouraged to follow the guides to further reading that will take you into the different literatures. One recent text about sociological method (which is particularly strong on the positivist/interpretivist debate) has a picture of a multi-coloured ball of twine on its cover that is probably intended to represent the Gordian Knot encountered by Alexander the Great (Hughes and Sharrock 2007). This may exaggerate the difficulties involved in studying these theories. Although there is no simple way of cutting through or simplifying the knot, it is possible to find your way around through understanding a few general debates.

In this concluding chapter, it seems appropriate to consider some general issues. The first section will consider whether law and society studies have a central question. The chapter will also consider debates about interdisciplinarity, the relationship between applied and scientific research, and offer some ideas on new topics and questions.

A central question

Does it make sense to see law and society research as having a central question or problem? As some law and society scholars have complained, sociology is organised into quite general, cross-cutting areas, such as the sociologies of work, organisations, the professions, stratification, gender relations, bureaucracy and racial and ethnic relations rather than recognising law as a distinctive phenomenon. This suggests that any sub-field should be considered a site for argument and debate between different theoretical traditions in the mainstream discipline, rather than as a bounded or distinctive field of enquiry in its own right. On the other hand, sociology has generated a number of sub-fields often through sociologists teaching within other programmes and subject areas. These include the sociologies of health and illness, science, organisations and management, crime and deviance, education and policing. The sub-fields usually draw on mainstream sociological theories, and debates within theories, but often develop their own questions and concepts.

Through reviewing a wide range of theoretical traditions, this book has demonstrated that law and society studies does have a central question or problem. It seeks to understand the relationship between law and society. This text has also demonstrated, however, that this does not necessarily create a simple or unified field of study around this question. It leads into sociological debates and arguments that depend on assumptions about the nature of society and how you can produce knowledge.

From the perspective of thinkers in the consensus tradition, law is seen as necessary for a complex industrial society. However, even here there are divergent views about the value of law and the state. Many classical sociological jurists were concerned about the growth of the state, and its effect on different areas of the living law (Chapter 2). On the other hand, other consensus traditions, ranging from the structural-functionalists to the new institutionalists have welcomed the growth of the state and seen regulation as beneficial. There are similar debates in the critical tradition. Some progressive thinkers place their faith in human rights legislation and a world government, whereas others are deeply suspicious of law and regulation as representing the interests of dominant economic groups.

A related question raised by many thinkers is whether one should see law and legal regulation as a good thing, or as suppressing human creativity and freedom. The interpretive thinker Harvey Sacks (1997) noted how the work of a lawyer involves potential disruption through questioning normal relations of trust:

> It is commonly said that where the lawyer participates in organizations that have on-going purposes he is constantly engaged in the uses of legalisms that interfere with the prosecuting of those purposes. From his perspective, however, it is taken to be the case that the organizations cannot hold together and perform their jobs 'on trust'. He fears that at each point ... there is a danger that the routineness by which goals may be accomplished and responsibilities assessed will break down. [This can only be maintained] it seems to him, by virtue of the care that goes into the drafting of organizational constitutions, rules of performance, codes of duties and the producing of the documents that attest to their being followed in every action. In short, the lawyer feels that he must give explicit concern to the production of the features of society which seem otherwise to be produced without any attendance to their production.
>
> (Sacks 1997, pp. 43–4)

This observation reminds one of Max Weber's fears about the growing burdens created by law and regulation in complex, modern societies. Many jurists have celebrated the achievements of law and its capacity to produce a better world. Thinkers in a variety of disciplines have seen law as potentially emancipatory, and favour developments such as human rights standards administered by a world government. Against this, there are sociologists who have sided romantically with what Habermas calls the 'lifeworld' against law and regulation, or written about the burdensome and time-consuming character of bureaucracy in everyday life. As an interpretivist, Sacks is not, however, advancing a general argument about the modern world, but asking us to appreciate the role of lawyers in helping businesses to draft rules and regulations. He seems to be inviting empirical study, using ethnographic methods, that looks at the detail of lawyers' work, without engaging in moral judgement or philosophising about an institution. There are, therefore, many ways of understanding the relationship between law and society. Asking this central question is useful, but it still means that one has to untangle the various theories, and understand the relationship between them.

Debates about inter-disciplinarity

There is a large secondary literature about the nature of sociology of law, and how it should develop. Some commentators have tended to complain about the state of the field, either by suggesting that it has not developed distinctive questions, or comparing the quality and diversity of research unfavourably with mainstream sociology. To give an example, Alan Hunt (1978, p. 2) noted that:

> The sociology of law has, to date, failed to develop a coherent theoretical framework within which to base its research activities. It has failed to achieve its explicit goal of overcoming the narrow and restrictive jurisprudential tradition within which the discussion and analysis of law has been confined.

Shortly after completing my doctorate, Richard Abel and Philip Lewis (1993) published a paper arguing that the sociology of lawyers needed more legal content. My response was that the sociology of law needed more *sociological* content (Travers 1993). For this to happen, law and society textbooks and journals would have to recognise the multi-perspectival character of sociology as an academic discipline, constituted around debates between different theoretical traditions.

Cotterrell argues, by contrast, that sociology of law should develop as a trans-disciplinary subject, not constrained by the various positions and specialisms within academic sociology:

> If sociology of law is portrayed, as this book has sought to portray it, not as an academic discipline or sub-discipline with specific methodological or theoretical commitments, but a continually self-reflective and self-critical enterprise of inquiry aspiring towards ever broader perspectives on law as a field or aspect of social experience, it follows that it cannot be constrained within particular social theories, concepts of system or structure, images of 'society', or, indeed, visions of 'truth'. Neither is sociology of law constrained methodologically by its drive to broaden partial perspectives on legal experience....
>
> (Cotterrell 1992, p. 310)

One response might be that it is, in fact, difficult to avoid adopting a recognisable sociological position as a sociological jurist, even if you believe that you have transcended debates in this discipline. Cotterrell, like many prominent law and society scholars in recent times, has been most influenced by critical theory. Because of this, his introduction to sociology of law did not engage with the more radical arguments made by feminists, postmodernists or ethnomethodologists, or he has tended to absorb or incorporate these into his own framework. One objective of this book has been to show that there is considerable diversity within sociology, and that any of these approaches can be used in researching law.

Although this book has a bias towards sociological perspectives on law, it will be apparent that the study of law and society is an inter-disciplinary subject. To give some examples, poststructuralist *philosophers* such as Foucault and Derrida have influenced writings on postmodern law, *political scientists* have contributed to our understanding of globalisation, and *critical sociolinguists* and *anthropologists* have studied law at the 'micro' level in addition to interpretive sociologists. My own approach has been to emphasise the distinctiveness of different disciplines, rather than suggesting that they should be merged into a trans-disciplinary subject.

There are some readers who may feel that this defence of traditional disciplines, and the dialogue and debate between them, sounds old-fashioned since we are in a postmodern world in which these barriers are breaking down. Immanuel Wallerstein (1996) has made this argument when writing on globalisation: that given our new conditions, disciplines formed in the modern world are irrelevant and should be replaced by inter-disciplinary clusters. This restructuring also appeals to universities faced with demographic and market forces ultimately caused by globalisation, since it offers greater flexibility in delivering courses. There is a certain irony in that we are being asked by a critical sociologist to celebrate the ceaseless, and often destructive, changes associated with the expansion of capitalism in the modern world, in the name of postmodernism.

From another perspective, inter-disciplinarity has already happened in law and society studies, and there is growing diversity within the field. Austin Sarat (2003) does not see this as necessarily liberating or leading to fruitful intellectual exchange. Instead, the field has lost its direction and purpose:

> The traditions of law and society scholarship are, as they should be, up for grabs as new scholars redefine the field. With growth has come greater inclusiveness, but also fragmentation. With every gain in inclusiveness, there will be an appropriate, though unsettling increase in uncertainty about what law and society scholarship is and what law and society scholars do. One measure of the progress of this field is uneasiness of what its boundaries are, what is orthodox and what is heresy.
>
> (Sarat 2003, p. 8)

This concern about fragmentation may indicate a sense of anxiety within the critical tradition rather than in law and society studies as a whole, since this has always contained a wide variety of theoretical traditions. In any event, what seems needed to combat fragmentation is greater awareness and appreciation of diversity and complexity within this inter-disciplinary field.

The relationship between scientific and applied research

The greatest challenge to traditional conceptions of doing academic research is not inter-disciplinarity but what Austin Sarat and Susan Silbey (1988) have termed 'the pull of the policy audience'. This arises from both a change in intellectual fashions, but also structural changes in universities as the institutions that produce knowledge. Broadly speaking, it means that some readers of this book may see the various approaches and theoretical traditions as interesting, but as not especially 'useful' in producing findings that government agencies can use. Some may also feel that this text has not provided enough information about quantitative methods, evaluation research and evidence-based policy; and that most of the research traditions reviewed have a liberal or left-wing bias. This again illustrates that there are many way of pursuing and conceptualising law and society research. It also, however, raises some interesting and difficult issues. How should one understand the relationship between scientific and applied research? Is the kind of open-ended intellectual enquiry represented by this text under threat, and if so why is this happening in contemporary universities?

Any academic field can be understood as a progression of cyclical fashions, and sometimes short-lived fads, around how to understand the modern world. Ideas are put forward, taken up, re-worked, forgotten and then re-surface in different guises later. There is scope for what Pitrim Sorokin (1956) termed the 'Columbus complex' in which a new generation feels it has discovered truths that were, in fact, already known by previous generations. In addition to these often short-lived intellectual movements, there are also deeper shifts in assumptions and political values. Although there are dangers in dividing the history of law and society studies into periods, a major development in the mid-twentieth century was the development of a progressive, liberal viewpoint in the United States. The law and society movement was progressive intellectually in demonstrating the openness of the law school to different social science perspectives. It also brought together scholars who despite the emergence of political differences during the 1960s and 1970s represented a liberal political consensus (Garth and Sterling 1998). They were committed to, and in many cases received their funding from, agencies associated with the New Deal that created the American welfare state.

After the oil shocks and other economic crises in the 1970s, there was a shift in political direction. The election of Margaret Thatcher in Britain and Ronald Reagan in America introduced what political historians and sociologists have come to call neo-liberalism (Harvey 2007). Governments in the developed world have tried to reduce the size of the state, remove welfare protections and increase competition. International institutions such as the World Bank and the International Monetary Fund have encouraged greater economic competition, both within Western countries and between the developed and underdeveloped world. Ironically, as society and politics moved to the right during the 1980s, European and American universities were, if anything, even more leftist and progressive than during the late 1960s. This was the era of feminism, post-Marxist critical theorists such as Foucault and Bourdieu, and postmodernism. Today, however, after a decade of occupation in Iraq that followed the terrorist attack on the World Trade Centre of 11 September 2001, there seems rather less of a critical voice in American universities. Partly because of the War on Terror, those with left-wing or liberal views can be denounced for being unpatriotic, and in rare cases have lost their jobs (Vaughan and Ensslin 2007).

This has not, however, just been a shift in political values. There have also been changes in the way universities are structured and financed. At the risk of over-simplifying, there is less funding for scientific or 'pure' research. Instead, researchers compete for grants that require applicants to pursue 'useful' research that produces clear-cut findings and policy recommendations. A number of epistemological positions inform the pure research programmes reviewed in this book, including positivism (the view that sociology should be like natural science), realism, interpretivism and postmodernism. However, the main way in which research has to be framed today to obtain support from funding agencies or government departments is empiricism. This can be defined as the assumption that too much reflection on theoretical debates or methodological issues is self-indulgent and harmful. Instead, researchers should seek to produce straightforward findings, preferably within a loose empiricist framework, that assist and can be understood by 'policy-makers', in other words managers in government agencies.

Although some texts do not distinguish between applied and scientific research, my own view is that each should be understood and appreciated in its own terms. One can employ different theoretical frameworks to strengthen an empiricist project, but in the end it is not concerned with reflecting on the relationship between law and society or pursuing some theoretically-derived question or problematic. It also makes sense to have separate courses on policy research and sociology of law taught on law degrees, or as part of inter-disciplinary programmes. This side-steps the question as to which is more important. There are some who believe strongly that universities should no longer be ivory towers, and instead seek to produce 'useful' findings that ordinary people can understand, or which help government agencies. There are others who are concerned that the state has undermined the independence of universities, and believe that society benefits from allowing academics and students to address intellectual questions for their own sake.

New topics and directions

In two previous collections, Reza Banakar and I offered some thoughts on how the law school curriculum should develop (Banakar and Travers 2002 and 2005a). We agreed with Karl Llewellyn (1965) that it was important for students to be exposed to more than black-letter law. One can debate whether or not it really makes a difference for law students to have read more than legal cases, or whether one could equally well acquire a general education or ethical awareness about the consequences of one's actions through reading novels outside formal education. Llewellyn believed that law schools should not leave this to chance. Exposure to a wide range of subjects would produce more rounded and capable lawyers, able to relate to clients from a wide range of backgrounds. One could also argue that, in the United States, students do general degrees before taking law at postgraduate level, so there is no need to broaden the law school curriculum.

This would not satisfy Llewellyn, who would argue that it is in their professional training that lawyers most need a broader perspective. He might also point to the fact that most law students in the United Kingdom and Australia, countries in which law is mainly taught on undergraduate degrees, can usually escape *any* contact with subjects outside the core curriculum, aside from a compulsory course in legal philosophy. In this respect, law seems out of step with other practical or professional subjects in which most students have to do some social science courses. It also seems to send the message, intentionally or otherwise, that law is a self-contained field of knowledge.

If one agrees that there is a problem, the next question is how one should reform the law school curriculum. There are various ways of doing this appropriate to different countries and institutions. What is most needed, however, is a cultural change of the kind recommended by Llewellyn: a recognition that law is part of society, and that social science approaches are relevant to students on law degrees. Finally, it goes without saying that, although students benefit from studying any contextual course, including legal philosophy and critical legal studies, sociology of law has much to offer. Through studying this subject, reading empirical studies and following through different analytic questions, you develop an understanding of the nature of law and legal practice that is intellectually stimulating, and politically balanced.

Another difficult problem lies in creating the conditions for researchers to publish more, and better studies. A traditional complaint in the United Kingdom is that socio-legal research uses a limited range of methods, and that applications to the Economic and Social Research Council do not match the quality of those in other areas of social science (Genn et al. 2006). This indicates that relatively few researchers in sociology departments are interested in studying law and legal phenomena. The main problem, however, lies in law schools. In the first place, there is a big difference between taking one contextual course on law, and doing a systematic programme that develops an expertise in doing sociological research, drawing on a range of theories and methods (see Banakar and Travers 2005a). In the second place, it is very rare to find a law degree where students are encouraged to do empirical research. To give an example, a friend with a background in law and sociology has started working in a law school in the United Kingdom. She was asked to teach a course on research methods: but with the proviso that the course should not cover empirical methods such as surveys or interviewing, but could only include general analytic perspectives on legal texts. British readers will recognise this as typical of an attempt to maintain the distinctiveness of the law school, but one that seems unlikely to result in producing new knowledge through conducting empirical research.

One can, perhaps, exaggerate these difficulties. Law and society studies is a growing inter-disciplinary field internationally. Sociology of law or related courses may only be viewed as electives of interest to relatively few students in most law schools, but there are centres with a critical mass of scholars and effective postgraduate programmes doing policy research or critical legal studies. There is also a large amount of empirical research published in law and society journals, increasingly by researchers based in law schools. Given that law and society researchers will continue to draw on sociological traditions and perspectives, where should this subject go now?

In some respects, this is a question for readers of this text to answer, by contributing to a new generation of scholarship. Although some are quite well-worked, none of the theoretical traditions reviewed in this book are exhausted. There are also new topics and questions that will concern us. There is, for example, a lot of concern today about global warming, and debates over whether regulation can help us to conserve resources are likely to become increasingly important internationally. There are also worries about the potentially far-reaching effects of scientific developments, such as genetic engineering, for everyday social relationships. One can conduct 'useful', policy-relevant studies on either topic. However, they quickly lead into more general questions, posed by classical thinkers, about our response to the modern world, and the relationship between law and society.

A question sometimes asked by undergraduate students is whether classical thinkers continue to have relevance today, or are simply studied out of respect for the founders of today's academic disciplines. My own view, after writing this book, is that they are even more important than you might imagine. This is partly because many later theorists draw on their ideas, even when this is not directly acknowledged. It is also because, despite emerging new problems, we are still living in a world that would be familiar to the classical sociologists but completely alien to anyone living before industrialisation. Social theorists today still either respond positively to modernity like Marx and Durkheim, or look sceptically at the achievements of the modern period like Weber. Even responses to new environmental problems, such as global warming, are influenced by eighteenth-century debates about whether science will save us or destroy the planet. The continuing rise of the regulatory state invites big questions, not about what lawyers do, or how regulation can be made more effective, but about how we should live in the modern world.

Further reading

There is a large secondary literature debating the nature and direction of sociology of law. See Hunt's *The Sociological Movement in Law* (Macmillan, London 1978), and any of the recent textbooks cited in Chapter 1. For debates on interdisciplinarity, see Cotterrell's *The Sociology of Law*, Chapter 9 (Butterworths, London 1992), and Travers' 'Putting Sociology Back into the Sociology of Lawyers' (*Journal of Law and Society* 1993. Vol. 20, No. 4, pp. 438–51). For arguments about the relationship between pure and applied research, see Sarat and Silbey's 'The Pull of the Policy Audience' (*Law and Policy*. Vol. 10, No. 2/3, pp. 97–166), and Genn, Partington and Wheeler's *Law in the Real World* (Nuffield Foundation, London 2006).

REFERENCES

Abel, R. 1988 *The Legal Profession in England and Wales*. Oxford: Blackwell.

Abel, R. and Lewis, P. 1993 'Putting law back into the sociology of lawyers', in R. Abel and P. Lewis (eds) *Lawyers in Society: Comparative Theories*. Berkeley, University of California Press, pp. 478–526.

Adams, B. and Sydie, R. 2002 *Classical Sociological Theory*. Thousand Oaks, California: Pine Forge.

Adorno, T. 1973 *Negative Dialectics*. London: Routledge, first published 1966.

Adorno, T. 1991 'Culture industry reconsidered', in J.M. Bernstein (ed.) *The Culture Industry: Selected Essays on Mass Culture*, London: Routledge, pp. 85–92; first published 1975.

Albrow, M. 1996 *The Global Age: State and Society Beyond Modernity*. Cambridge: Polity Press.

Althusser, L. 1969 *For Marx*. London: Allen Lane.

Althusser, L. 1984 'Ideology and ideological state apparatuses', in L. Althusser (ed.) *Essays on Ideology*. London: Verso, pp. 1–60, first published 1971.

Anderson, R., Hughes, J. and Sharrock, W. 1978 *The Sociology Game: An Introduction to Sociological Reasoning*. London: Longman.

Atkinson, J. and Drew, P. 1979 *Order in Court: The Organisation of Verbal Interaction in Judicial Settings*. London: Macmillan.

Bagaric, M. 2008 'Compassionate torture an essential life saving tool', *The Australian*. 7th January, p. 6.

Banakar, R. 2002 'Sociological jurisprudence', in R. Banakar and M. Travers (eds) *An Introduction to Law and Social Theory*. Oxford: Hart, pp. 33–44.

Banakar, R. 2003 *Merging Law and Sociology*. Berlin: Galda and Wilch.

Banakar, R. and Travers, M. (eds) 2002 *An Introduction to Law and Social Theory*. Oxford: Hart.

Banakar, R. and Travers, M. (eds) 2005a *Theory and Method in Socio-Legal Research*. Oxford: Hart.

Banakar, R. and Travers, M. 2005b 'Law, sociology and method', in R. Banakar and M. Travers (eds) *Theory and Method in Socio-Legal Research*. Oxford: Hart, pp. 1–26.

Bankowski, Z. and Mungham, G. 1976 *Images of Law*. London: Routledge.

Barnett, H. 1997 *Sourcebook on Feminist Jurisprudence*. London: Cavendish.

Barnett, H. 1998 *An Introduction to Feminist Jurisprudence*. London: Cavendish.

Barthes, R. 1982 *A Barthes Reader*. London: Cape.

Baudrillard, J. 1988 *Selected Writing*. Cambridge: Polity Press.

Bauman, Z. 2000 *Liquid Modernity*. Cambridge: Polity Press.

Beck, U. 1992 *Risk Society: Toward a New Modernity*. London: Sage.

Becker, H. 1951 *Role and Career Problems of the Chicago Public-School Teacher*. Phd dissertation. University of Chicago.

Becker, H. 1966 *Outsiders*. New York: The Free Press.

Becker, H., Hughes, E., Geer, B. and Strauss, A. 1961 *Boys in White: Student Culture in a Medical School*. Chicago: University of Chicago Press.

Bentham, J. 1973 *An Introduction to the Principles of Morals and Legislation*. New York: Hafner Press, first published 1789.

Benton, T. 2006 'Do we need rights? If so, what sort?' in L. Morris (ed.) *Rights: Sociological Perspectives*. London: Routledge, pp. 21–36.

Best, J. 1989 *Images of Issues: Typifying Contemporary Social Problems*. New York: Aldine.

Best, S. and Kellner, D. 1991 *Postmodern Theory: Critical Interrogations*. Basingstoke: Macmillan.

Best, S. and Kellner, D. 2001 *Postmodern Theory*. Basingstoke: Macmillan.

Bhaskar, R. 1979 *A Realist Theory of Science*. Hemel Hempstead: Harvester Wheatsheaf.

Black, D. 1972 'Review of law, society and industrial justice by Philip Selznik'. *American Journal of Sociology*. Vol. 78, No. 3, pp. 709–14.

Black, D. 1989 *Sociological Justice*. Oxford: Oxford University Press.

Blumer, H. 1969 *Symbolic Interactionism: Perspective and Method*. Berkeley: University of California Press.

Bodichon, B.L.S. 1854 *A Brief Summary of the Laws of England Concerning Women*. London: John Chapman.

Bottomley, A. 2002 *Feminist Perspectives on the Foundational Subjects of Law*. London: Cavendish.

Bourdieu, P. 1977 *Outline of a Theory of Practice*. Cambridge: Cambridge University Press.

Bourdieu, P. 1984 *Distinction: A Social Critique of the Judgement of Taste*. London: Routledge, first published 1979.

Bourdieu, P. 1987 'The force of law: Toward a sociology of the juridical field'. *Hastings Law Journal*, Vol. 38 No. 5, pp. 805–53.

Bourdieu, P. et al. 2000 *The Weight of the World: Social Suffering in Contemporary Society*. Cambridge: Polity.

Braithwaite, J. and Drahos, P. 2000 *Global Business Regulation*. Cambridge: Cambridge University Press.

Bredemeier, H. 1962 'Law as an integrative mechanism', in W. Evan (ed.) *Law and Sociology*. New York: The Free Press, pp. 73–90.

Brown, C. 2003 'A world gone wrong?' in D. Held and T. McGrew (eds) *The Global Transformations Reader*. Cambridge: Polity, pp. 564–76.

Bucher, R. and Strauss, A. 1961 'Professions in process', *American Journal of Sociology*, Vol. 66, pp. 325–34.

Burns, S. 2005 *Ethnographies of Law and Social Control*. Amsterdam: Elsevier.

Butler, J. 1990 *Gender Trouble: Feminism and the Subversion of Identity*. New York: Routledge.

Cain, M. 1983 'The general practice lawyer and the client: Towards a radical conception', in R. Dingwall and P. Lewis (eds) *The Sociology of the Professions: Doctors, Lawyers and Others*. London: Macmillan, pp. 106–30.

Campbell, C. and Wiles, P. 1976 'The study of law in society in Britain', *Law and Society Review*, Vol. 10, pp. 547–78.

Carlin, J. 1962 *Lawyers on Their Own: A Study of Individual Practitioners in Chicago*. New Brunswick: Rutgers University Press.

Charon, J. 2006 *Symbolic Interactionism: An Introduction, An Interpretation* (9th edn). New York: Prentice-Hall.

Chodorow, N. 1978 *The Reproduction of Mothering*. Berkeley: University of California Press.

Clifford, J. and Marcus, G. 1986 *Writing Culture*. Berkeley: University of California Press.

Comte, A. 1975 *Auguste Comte and Positivism* (edited by G. Lenzer). Chicago: University of Chicago Press, first published 1853.

Conley, J. and O'Barr, M. 1990 *Rules Versus Relationships*. Chicago: University of Chicago Press.

Conley, J. and O'Barr, M. 2005 *Just Words: Language, Law and Power* (2nd edn). Chicago: University of Chicago Press.

Connell, R. 2007 *Southern Theory: The Global Dynamics of Knowledge in Social Science*. Cambridge: Polity Press.

Coppola, S. 2003 *Lost in Translation*. Focus Features.

Cornell, D. 1991 *Beyond Accommodation: Ethical Feminism, Deconstruction and the Law*. New York: Routledge.

Cotterrell, R. 1989 *The Politics of Jurisprudence: A Critical Introduction to Legal Philosophy*. London: Butterworths.

Cotterrell, R. 1992 *The Sociology of Law: An Introduction*. London: Butterworths.

Cotterrell, R. 1995 *Law's Community: Legal Theory in Sociological Perspective*. Oxford: Oxford University Press.

Cotterrell, R. 2000 *Emile Durkheim: Law in a Moral Domain*. Stanford: Stanford University Press.

Cotterrell, R. 2005 *The Sociology of Law: An Introduction* (2nd edn). Oxford: Oxford University Press.

Cuff, E., Sharrock, W. and Francis, D. 2006 *Perspectives in Sociology* (5th edn). London: Routledge.

Davis, K. and Moore, W. 1945 'Some principles of stratification', *American Sociological Review*, Vol. 10, pp. 242–9.

de Sousa Santos, B. 2002 *Toward a New Legal Common Sense: Law, Globalization and Emancipation*. London: Butterworths.

Deflem, M. 2008 *The Sociology of Law: Visions of a Scholarly Tradition*. Cambridge: Cambridge University Press.

Derrida, J. 1986 *Glas*. Nebraska: University of Nebraska Press.

Derrida, J. 1988 *Writing and Difference*. Chicago: University of Chicago Press.

Derrida, J. 1992 'Force of law', in D. Cornell, M. Rosenfeld and D. Carlson (eds) *Deconstruction and the Possibility of Justice*. New York: Routledge.

Dezalay, Y. and Garth, B. 1996 *Dealing in Virtue: International Commercial Arbitration and the Construction of a Transnational Legal Order*. Chicago: University of Chicago Press.

Dezalay, Y. and Garth, B. 2002 *The Internationalization of Palace Wars: Lawyers, Economists and the Contest to Transform Latin American States*. Chicago: University of Chicago Press.

DiMaggio, P. and Powell, W. 1991a *The New Institutionalism in Organizational Analysis*. Chicago: University of Chicago Press.

DiMaggio, P. and Powell, W. 1991b 'The iron cage revisited: Institutional isomorphism and collective rationality', in P. DiMaggio and W. Powell (eds) *The New Institutionalism in Organizational Analysis*, Chicago: University of Chicago Press, pp. 63–82.

Donnelly, J. 2003 *Universal Human Rights*. Ithaca: Cornell University Press.

Douzinas, C., Goodrich, P. and Hachamovitch, Y. (eds) 1994 *Politics, Postmodernity and Critical Legal Studies: The Legality of the Contingent*. London: Routledge.

Drew, P. 1997 'Contested evidence in courtroom cross-examination: The case of a trial for rape', in M. Travers and J. Manzo (eds) *Law in Action: Ethnnomethodological and Conversation Analytic Approaches to Law*. Ashgate: Aldershot, pp. 51–76.

Drummond, M. 1996 'Bond jailed for three years for fraud'. *Sydney Morning Herald*. 20 August, p. 1.

Durkheim, E. 1951 *Suicide*. London: Routledge, first published 1897.

Durkheim, E. 1966 *The Rules of Sociological Method*. New York: The Free Press, first published 1895.

Durkheim, E. 1984 *The Division of Labour in Society*. London: Macmillan, first published 1893.

Durkheim, E. 1985 'Two laws of penal evolution', in P. Hamilton (ed.) *Readings from Emile Durkheim*. London: Routledge, pp. 58–62; first published 1900.

Dworkin, A. 1987 *Intercourse*. London: Secker and Warburg.

Edelman, L. and Suchman, M. 1997 'The legal environment of organizations', *Annual Review of Sociology*, Vol. 23, pp. 479–515.

Edelman, L., Erlanger, H. and Lande, J. 1993 'Internal dispute resolution: The transformation of civil rights in the workplace', *Law and Society Review*, Vol. 27, No. 3, pp. 497–534.

Emmelman, D. 2003 *Justice for the Poor: A Study of Criminal Defence Work*. Aldershot: Ashgate.

Engels, F. 1972 *The Origin of the Family, Private Property and the State*. New York: International Publishers, first published 1844.

Engels, F. 1993 *The Condition of the Working Class in England*. Oxford: Oxford University Press, first published 1887.

Erhlich, E. 1936 *Fundamental Principles of the Sociology of Law*. New York: Arno Press.

Evan, W. (ed.) 1962 *Law and Sociology*. New York: The Free Press.

Evan, W. 1980 'Law as an instrument of social change', in W. Evan (ed.) *The Sociology of Law: A Social-Structural Perspective*. New York: The Free Press, pp. 554–62.

Ewick, P. and Silbey, S. 1998 *The Common Place of Law*. Chicago: University of Chicago Press.

Fine, R. 2002 'Marxism and the social theory of law', in R. Banakar and M. Travers (eds) *An Introduction to Law and Social Theory*. Oxford: Hart, pp. 101–18.

Finnis, J. 1980 *Natural Law and Natural Rights*. Oxford: The Clarendon Press.

Fish, S. 1989 *Doing What Comes Naturally: Interpretation and Theory in Literature and the Law*. Durham, North Carolina: Duke University Press.

Flood, J. 1983 *Barrister's Clerks: The Law's Middlemen*. Manchester: Manchester University Press.

Flood, J. 1996 'Megalawyering in the global order: The cultural, social and economic transformation of global legal practice', *International Journal of the Legal Profession*, Vol. 3, pp. 169–214.

Flood, J. 2002 'Globalisation and law', in R. Banakar and M. Travers (eds) *An Introduction to Law and Social Theory*. Oxford: Hart, pp. 311–28.

Flood, J. and Caiger, A. 1993 'Lawyers and arbitration: The juridification of construction disputes', *Modern Law Review*, Vol. 56, pp. 412–40.

Foucault, M. 1967 *Madness and Civilisation*. London: Tavistock.

Foucault, M. 1970 *The Order of Things*. London: Tavistock.

Foucault, M. 1973 *The Birth of the Clinic*. London: Tavistock.

Foucault, M. 1977 *Discipline and Punish*. London: Tavistock.

Foucault, M. 1978 *The History of Sexuality Vol.1*. New York: Pantheon.

Francis, D. and Hester, S. 2004 *An Invitation to Ethnomethodology*. London: Sage.

Frank, A. 1967 *Capitalism and Underdevelopment in Latin America*. New York: Monthly Review Press.

Freeman, M. 2001 *Lloyds Introduction to Jurisprudence* (7th edn). London: Sweet and Maxwell.

Friedan, B. 1974 *The Feminine Mystique*. New York: Dell.

Friedrichs, D. 2006 *Law in Our Lives* (2nd edn). Los Angeles: Roxbury.

Frohman, L. 1991 'Discrediting victims' allegations of sexual assault: Prosecutorial accounts of case rejections', *Social Problems*, Vol. 38, pp. 218–24.

Fukuyama, F. 1992 *The End of History and the Last Man*. New York: Free Press.

Gabel, P. and Kennedy, D. 1984 'Roll over Beethoven', *Stanford Law Review*, Vol. 36, No. 1/2, pp. 1–55.

Galanter, M. 1983 'Mega-law and mega-lawyering in the contemporary United States', in R. Dingwall and P. Lewis (eds) *The Sociology of the Professions: Lawyers, Doctors and Others*. London: Macmillan, pp. 152–76.

Garcia, A. 1991 'Dispute resolution without disputing: How the interactional organization of mediation hearings minimizes argument', *American Sociological Review*, Vol. 56, pp. 818–35.

Garfinkel, H. 1984 'Some rules of correct decisions that jurors respect', in H. Garfinkel, *Studies in Ethnomethodology*. Cambridge: Polity Press, pp. 104–15, first published 1967.

Garfinkel, H. 1997 'Practical sociological reasoning: Some features in the work of the Los Angeles suicide prevention center', in M. Travers and J. Manzo (eds) *Law in Action: Ethnomethodological and Conversation Analytic Approaches to Law*. Aldershot: Ashgate, pp. 25–42, first published 1967.

Garth, B. and Sterling, J. 1998 'From legal realism to law and society: Reshaping law for the last stages of the social activist state', *Law and Society Review*, Vol. 32, No. 2, pp. 409–72.

Genn, H., Partington, M. and Wheeler, S. 2006 *Law in the Real World: Improving Our Understanding Of How Law Works*. London: Nuffield Foundation.

Giddens, A. 1976 *New Rules of Sociological Method: A Positive Critique of Interpretivist Sociologies*. London: Hutchinson.

Giddens, A. 1991 *The Consequences of Modernity*. Cambridge: Polity Press.

Giddens, A. 1999 *A Runaway World: How Globalisation is Shaping our Lives*. London: Profile Books.

Gilligan, C. 1982 *In a Different Voice*. Cambridge: Harvard University Press.

Glaser, B. and Strauss, A. 1967 *The Discovery of Grounded Theory*. New York: Aldine.

Goffman, E. 1989 'On fieldwork' (transcribed and edited by L. Lofland), *Journal of Contemporary Ethnography*, Vol. 18, No. 2, pp. 123–32.

Golder, B. and Fitzpatrick, P. 2009 *Foucault's Law*. London: Routledge.

Goodrich, P. 1995 *Oedipus Lex: Psychoanalysis, History, Law*: Berkeley: University of California Press.

Gouldner, A. 1970 *The Coming Crisis of Western Sociology*. New York: Basic Books.

Gouldner, A. 1980 *The Two Marxisms*. London: Macmillan.

Gramsci, A. 1971 *Selections from the Prison Notebooks of Antonio Gramsci*. London: Lawrence and Wishart, first published 1932.

Green, P. 1990 *The Enemy Without: Policing and Class Consciousness in the Miners' Strike*. Milton Keynes: Open University Press.

Griffith, J., Bood, D. and Heleen, W. 1998 *Euthanasia and the Law in Netherlands*. Amsterdam: Amsterdam University Press.

Griffith, A. 2002 'Pluralism', in R. Banakar and M. Travers (eds) *An Introduction to Law and Social Theory*. Oxford: Hart, pp. 289–310.

Gubrium, J. and Holstein, J. 2003 *Postmodern Interviewing*: Thousand Oaks, California: Sage.

Habermas, J. 1984 *The Theory of Communicative Action Vol. 1*. Cambridge: The Polity Press.

Habermas, J. 1986a *The Theory of Communicative Action Vol. 2*. Cambridge: The Polity Press.

Habermas, J. 1986b *Legitimation Crisis*. London: Heinemann, first published 1975.

Habermas, J. 1996 *Between Facts and Norms*. Cambridge, MA: MIT Press.

Hagan, J. and Kay, F. 1995 *Gender in Practice: A Study of Lawyers' Lives*. New York: Oxford University Press.

Harding, S. 1986 *The Science Question in Feminism*. Ithaca, New York: Cornell University Press.

Hardt, M. and Negri, A. 2000 *Empire*. Cambridge: Harvard University Press.

Harper, R. 2000 'The social organisation of the IMF's mission work: An examination of international accounting', in M. Strathern (ed.) *Audit Cultures: Anthropological Studies in Accountability, Ethics and the Academy*. London: Routledge, pp. 21–54.

Harrington, C. 1985 *Shadow Justice: The Ideology and Institutionalization of Alternatives to Court*. Westport, CT: Greenwood Press.

Harvey, D. 2007 *A Brief History of Neoliberalism*. Oxford: Oxford University Press.

Head, M. 2007 *Evgeny Pashukanis: A Critical Reappraisal*. London: Routledge.

Heinz, J. and Laumann, E. 1994 *Chicago Lawyers: The Social Structure of the Bar.* Illinois: Northwestern University Press, first published 1982.

Held, D. and McGrew, A. (eds) 2003 *The Global Transformations Reader.* Cambridge: Polity.

Heritage, J. 1984 *Garfinkel and Ethnomethodology.* Cambridge: Polity.

Hermer, J. 2008 *Policing Compassion: Begging, Law and Power in Public Spaces.* Oxford: Hart.

Hester, S. and Eglin, P. 1992 *A Sociology of Crime.* London: Routledge.

Hirst, P. and Thompson, G. 2003 'Globalization – a necessary myth', in D. Held and A. McGrew (eds) *The Global Transformations Reader.* Cambridge: Polity, pp. 98–105.

Hobbes, T. 1996 *Leviathan.* Cambridge: Cambridge University Press, first published 1660.

Hochschild, A. 1983 *The Managed Heart: Commercialisation of Human Feeling.* Berkeley: University of California Press.

Holmes, O.W. 1923 *The Common Law.* Boston: Little, Brown, first published 1881.

Hopgood, S. 2006 *Keepers of the Flame: Inside Amnesty International.* Cornell: Cornell University Press.

Hughes, E. 1971 *The Sociological Eye.* Chicago: Aldine.

Hughes, E. 1994 *On Work, Race and the Sociological Imagination* (edited by L. Coser). Chicago: University of Chicago Press.

Hughes, J. and Sharrock, W. 2007 *Theory and Methods in Sociology.* Basingstoke: Palgrave.

Hughes, J., Sharrock, W. and Martin, P. 2003 *Understanding Classical Sociological Theory.* London: Sage.

Hull, K. 2006 *Same-Sex Marriage: The Cultural Politics of Love and Law.* Cambridge: Cambridge University Press.

Humm, M. 1992 *Modern Feminisms.* New York: Columbia University Press.

Hunt, A. 1978 *The Sociological Movement in Law.* London: Macmillan.

Hunt, A. 1990 'The big fear: Law confronts postmodernism', *McGill Law Journal,* Vol. 35, No. 3, pp. 507–40.

Hunt, A. 1992 'Foucault's expulsion of law: Towards a retrieval', *Law and Social Inquiry,* Vol. 17, pp. 1–38.

Hunt, A. 2006 'On Georges Gurvitch sociology of law', in J. Trevino (ed.) *Classic Writings in Law and Society,* New Jersey: Transaction, pp. 131–60.

Hunt, A. and Wickham, G. 1994 *Foucault and Law: Towards a Sociology of Law as Governance.* London: Pluto Press.

Johnson, T. 1972 *Professions and Power.* London: Macmillan.

Kaufman, J. and Hymowitz, C. 2008 'Women feel the Clinton backlash', *The Australian,* 31 March, p. 15.

Kennedy, D. 1979 'The structure of Blackstone's commentaries', *Buffalo Law Review,* Vol. 28, pp. 205–362.

Kidder, R. 1983 *Connecting Law and Society.* Englewood Cliffs, NJ: Prentice-Hall.

King, M. and Piper, C. 1980 *How the Law Thinks About Children.* Aldershot: Gower.

Lacan, J. 1994 *The Four Fundamental Concepts of Psycho-Analysis.* London: Penguin.

Latour, B. 2009 *The Making of Law: An Ethnography of the Conseil d'Etat.* Cambridge: Polity Press.

Levi-Strauss, C. 1963 *Structural Anthropology*. New York: Basic Books.

Livingston, E. 1987 *Making Sense of Ethnomethodology*. London: Routledge.

Llewellyn, K. 1930 'A realistic jurisprudence: The next step', *Columbia Law Review*, Vol. 30, No. 4, pp. 431–65.

Llewellyn, K. 1931 'Some realism about realism: Responding to Dean Pound', *Harvard Law Review*, Vol. 44, No. 8, pp. 1222–64.

Llewellyn, K. 1965 'What law is about', in K. Llewellyn (ed.) *Bramble Bush*. New York: Oceana.

Llewellyn, K. and Hoebel, E. 1941 *The Cheyenne Way: Conflict and Case Law in Primitive Jurisprudence*. Oklahoma: University of Oklahoma Press.

Luhmann, N. 1985 *A Sociological Theory of Law*. London: Routledge.

Lumet, S. 1957 *Twelve Angry Men*. United Artists.

Lyotard, J. 1984 *The Postmodern Condition: A Report on Knowledge*. Manchester: Manchester University Press.

Macauley, S. 1963 'Non-contractual relations in business: A preliminary study'. *American Sociological Review*, Vol. 28, pp. 55–67.

McConville, M., Hodgson, J., Bridges, L. and Pavlovic, A. 1994 *Standing Accused: The Organisation and Practices of Criminal Defence Lawyers in Britain*. Oxford: Clarendon Press.

McGoldrick, D. 1996 *Human Rights And Religion: The Islamic Headscarf Debate in Europe*. Oxford: Hart.

MacKinnon, C. 1989 *Toward a Feminist Theory of the State*. Cambridge: Harvard University Press.

MacKinnon, C. 1995a 'Reflections on law in the everyday life of women', in A. Sarat and T. Kearns (eds) *Law in Everyday Life*. Michigan: University of Michigan Press, pp. 109–22.

MacKinnon, C. 1995b *Only Words*. New York: HarperCollins.

McLuhan, M. 1962 *The Gutenberg Galaxy*. London: Routledge.

McVeigh, S. 2002 'Postmodernism', in R. Banakar and M. Travers (eds) *An Introduction to Law and Social Theory*. Oxford: Hart, pp. 267–84.

Madsen, M. and Dezalay, Y. 2002 'The power of the legal field', in R. Bankar and M. Travers (eds) *An Introduction to Law and Social Theory*. Oxford: Hart, pp. 189–204.

Malinowski, B. 1926 *Crime and Custom in a Savage Society*. Paterson, NJ: Littlefield Adams.

Mansbridge, J. 1986 *Why We Lost The ERA*. Chicago: University of Chicago Press.

Mansell, W., Meteyard, B. and Thomson, A. 1999 *A Critical Introduction to Law*. London: Cavendish.

March. J. and Olsen, J. 1984 'The new institutionalism: Organizational factors in political life', *American Political Science Review*, Vol. 78, pp. 738–49.

Marcuse, H. 1964 *One Dimensional Man*. London: Routledge.

Martin, P. 1997 *Sounds and Society: Themes in the Sociology of Music*. Manchester: University of Manchester Press.

Marx, K. 1970 *A Contribution to the Critique of Political Economy*. New York: International Publishers, first published 1859.

Marx, K. 1975 'On the Jewish question', in K. Marx and F. Engels *Collected Works: Vol. III*. New York: International Publishers, first published 1844.

Marx, K. 1976 *Capital: A Critique of Political Economy Vol. I.* Harmondsworth: Penguin, first published 1867.

Marx, K. and Engels, F. 1967 *The Communist Manifesto.* Harmondsworth: Penguin, first published 1848.

Matoesian, G. 1993 *Reproducing Rape: Domination Through Talk in the Courtroom.* Chicago: University of Chicago Press.

Maturana, H. 1981 'Autopoesis', in M. Zeleney (ed.) *Autopoesis: A Theory of Living Systems.* New York: North Holland, pp. 21–33.

Mayhew, L. 1982 'Introduction', in T. Parsons (ed.) *On Institutions and Social Evolution.* Chicago: University of Chicago Press, pp. 1–64.

Maynard, D. and Manzo, J. 1997 'Justice as a phenomenon of order: Notes on the organization of a jury deliberation', in M. Travers and J. Manzo (eds) *Law in Action: Ethnomethodological and Conversation Analytic Approaches to Law.* Aldershot: Ashgate, pp. 209–38.

Mead, G.H. 1934 *Mind, Self and Society.* Chicago: University of Chicago Press.

Merry, S. 1988 'Legal Pluralism', *Law and Society Review*, Vol. 22, No. 5, pp. 869–96.

Merry, S. 1990 *Getting Justice and Getting Even: Legal Consciousness Among Working Class Americans.* Chicago: University of Chicago Press.

Merton, R., Reader, G. and Kendall, P. (eds) 1957 *The Student-Physician: Introductory Studies in the Sociology of Medical Education.* Cambridge: Harvard University Press.

Mertz, E. 2007 *The Language of Law School: Learning to 'Think Like a Lawyer'.* Oxford: Oxford University Press.

Milovanovic, D. 2003 *An Introduction to the Sociology of Law.* Monsey, NY: Criminal Justice Press.

Mill, J.S. 1989 *The Subjection of Women.* Cambridge: Cambridge University Press, first published 1869.

Mills, C.W. 1959 *The Sociological Imagination.* Harmondsworth: Penguin.

Moore, S. 1973 'Law and social change: The semi-autonomous social field as an appropriate subject of study', *Law and Society Review.* Vol. 7, pp. 719–46.

Naffine, N. and Owens, R. (eds) 1997 *Sexing the Subject of Law.* London: Sweet and Maxwell.

Nelken, D. (ed.) 2000 *Contrasting Criminal Justice: Getting from Here to There.* Aldershot: Ashgate.

Nelken, D. 2002 'Comparative sociology of law', in R. Banakar and M. Travers (eds) *An Introduction to Law and Social Theory.* Oxford: Hart, pp. 329–43.

Nietzche, F. 1968 *The Will to Power.* New York: Random House.

Odeh, L. 1993 'Post-colonial feminism and the veil: Thinking the difference', *Feminist Review*, No. 43, pp. 26–37.

Parsons, T. 1937 *The Structure of Social Action.* Boston: McGraw-Hill.

Parsons, T. 1951 *The Social System.* New York: The Free Press.

Parsons, T. 1954 'A sociologist looks at the legal profession', in T. Parsons *Essays in Sociological Theory.* New York: The Free Press, pp. 370–85.

Parsons, T. 1967 *Sociological Theory and Modern Society.* New York: The Free Press.

Pashukanis, E. 1978 *Law and Marxism: A General Theory.* London: Ink Links, first published 1924.

Paterson, A. 1982 *The Law Lords*. London: Macmillan.

Paterson, J. and Teubner, G. 2005 'Changing maps: Empirical legal autopoesis', in R. Banakar and M. Travers (eds), *Theory and Method in Socio-Legal Research*. Oxford: Hart, pp. 215–38.

Patterson, D. 1994 *Postmodernism and Law*. New York: New York University Press.

Peters, G. 1999 *Institutional Theory in Political Science*. London: Pinter.

Petrazycki, L. 1955 *Law and Morality*. Harvard: Harvard University Press.

Philips, S. 1998 *Ideology in the Language of Judges: How Judges Practice Law, Politics, and Courtroom Control*. Oxford: Oxford University Press.

Philippopoulos-Mihalopoulos, A. 2009 *Niklas Luhmann: Law, Justice, Society*. London: Routledge.

Pierce, J. 1995 *Gender Trials*. Berkeley: University of California Press.

Poulantzas, N. 1978 *State, Power, Socialism*. London: New Left Books.

Pound, R. 1926 *Law and Morals*. Chapel Hill: University of North Carolina Press.

Pound, R. 1931 'The call for a realist jurisprudence', *Harvard Law Review*, Vol. 44, No. 5, pp. 697–711.

Power, M. 1997 *The Audit Society: Rituals of Verification*. Oxford: Oxford University Press.

Prus, R. 1996 *Symbolic Interaction and Ethnographic Research: Intersubjectivity and the Study of Human Lived Experience*. New York: State University Press of New York.

Riles, A. 2000 *The Network Inside Out*. Ann Arbor: University of Michigan Press.

Ritzer, G. 2007 *Sociological Theory*. New York: McGraw-Hill.

Ritzer, G. 1995 *The McDonaldization of Society: An Investigation into the Changing Character of Contemporary Social Life*. California: Pine Forge Press.

Roach Anleu, S. 2000 *Law and Social Change*. London: Sage.

Robertson, R. 1992 *Globalization: Social Theory and Global Culture*. London: Sage.

Rose, N. 1996 'The death of the social? Re-figuring the territory of government', *Economy and Society*, Vol. 25, No. 3, pp. 327–56.

Rose, N. and Miller, P. (1992) 'Political power beyond the state: Problematics of government', *British Journal of Sociology*, Vol. 43, No. 2, pp. 173–205.

Sacks, H. 1992 *Lectures on Conversation*. Oxford: Blackwell.

Sacks, H. 1997 'The lawyer's work', in M. Travers and J. Manzo (eds) *Law in Action: Ethnomethodological and Conversation Analytic Approaches to Law*. Aldershot: Ashgate, pp. 34–50.

Said, E. 1979 *Orientalism*. London: Routledge.

Saint-Simon, H. 1975 *Henri Saint-Simon: Selected Writings on Science, Industry and Social Organisation* (edited by K. Taylor) New York: Holmes and Meier, first published 1815.

Sarat, A. 2003 'Vitality amidst fragmentation: On the emergence of postrealist law and society scholarship', *The Blackwell Companion to Law and Society*. Oxford: Blackwell, pp. 1–12.

Sarat, A. and Felstiner, W. 1986 'Law and strategy in the divorce lawyer's office', *Law and Society Review*, Vol. 20, pp. 94–134.

Sarat, A. and Silbey, S. 1988 'The Pull of the Policy Audience', *Law and Policy*, Vol. 10, No. 2/3, pp. 97–166.

Sarat, A. and Felstiner, W. 1996 *Divorce Lawyers and Their Clients: Power and Meaning in the Divorce Process*. Oxford: Oxford University Press.

Savigny, F. von 1975 *Of the Vocation of our Age for Legislation* (translated by A. Hayward). New York: Arno Press, first published 1831.

Scheffer, T. 2005 'Courses of mobilisation: Writing systematic micro-histories of legal discourse', in R. Banakar and M. Travers (eds) *Theory and Method in Socio-Legal Research*, Oxford: Hart, pp. 75–90.

Schutz, A. 1962 *Collected Papers: Vol. I*. The Hague: Martinus Nijhoff.

Selznik, P. 1949 *TVA and the Grass Roots*. California: University of California Press.

Selznik, P. 1957 *Leadership in Administration*. New York: Harper and Row.

Selznik, P. 1996 'Institutionalism "Old" and "New"', *Administrative Science Quarterly*, Vol. 41, No. 2, pp. 270–7.

Skolnick, J. 1975 *Justice Without Trial: Law Enforcement in Democratic Society*. New York: Wiley.

Smart, C. 1984 *The Ties that Bind: Law, Marriage and the Reproduction of Patriarchal Relations*. London: Routledge.

Smart, C. 1989 *Feminism and the Power of Law*. London: Routledge.

Smith, A. 1970 *The Wealth of Nations*. Harmondsworth: Penguin, first published 1776.

Smith, D. 1987 *The Everyday World as Problematic*. Toronto: University of Toronto Press.

Smith, D. 2005 *Institutional Ethnography: A Sociology for People*. Lanham: Rowman and Littlefield.

Sommerlad, H. and Sanderson, P. 1998 *Gender, Choice and Commitment: Women Solicitors in England and Wales and the Struggle for Equal Status*. Aldershot: Ashgate.

Sorokin, P. 1956 *Fads and Foibles in Sociology and Related Sciences*. Chicago: Regnery.

Spencer, H. 1965 *The Study of Sociology*. New York: Free Press, first published 1873.

Stacy, H. 2001 *Postmodernism and Law: Justice in a Fragmenting World*. Aldershot: Ashgate.

Stewart, A. and Williams, G. 2007 *Work Choices: What the High Court Said*. Sydney: Federation Press.

Stonequist, E. 1937 *The Marginal Man: A Study in Personality and Culture Conflict*. New York: Russell & Russell.

Stychin, C. 1995 *Law's Desire: Sexuality and the Limits of Justice*. London: Routledge.

Suchman, M. and Edelman, L. 1996 'Legal-rational myths: Lessons for the new institutionalism from the law and society tradition', *Law and Social Inquiry*. Vol. 21, No. 4, pp. 903–41.

Sudnow, D. 1965 'Normal crimes: Sociological features of the penal code', *Social Problems*, Vol. 12, No. 4, pp. 255–64.

Sumner, W. 1906 *Folkways*. New York: New American Library.

Sutton, J. 2001 *Law/Society*. Thousand Oaks, California: Sage.

Tamanaha, B. 1993 'The folly of the 'Social scientific concept' of legal pluralism', *Journal of Law and Society*, Vol. 20, pp. 192–217.

Taylor, I., Walton, P. and Young, J. 1973 *The New Criminology*. London: Routledge.

Ten Have, P. 1999 *Doing Conversation Analysis: A Practical Guide*. London: Sage.

Teubner, G. 1993 *Law as an Autopoetic System*. Oxford: Blackwell.

Thompson, E. 1975 *Whigs and Hunters: The Origins of the Black Act*. Harmondsworth: Penguin.

Thornton, M. 1996 *Dissonance and Distrust: Women in the Legal Profession*. Melbourne: Oxford University Press.

Tong, R. 1989 *Feminist Thought*. London: Routledge.

Tonnies, F. 1974 *Community and Association*. London: Routledge, first published 1887.

Travers, M. 1993 'Putting sociology back into the sociology of law', *Journal of Law and Society*, Vol. 20, No. 4, pp. 438–51.

Travers, M. 1997 *The Reality of Law: Work and Talk in a Firm of Criminal Lawyers*. Aldershot: Ashgate.

Travers, M. 1999 *The British Immigration Courts: A Study of Law and Politics*. Bristol: Policy Press.

Travers, M. 2002 'Symbolic interactionism', in R. Banakar and M. Travers (eds) *An Introduction to Law and Social Theory*. Oxford: Hart, pp. 209–26.

Travers, M. 2006 'Understanding talk in legal settings: What law and society studies can learn from a conversation analyst', *Law and Social Inquiry*, Vol. 31, No. 2, pp. 447–65 (published with replies by John Conley and Doug Maynard).

Travers, M. 2007 *The New Bureaucracy: Quality Assurance and its Critics*. Bristol: Policy Press.

Travers, M. 2008 'Understanding comparison in criminal justice research: An interpretive perspective', *International Criminal Justice Review*, Vol. 18, No. 4, pp. 389–405.

Trevino, J. 2006 *Classic Writings in Law and Society: Contemporary Comments and Criticisms*. New Jersey: Transaction.

Trevino, J. (ed.) 2008 *Parsons on Law and the Legal System*. Cambridge: Cambridge Scholars Press.

Twining, W. 2000. *Globalisation and Legal Theory*. London: Butterworths.

Unger, M. 1976 *Law in Modern Society: Towards a Criticism of Social Theory*. New York: The Free Press.

Vago, S. 2005 *Law and Society* (8th edn). Englewood Cliffs, NJ: Prentice-Hall.

Vaughan, K. and Ensslin, J. 2007 'CU Regents fire Ward Churchill', *Rocky Mountain News*. Denver, 25 July, p 1.

Wallerstein, I. 1996 *Open the Social Sciences: Report of the Gulbenkian Commission on the Restructuring of the Social Sciences*. Stanford: Stanford University Press.

Walters, M. 2006 *Feminism: A Very Short Introduction*. Oxford: Oxford University Press.

Weber, M. 1930 *The Protestant Ethic and the Spirit of Capitalism*. London: Unwin Hyman, first published 1921.

Weber, M. 1968 *Max Weber on Law in Economy and Society* (translated by E. Shils and M. Rheinstein). New York: Simon and Schuster, first published 1921.

Weber, M. 1978 *Economy and Society*. Berkeley: University of California Press, first published 1921.

Weber, M. 2007 'Class, status and party', in H. Gerth and C. Wright Mills (eds) *From Max Weber: Essays in Sociology*. London: Routledge, pp. 180–95; first published 1921.

Wickham, G. 2002 'Foucault and law', in R. Banakar and M. Travers (eds) *An Introduction to Law and Social Theory*, Oxford: Hart, pp. 249–66.

Wilson, A. and Pence, E. 2006 'U.S. legal interventions into the lives of battered women: An indigenous assessment', in D. Smith (ed.) *Institutional Ethnography as Practice*, Lanham: Rowman and Littlefield, pp.199–226.

Wollstonecraft, M. 1975 *A Vindication of the Rights of Women*. New York: W.W. Norton, first published 1792.

Yngvesson, B. 1988 'Making law at the doorway: The Clerk, the Court, and the construction of community in a New England town', *Law and Society Review*, Vol. 22 No. 3, pp. 409–47.

Ziegert, K. 2002 'The thick description of law: An introduction to Niklas Luhmann's Theory', in R. Banakar and M. Travers (eds) *An Introduction to Law and Social Theory*. Oxford: Hart, pp. 55–76.

Ziegert, K. 2006 'On Eugen Ehrlich, fundamental principles of the sociology of law', in J. Trevino (ed.) *Classic Writings in Law and Society*. New Jersey: Transaction, pp. 103–30.

Index

Abel, Richard 83, 193
actor-network theory 136
Adorno, Theodor 34, 144
agency concept 12, 56, 60, 70, 118
AGIL model of society 44, 46
Al-Qaeda 87, 158
Alternative Dispute Resolution 130
Althusser, Louis 69–73, 146–7
Animal Rights Front 93
anthropology 117, 168–73, 186
arbitration, international 178–80, 185
Asian financial crisis (1997) 177
Atkinson, J. 132
Australia 78–80, 105, 185, 197
Austria 29
autoethnography 118
autopoesis theory 41–2, 49–55, 136

Banakar, Reza 12, 28, 197
Barings Bank 177
Barnett, Hilaire 94, 99, 156–7
Barthes, Roland 146
base-superstructure model 22, 24
battered women 101–2
Baudrillard, Jean 142–6
Bauman, Z. 32
Beck, Ulrich 32
Becker, Howard 117, 120–5
Benjamin, Walter 149
Bentham, Jeremy 20, 95, 152
Bhaskar, Roy 34
bio-power 154
Bismarck, Otto von 24
Black, Donald 59–60
'black-letter law' 6–10, 13–14, 52, 85, 116, 121, 150, 197
Blood, Diana 99

Blumer, Herbert 62, 117, 119
Bodichon, Barbara Leigh Smith 93
Bonaparte, Napoleon 26–7
Bond, Alan 67
Bourdieu, Pierre 12, 14, 32–3, 51, 74, 87, 178–80, 196
Bredemeier, Harry 47, 58
British Gas 181
Brown, Chris 177
Bucher, R. 83
Bush, George W. 81
Butler, Judith 156

capitalism 11, 14, 20–2, 33, 43, 45, 61, 67–75, 78, 85–7, 96, 143, 155, 168, 176, 194
Carlin, Jerome 62, 121
case law 3
Castels, Manuel 32
Cheyenne tribe 170
Chicago 84
Chicago Schools, *first* and *second* 117, 119
China 68, 96, 184
Chodorow, Nancy 96, 109
civil law 3–4, 47
class divisions 21–3, 143, 155–6
climate change 73, 186–7; *see also* global warming
Clinton, Bill 81
Clinton, Hilary 91, 109
comparative legal research 185–6
Comte, Auguste 10, 19, 33, 41–5, 48, 59, 61, 94
Condorcet, Marquis de 92
conflict sociology 11, 95, 100–1, 109
Conley, J. 136

'conscience collective' (Durkheim) 23–4
consensus tradition in sociology 31,
    59–61, 95, 101, 109, 160, 192
conversation analysis 125, 130, 132,
    136
conveyancing work 82–3
Cornell, D. 150
Cotterrell, Roger 27–8, 35, 53–4,
    193–4
criminal law 3–4, 29, 47, 116, 123
Critical Legal Studies move-ment 72,
    150, 160, 162
critical theory 12–14, 35, 59–60,
    66–88, 109, 115, 157, 160–2,
    173–4, 192–6; assessment of 85–8;
    and the legal profession 82–5
Cuff, E. 148
cultural capital 74, 179

deconstruction 148–51
democracy 61, 176
dependency theory 168
Derrida, Jacques 141–3, 147–51,
    160, 194
Descartes, René 146
de Sousa Santos, Bonaventura 173–4
deviance 124
Dezalay, Yves 178–80, 185
differance, concept of 148
DiMaggio, P. 56–7
discourse analysis 130
divorce law 93, 100–1
documentary method of interpretation
    126
domestic violence 102–3
Douzinas, Costas 150
Drew, Paul 132–5
Durkheim, Emile 10, 19–20, 23–5,
    33–5, 41–5, 51, 55, 59, 61, 115–16,
    135, 185, 199
duty of care 7
Dworkin, Andrea 96–7
Dworkin, Ronald 8

Economic and Social Research Council
    198
Edelman, Lauren 57–8
Ehrlich, Eugene 26, 29, 31, 43, 49, 57,
    72–3, 169, 172–3
Emmelman, Debra 122–3
empiricism 196
employment law 76–80

Engels, Friedrich 21, 76–7, 96, 143, 176
'English Question' 20, 25
Enlightenment thinking 146–7, 151–3;
    Foucault's criticisms of 152–3
environmental degradation 177
epistemology 101, 115, 147
ethnography 62, 101–2, 107, 117–22,
    125, 128–9, 151–4, 168, 192–3
ethnomethodology 14–15, 56–7, 62,
    101, 124–9, 135–7; first use of term
    127
euthanasia 125
Evan, William 28, 47–9
Ewick, Patricia 77

feedback forms in higher education 155
Felstiner, W. 100, 136
feminism 91–110, 155, 196; backlash
    against 110; empirical studies
    informed by 100–3; and jurisprudence
    94–100; postmodern 110, 156–7; as
    a social move-ment 92–4
fertility treatment 99
financial crisis starting in 2008 51,
    154; see also Asian financial crisis
Finnis, John 8
Fish, Stanley 150
Flood, John 121–2, 180–2
'folkways' (Sumner) 27
formalism, legal 30, 32, 46, 54, 60
Foucault, Michel 13, 32–4, 51, 101,
    103, 141–3, 147–8, 151–62, 194,
    196
France 158–60; see also French
    Revolution
Frank, Jerome 30
Frankfurt School 69, 72–3, 143–4
French Revolution 26–7, 43, 48, 152
Freud, Sigmund (and Freudianism)
    44, 147
Friedan, Betty 95–6
Fukuyama, Francis 68, 168
Fuller, Lon 8

Gabel, Peter 150
Garcia, Angela 130–2
Garfinkel, Harold 125–9, 135
Garth, Bryant 178–80, 185
Gay Rights movement 80–1, 86–7
Genet, Jean 148
Germany 24–7, 186
Giddens, Anthony 12, 32–3, 135, 143

Gilligan, Carol 96, 109
Glaser, Barney 118
global warming 87, 198–9; *see also* climate change
globalisation 122, 167–8, 194; academic literature on 184; debates on 175–8, 186; failures of 177; and law 173–84
Goffman, Erving 117, 121
Goodrich, Peter 150
Gouldner, Alvin 61
Gramsci, Antonio 69–72
'grand narratives' 144, 147, 157
Gregson, Jane 129
Griffiths, Anne 171, 173
grounded theory 59, 118, 123
Gurvitch, Georges 26, 28, 35–6

Habermas, Jurgen 32, 51, 72–3, 85, 87, 144, 192
Harding, Sandra 100–1, 105
Hardt, Michael 168
Hart, H.L.A. 8
Hegel, G.W.F. 70, 148
hegemony, concept of 72, 77
Heinz, John 83–4
Hirst, P. 175
historical materialism, theory of 21–2
Hobbes, Thomas 43
Hochschild, Arlie 108
Hoebel, E. Adamson 170
Holmes, Oliver Wendell 30–1
homosexuality 80–2, 86–7, 155–8
House of Commons 4
Hughes, Everett 117–20
human rights 86, 159, 182–4, 192
humanism 70–1
Hunt, Alan 35–6, 160–2, 193
hyperreality 144

idealised view of law 61–2
'Ideological State Apparatus' (ISA) (Althusser) 70–1
ideology 21, 75, 79–80, 173; concept of 21; and legal consciousness 77; reproduction of 85
Immigration Appeals Tribunal 183–4
indigenous peoples and law 102–3, 169–72
individualism 33, 61
industrialisation 20–5, 30, 43, 73, 96
institutional ethnography 101

institutionalism 54–8; *old* and *new* 55–7; *see also* new institutionalism
inter-disciplinarity 193–6
International Chamber of Commerce (ICC) 179
International Covenant on Civil and Political Rights 182
International Criminal Court 4
international law and the international legal system 177–8
International Sociological Association 184
interpretive sociology 12, 35, 56, 59–61, 113–37; assessment of 135–7; as a theoretical perspective 115–17
interviews for data collection purposes 116–22
Iraq War (2003) 10, 183
Islamic headscarves 158–9
isomorphism 57–8
Italy 186

Johnson, Lyndon B. 50
Johnson, T. 83
'juridification' (Habermas) 73
jurisprudence 8, 10, 21; and feminism 94–100; *see also* sociological jurisprudence
jury deliberations 126–7
justice, Derrida's view of 149

Kelsen, Hans 8
Kennedy, Duncan 150

labelling theory 123–5
Lacan, Jacques 141, 147–50
late modernity 143
Latour, Bruno 136
Laumann, Edwin 83–4
law: as encountered in everyday life 102; function of 45–6, 51–2; measurement of effectiveness of 47–9, 59–60; sources of 3
law and society, relationship between 5–6, 141, 172
law and society studies 15, 35, 60, 115, 151, 153, 169, 185–6, 194–8; alternative names for the study of 3; central question of 191–3
law firms, global 180–2
law in context tradition 8–9

Law Lords 121
law schools 85, 121, 162, 195;
    curriculum of 197–8
Law Society 104, 181
legal institutions 3–5, 121
legal phenomena 5
legal practice, studies of 121–3
legal profession 82–5; criticisms of 46;
    mergers in 181; as seen by Parsons
    45–6; women in 91, 103–9, 156
legal terminology 52–3
legal texts, deconstruction of 149–50
Levi-Strauss, Claude 146
Lewis, Philip 193
liberalism, political 95–6
'lifeworld' concept (Habermas) 72–3,
    192
Llewellyn, Karl 30–2, 41, 43, 60, 170,
    197
Luhmann, N. 32, 41, 51–3, 59, 136,
    144
Lyotard, Jean-François 141–7, 155

Macauley, Stewart 169
McConville, M. 128
McGoldrick, D. 158, 160
MacKinnon, Catherine 96–8, 109
McLuhan, Marshall 173
McVeigh, Sean 150
Malinowski, B. 41, 168
Manzo, John 127
March, James 56
Marcuse, H. 144
marriage, same-sex 80–2, 157
Marx, Karl 12, 19–25, 33–5, 68–71,
    74–82, 86, 97, 143, 151–3, 174–8,
    199
Marxism 12, 14, 26, 69–75, 79, 82–7,
    91, 96, 141, 144, 151, 155, 160–2;
    cultural 71–2, 144; structural 69–71
Maturana, Humberto 52
Mayhew, L. 45
Maynard, Doug 127
Mead, George Herbert 117–19, 123
mediation hearings 130–2
medical sociology 62
membership categorisation analysis 130
Merry, Sally 136, 153–4
Merton, Robert 42
Mertz, Elizabeth 85, 136
'micro' level of society 116–18,
    135, 168

migration 158, 175
Mill, John Stuart 95
Miller, P. 154
Miners' Strike (1984) 78–9
Minnesota 97
modernisation theory 168
modernism 199
Montaigne, Michel de 92
Moore, Sally Falk 171
'mores' (Sumner) 27–8
multiculturalism 158–9
multinational corporations 176

Nader, Laura 59
natural law 5, 8, 26–7, 30
Negri, Antonio 168
Nelken, David 186
neo-liberalism 8, 74, 154, 196
Netherlands, the 80–1
new institutionalism 42, 58, 179, 192
Nietzsche, Friedrich 146, 152
Nixon, Richard 50
Nonet, Philippe 60

O'Barr, M. 136
Odeh, Lena 159
Olsen, Johan 56
ontology 101, 115
order, problem of 43–4
organisations, legal environment
    of 57–8
outsourcing 78

Park, Robert 117, 158
parliamentary draughtsmen 4
Parsons, Talcott 4, 9–15, 41–7,
    51–8, 61–2, 67, 82, 101, 126, 167–8;
    on the legal profession 45–6
participant observation 120–3
partnerships, legal 83, 103–4
Pashukanis, Evgeny 85–6
Paterson, Alan 121
Pence, E. 102–3
Peter the Great 28
Peters, G. 55
Petrazycki, Leon 26, 28, 36
Philips, Susan 136
Pierce, Jennifer 107–9
plea-bargaining 123, 129, 169
pluralism, legal 167–73; and the
    classical tradition 172–3; *weak* and
    strong versions of 171–2

Podogecki, Adam 28
policy-oriented research 8–10, 196, 198
pornography 96–9
positivism 8, 26, 29–30, 35, 42, 53–4, 59, 62, 115, 150, 162, 196
postmodern feminism 110, 156–7
postmodernism 12–13, 59, 72, 87, 98, 141–50, 160–2, 194, 196; assessment of 160–1; and empirical research 162; in relation to law 142–8
poststructuralism 142–51, 155–61, 194
Poulantzas, Nicos 71
Pound, Roscoe 30–1, 35, 41, 43, 46, 51, 57, 60, 169, 172–3
Powell, W. 56–7
pragmatism 30
precedents 7
pressure groups 125
professionals: power of 101; relationships with clients 119; restrictive practices of 82–3; special characteristics of 120; use of practical reasoning by 127, 129

qualitative research 59, 105, 115–20
quality assurance 33–4, 155
queer theory 87, 157–8

radical feminism 96–100, 109–10, 156
rape cases 98–100, 109, 132–3, 136
rational choice theory 55–6
Reagan, Ronald 196
realism, legal 29–34, 62, 137, 150
regulation 34, 45, 50–1, 58, 73, 78, 125, 154–5, 169, 174, 177, 199; international 186–7
relativism, problem of 160–1
'Repressive State Apparatus' (Althusser) 70–1
research, *scientific* versus *applied* 195–7
revolutionary movements 68–72, 87, 92, 176
Rice, Condoleeza 91
rights: problem of 85–6; of women 92–6
Roosevelt, Franklin D. 31
Rose, N. 154

Rousseau, Jean-Jacques 92, 94
rule of law 20–1
Russia 28, 96
Russian Revolution 68

Sacks, Harvey 6, 125, 130, 192–3
Said, Edward 158
Sarat, Austin 100, 136, 194–5
Savigny, Friedrich Karl von 26–7, 49
Scargill, Arthur 79
Scheffer, Thomas 136
Schutz, Alfred 126, 128
science, sociology of 151
scientific method 116, 146
Selznik, Philip 42, 55–60
September 11th 2001 attacks 87, 158, 196
sexism 105–7
shared values 11, 23, 31, 41–4, 55, 67–8, 95
Silbey, Susan 77, 195
Simpson, O.J. 117
Skolnick, Jerome 124
Smart, Carol 99–100
Smith, Adam 20
Smith, Dorothy 100–5, 109
smoking 125
social democracy 51, 154
social norms 5–6
social problems tradition in sociology 125
social systems 44
social worlds 119
socialisation 11, 43–4, 62, 74, 118, 126
sociological jurisprudence 25–31, 35–6, 45–6, 52, 60, 173, 194; first use of term 30–1; legacy of 35–6
sociology: classical 19–25, 32–6, 61, 198–9; debates in 10–13, 33, 142, 191; first use of term 19; structural 101, 115–16, 123, 135; subfields of 191
sociology of law 7–15, 74, 150, 156–7, 162, 196–8; classical tradition of 19–25
Sommerlad, Hilary 103–5
Sophocles 150
Sorokin, Pitrim 195
Soviet Union 68, 86, 155
speech-exchange systems 131
Spencer, Herbert 20, 27

Stacy, H. 147
Stalin, Joseph 155
standpoint theory 100–1, 105
states: power of 25–7, 78; role of 49–50
Stonequist, Everett 158
Strange, Susan 177
Strauss, Anselm 83, 117–18
structural-functionalism 11–12, 41–4, 49–50, 53–62, 67, 171, 192
'structuration' (Giddens) 135
Stychin, Carl 157
Suchman, Mark 57–8
Sudnow, David 62, 129
Sumner, William Graham 26–8, 31, 43, 49
surplus value, theory of 75
Sutton, John 49–50
symbolic interactionism 59–62, 101, 117–26, 135–7; central assumption of 118
systems theory 44, 51–2, 60–2, 72

Tamanaha, Brian 173
terrorism 87, 158, 196
Teubner, G. 53
Thatcher, Margaret 75, 109, 196
Thompson, Edward 86
Thompson, G. 175
Thornton, Margaret 105–6, 109
Timasheff, Nicholas 28
Tocqueville, Alexis de 144–5

Tonnies, Ferdinand 23
torture 152, 183
Travers, Max 12, 34
tribunals 14; see also Immigration Appeals Tribunal
truth, concept of 146–9

United Nations 4–5, 182–3, 186
United States 30, 43, 48–50, 58, 81, 179–80, 183, 197; Civil Rights Act (1964) 50; Constitution and Supreme Court 48, 92–7
universities, role of 196–7
utilitarianism 20–1, 43, 55

verstehen methodology 116
vested interests 58
Voltaire 92

Wallerstein, Immanuel 194
Weber, Max 10, 14, 19–21, 24–5, 33–5, 43, 51, 69, 74, 82, 100–3, 115–19, 126, 144, 146, 152–3, 156, 176–9, 192, 199
Wilson, A. 102–3
Wollstonecraft, Mary 94–6
women lawyers 91, 103–9, 156
women's rights 92–6
World Trade Organisation (WTO) 11, 177

Ziegert, K. 54

Printed in the USA/Agawam, MA
January 13, 2014

584107.048